D0890136

"This book is compelling reading, not only because of its intellectual rigor and the fact that it is beautifully written but also because of its honest, empathetic humanity. Readers will find themselves expertly guided on a journey that involves them not only in confronting Christianity but also in confronting themselves—their worldviews, hopes, fears, failures, and search for identity and satisfaction—and, finally, in confronting Christ as the altogether credible source of life as God means it to be."

John C. Lennox, Emeritus Professor of Mathematics, University of Oxford

"McLaughlin probes some of the trickiest cultural challenges to Christianity of our day and clearly demonstrates the breadth and richness of a Christian response. *Confronting Christianity* is well worth reading and pondering."

Tyler J. VanderWeele, John L. Loeb and Frances Lehman Loeb Professor of Epidemiology and Director of the Human Flourishing Program, Harvard University

"In the West, many people are persuaded by dominant secular narratives and think they already know what Christianity is about. In this bombshell of a book packed with myth-busting statistics, McLaughlin reveals the many surprises in authentic Christianity."

Peter J. Williams, Principal, Tyndale House, Cambridge; author, *Can We Trust the Gospels?*

"A deep and caring response to current criticisms and confrontations of the Christian faith fills Rebecca McLaughlin's book. She speaks from real-life experience of the personal and intellectual challenges we encounter today in considering the claims of Jesus Christ. Her open and faithful answers to serious questions provide not an easy stroll through imagined virtual reality but an adventurous rocky pathway through true and abundant life."

Ian Hutchinson, Professor of Nuclear Science and Engineering, Massachusetts Institute of Technology; author, *Can a Scientist Believe in Miracles?*

"Apologetics with heart, discernment, empathy, and rigorous study. *Confronting Christianity* will help you understand the hard questions of the Christian faith while also igniting a love for neighbor. McLaughlin doesn't shy away from tough questions about diversity and the nations, as well as slavery and facing America's past and present. Her answers are not only insightful; they have the potential to transform a heart of stone to a heart of flesh. Take up and read."

Trillia Newbell, author, *If God Is For Us*; *Fear and Faith*; and *United*

"Rebecca McLaughlin refuses to duck the biggest challenges to the Christian faith and takes on the hardest questions with empathy, energy, and understanding. She has studied widely, thinks deeply, and argues very persuasively. This is an outstanding resource for the skeptic, the doubter, and anyone who is ready to engage with some compelling thinking."

Sam Allberry, Speaker, Ravi Zacharias International Ministries; author, *Is God Anti-Gay?* and *7 Myths about Singleness*

"Rebecca McLaughlin's defense of the Christian faith is what all defenses should be: sensitive, smart, and sound. This is apologetics done right—and exactly right for this age in which we live. *Confronting Christianity* is a book I will draw upon myself and will recommend widely to believers and skeptics alike."

Karen Swallow Prior, author, *On Reading Well* and *Fierce Convictions*

"Rebecca McLaughlin addresses the most frequent and pressing objections to Christianity in our time with unflinching honesty, rigorous clarity, and deep compassion. This book is written not merely for skeptics but also for those who have suffered much in this sin-sick, destructive world. It is brimming with hope and will surprise you—and likely change the way you think about Jesus."

Jon Bloom, Cofounder, Desiring God; author, *Not by Sight*

"What Christianity has to offer the world is bound up in its strangeness. Only a distinctive word can be truly good news in a world like this. In a secularizing age, though, Christianity is often not simply odd to the world but also unexplained and seemingly inexplicable. In this book, Rebecca McLaughlin takes seriously both the Bible and the questions of nonbelievers. If you're a non-Christian and have wondered why Christians think and do as they do, this book will be a good start to exploring those questions. If you're a believer, this book will not only equip you intellectually but also call you to compassion and empathy for your questioning, unbelieving neighbor, as well as prepare you to bear witness to the Light that has come into the world."

Russell Moore, President, The Ethics and Religious Liberty Commission of the Southern Baptist Convention

"A fresh voice, arresting arguments, and an easy-to-read style. McLaughlin writes for curious thinkers everywhere and handsomely repays the open-minded reader."

Os Guinness, author, *The Call*

Confronting Christianity

Other Gospel Coalition Books

Confronting Christianity

12 Hard Questions for the World's Largest Religion

Rebecca McLaughlin

CROSSWAY®

WHEATON, ILLINOIS

Library of Congress Cataloging-in-Publication Data

Names: McLaughlin, Rebecca, 1980– author.
Title: Confronting Christianity: 12 hard questions for the world's largest religion / Rebecca McLaughlin.
Description: Wheaton: Crossway, 2019. | Includes bibliographical references and index.
Identifiers: LCCN 2018041912 (print) | LCCN 2018056552 (ebook) | ISBN 9781433564246 (pdf) | ISBN 9781433564253 (mobi) | ISBN 9781433564260 (epub) | ISBN 9781433564239 (hc)
Subjects: LCSH: Apologetics. | Bible—Theology.
Classification: LCC BT1103 (ebook) | LCC BT1103 .M353 2019 (print) | DDC 239—dc23
LC record available at https://lccn.loc.gov/2018041912

Crossway is a publishing ministry of Good News Publishers.

LB			29	28	27	26	25	24	23	22	21	20	19
16	15	14	13	12	11	10	9	8	7	6	5	4	3	2

For Natasha,
and for all my other fiercely intelligent friends
who disagree with me, but will do me the
honor of reading this book

Contents

Introduction

In 1971, Beatles star John Lennon had a dream. Closing his eyes to the atheist regimes of his day, he dreamed of a brotherhood of man with no heaven, no hell, no countries, no possessions, "nothing to kill or die for," and "no religion." This dream persists. "Imagine" was sung reverentially at the opening ceremony of the 2018 Winter Olympics in South Korea. Despite prescribing an antireligious pill swallowed by only a tiny fraction of the world, it is seen as an anthem of unity across ideological differences. As its notes rang out in PyeongChang, the sister of the supreme leader of North Korea—a state that has tried "no religion" and still found much to kill and die for—graced the crowd.

Eight years before "Imagine" was released, another prophet shared another dream. He dreamed that "one day in Alabama . . . little black boys and black girls [would] be able to join hands with little white boys and white girls as sisters and brothers."[1] But in the Reverend Dr. Martin Luther King's vision, peace and brotherhood sprang not from the loss of faith but from its fulfillment. King dreamed that "one day every valley shall be exalted, every hill and mountain shall be made low. The rough places will be made plain, and the crooked places will be made straight. And the glory of the Lord shall be revealed" (Isa. 40:4).

Who was right?

At the time John Lennon dreamed, another set of prophets spoke. Sociologists of religion foretold that global modernization would drive

---

1. Martin Luther King Jr., "I Have a Dream . . ." (speech delivered at the "March on Washington for Jobs and Freedom," August 28, 1963), https://www.archives.gov/files/press/exhibits/dream-speech.pdf.

secularization. As the world became more educated, more advanced, more scientific, religious belief would retreat. It had happened in Western Europe, so the rest of the world would follow. There was only one problem with the so-called secularization hypothesis. It failed.

In Western Europe and North America, the proportion of people identifying as religious has certainly shrunk. But at a global level, not only has religion failed to decline, but sociologists are now predicting an *increasingly* religious world.[2] While numbers do not tell the whole story, by 2060, the latest projections suggest, Christianity will still be the largest global belief system, having increased slightly, from 31 percent to 32 percent of the world's population.[3] Islam will have grown substantially, from 24 percent to 31 percent. Hinduism is set for marginal decline, from 15 percent to 14 percent, and Buddhism from 7 percent to 5 percent. Judaism will hold stable at 0.2 percent. And by 2060, the proportion of humanity identifying as atheists, agnostics, or "none" will have declined from 16 percent to 13 percent. Yes, declined.[4] For those of us who grew up under the secularization hypothesis, this comes as a surprise—pleasant or otherwise. So, what is happening?

Part of the answer lies in the link between theology and biology: Muslims, Christians, Hindus, and Jews outbreed the nonreligious.[5] Sixty percent of the world's religiously unaffiliated live in China, where fertility rates have been deliberately controlled. But even within the United States, religiosity correlates with fertility.[6] This may be a comfort to secularists, who would rather imagine believers outbreeding them than outthinking them. But the presumed link between education and secu-

---

2. See "The Future of World Religions: Population Growth Projections, 2010–2050," Pew Research Center, April 2, 2015, http://www.pewforum.org/2015/04/02/religious-projections-2010-2050/.

3. See "Projected Change in Global Population, 2015–2060," Pew Research Center, March 31, 2017, http://www.pewforum.org/2017/04/05/the-changing-global-religious-landscape/pf_17-04-05_projectionsupdate_changepopulation640px/.

4. See "Size and Projected Growth of Major Religious Groups, 2015–2060," Pew Research Center, April 3, 2017, http://www.pewforum.org/2017/04/05/the-changing-global-religious-landscape/pf-04-05-2017_-projectionsupdate-00-07/.

5. Global fertility rates are as follows: Muslims (3.1), Christians (2.7), Hindus (2.4), Jews (2.3), unaffiliated (1.7), Buddhists (1.6). See "Total Fertility Rate by Religion, 2010–2015," Pew Research Center, March 26, 2015, http://www.pewforum.org/2015/04/02/religious-projections-2010-2050/pf_15-04-02_projectionsoverview_totalfertility_640px/.

6. See, for example, Sarah Hayford and S. Philip Morgan, "Religiosity and Fertility in the United States: The Role of Fertility Intentions," *Social Forces* 86, no. 3 (2008): 1163–88.

larization is weak. While the gaps are closing for younger generations, Jews and Christians are still the most educated groups, with the smallest educational gap between men and women.[7] In the US, while nominally religious people are more likely to declare themselves nonreligious if they are more educated, professing Christians with higher levels of education appear to be just as religious as those with less schooling. Indeed, highly educated Christians are *more* likely to be weekly churchgoers.[8]

Furthermore, while many Americans are becoming nonreligious, the traffic flows both ways. A recent study found that nearly 40 percent of Americans raised nonreligious become religious (typically Christian) as adults, while only 20 percent of those raised Protestant switch.[9] If that trend continues, my secular friends are twice as likely to raise children who become Christians as I am to raise children who become nonreligious.[10] And the kind of religious beliefs people hold today are not the kind that fit comfortably into the "Coexist" bumper sticker. In North America, partly thanks to immigrant believers, full-blooded Christianity is outcompeting theologically liberal faith.[11]

But perhaps the biggest shock to the secular system is China, a country that has tried hard to imagine and enforce no religion. Conservative estimates from 2010 put China's Christian population at over sixty-eight million, representing 5 percent of its vast population.[12] But Christianity is spreading so fast that experts believe China could have more Christians than the US by 2030, and that it could be a majority-Christian country by 2050.[13]

7. See "Religion and Education around the World," Pew Research Center, December 13, 2016, http://www.pewforum.org/2016/12/13/religion-and-education-around-the-world/.

8. See "In America, Does More Education Equal Less Religion?," Pew Research Center, April 26. 2017, http://www.pewforum.org/2017/04/26/in-america-does-more-education-equal-less-religion/.

9. See "One-in-Five U.S. Adults Were Raised in Interreligious Homes," Pew Research Center, October 26, 2016, http://www.pewforum.org/2016/10/26/one-in-five-u-s-adults-were-raised-in-interfaith-homes/.

10. "Religious Switching and Intermarriage," in *America's Changing Religious Landscape*, Pew Research Center, May 12, 2015, http://www.pewforum.org/2015/05/12/chapter-2-religious-switching-and-intermarriage/.

11. "The Changing Religious Composition of the U.S.," in *America's Changing Religious Landscape*, Pew Research Center, May 12, 2015, http://www.pewforum.org/2015/05/12/chapter-1-the-changing-religious-composition-of-the-u-s/.

12. Pew Research Center Global Religious Survey, 2010, cited by Eleanor Albert, "Christianity in China," Council on Foreign Relations (website), March 9, 2018, https://www.cfr.org/backgrounder/christianity-china.

13. See Antonia Blumberg, "China on Track to Become World's Largest Christian Country by 2025, Experts Say," *Huffpost*, April 22, 2014, http://www.huffingtonpost.com/2014/04/22/china-largest-christian-country_n_5191910.html.

Fenggang Yang, a leading sociologist of religion in China, argues that we need to undergo a paradigm shift akin to a scientific revolution as we adjust to the failure of the secularization hypothesis.[14] Much academic discourse rests on the assumption that religion is withering under the scorching heat of modernization. Secular humanism is seen as the shared ground on which we all can stand. But this framework has crumbled. Today, we must wake up to the fact that Lennon's dream was a fantasy. What is worse, it was a fantasy fueled by white Western bias and grounded on the assumption that the world would follow where Western Europe led. The question for the next generation is not *How soon will religion die out?* but *Christianity or Islam?*

For many, this is a troubling thought. Full-blooded religious belief worries us. We envisage extremism and violence, the stifling of free thought, and the subjugation of women. In some parts of the world, the resurgence of traditionalist Islam has borne this unappealing fruit. But for many raised in the secularizing West, biblical Christianity also triggers moral and intellectual objections: What about science, suffering, and sexuality? What about the Crusades? How can you say there is one true faith? How can you take the Bible literally? Doesn't the Bible justify slavery? How could a loving God send people to hell?

If you resonate with these questions, this book is for you. I feel their weight. If I give smug, simplistic answers, I have failed. I have spent decades of my life engaging with brilliant friends who have principled reasons for dismissing Christianity. But I have also spent years working with Christian professors at leading secular universities in fields ranging from physics to philosophy. Some grew up in the church. Others encountered Christianity later. All have found that their faith has stood the test of their research and left them more convinced that Christianity represents our tightest grasp on truth and our best hope for the world. This book aims to look closely at important questions through the lenses these friends have given me, and to share that experience with you.

---

14. See Fenggang Yang, "Response by Fenggang Yang—Agency-Driven Secularization," in Peter L. Berger, *The Many Altars of Modernity: Toward a Paradigm for Religion in a Pluralist Age* (Boston: De Gruyter Mouton, 2014), 128.

Often, when we observe from a distance, we misinterpret. Look up at the night sky and you will see much darkness. But train a telescope on the blackest patch, and a million galaxies explode into view. John Lennon dreamed of a religion-free world where there would be "nothing to kill or die for." Staring into the dark night of segregation, Martin Luther King preached an antithetical message: that "there are some things so dear, some things so precious, some things so eternally true, that they are worth dying for. And I submit to you that if a man has not discovered something that he will die for, he isn't fit to live."[15]

---

15. Martin Luther King Jr. (address at a freedom rally, Detroit, Michigan, June 23, 1963), Stanford University (website), accessed August 27, 2018, https://kinginstitute.stanford.edu /king-papers/documents/address-freedom-rally-cobo-hall.

1

Aren't We Better Off
without Religion?

Most college freshmen try to blend in. I stuck out. My English-major classmates were preternaturally cool. Some modeled; others starred in films. I did neither. But it wasn't just my lack of time in front of a camera that set me apart: I showed up to college with a three-inch wooden cross around my neck.

One guy assumed I was being ironic, and we struck up an unlikely friendship. He was into drugs. I was into Jesus. We both loved books. I could have increased my credibility to no end by confessing that I was quietly falling in love with a succession of girls. But I didn't. I was still hoping it was a phase I would grow out of.[1] So, for the time being, I was just one of a handful of Bible-clinging oddities among my mystified, secularized, and occasionally scandalized peers.

The Christian student group at Cambridge was larger and more active than people imagined. We knocked on dorm-room doors to deliver gospel booklets and discuss Jesus. But most casual observers of the Cambridge scene at the turn of the millennium would have bet these groups would subside: full-bodied Christian belief was simply no longer viable in a world-class university.

---

1. We will explore this puzzle piece in chap. 9, "Isn't Christianity Homophobic?"

New Atheist Narratives

Since then, New Atheists have spun a credibility-killing web around faith. In 2004, Sam Harris published *The End of Faith: Religions Terror, and the Future of Reason*, followed in 2006 by *Letter to a Christian Nation*. That same year, Richard Dawkins released *The God Delusion*, which remained on the *New York Times* best seller list for fifty-one weeks. In 2008, the late Christopher Hitchens launched his tour de force of new atheist persuasion, *God Is Not Great: How Religion Poisons Everything*. These rhetorically gifted men preached that Christianity was neither plausible nor desirable. Dawkins ridiculed a faith disproved by science. Hitchens sought to puncture the sagging balloon of public opinion that imagined Christianity was a force for good.

Invigorated by these triumphs, atheists have boldly claimed the moral and intellectual high ground—even when that has meant trespassing. In a popular 2011 TED talk, "Atheism 2.0," School of Life founder Alain de Botton advocated a new kind of atheism that could retain the goods of religion without the downside of belief. He salivated over the black American preaching tradition and the enthusiastic response of congregants: "Thank you Jesus, thank you Christ, thank you Savior!" Rather than abandoning rapture, de Botton suggested secular audiences respond to atheist preaching by lauding *their* heroes: "Thank you Plato, thank you Shakespeare, thank you Jane Austen!"[2] One wonders how Shakespeare, whose world was fundamentally shaped by Christianity, would have felt about being cast as an atheist icon. But when it comes to Jane Austen, the answer is clear: a woman of deep, explicit, and abiding faith in Jesus, she would be utterly appalled.[3]

Likewise, at the 2016 "Reason Rally," designed to mobilize atheists, agnostics, and "nones," multiple speakers invoked Martin Luther King's March on Washington—as if a rally that despised Christianity would have pleased one of the most powerful Christian preachers in American history. In the same year, I stumbled upon an *Atlantic* article that promised to explain "Why the British Tell Better Children's

---

2. Alain de Botton, "Atheism 2.0," TEDGlobal (video), July 2011, https://www.ted.com/talks/alain_de_botton_atheism_2_0.

3. See Rebecca McLaughlin, "Jane Austen's Answer to Atheism 2.0," The Gospel Coalition, January 22, 2018, https://www.thegospelcoalition.org/article/jane-austens-answer-atheism-2-0/.

Stories."[4] As a Brit living in America, I read it eagerly, only to find it arguing that American children's stories are *less* compelling because they are *more* Christian. The author cited *The Lord of the Rings* and *The Chronicles of Narnia* as examples of stories shaped by paganism, failing to note that Tolkien and Lewis were passionate Christians who grounded their stories in the death-and-resurrection truth claims of Jesus. J. K. Rowling, another author referenced on the side of good-old British paganism, chose not to disclose her fragile Christian faith until the last Harry Potter book was published, precisely because of its Christian influence: she feared it would give the story away.[5] The trend persists. In an oddly appropriating act, the 2018 film version of Madeleine L'Engle's *A Wrinkle in Time* expunged its many Christian references.

Meanwhile, brilliant skeptical storytellers have captured our imaginations. Margaret Atwood's 1985 dystopian novel, *The Handmaid's Tale*, has been revivified in a popular Hulu dramatization. It imagines New England ruled by a pseudo-Christian sect, the Sons of Jacob. Women's bank accounts are suspended. Women are forbidden to read or work jobs. Those still fertile after a nuclear fallout are assigned to male "Commanders," who seek to impregnate them in a monthly ceremony, supposedly modeled on Abraham's impregnation of his wife Sarah's handmaid. Partly inspired by the 1980 Islamic Revolution in Iran, Atwood envisages a similarly repressive, supposedly Christian regime.

Back in my own motherland, the iconic sci-fi series *Doctor Who* takes viewers on breathless sprints between the moving, the witty, and the profound. The Doctor is in many ways deeply Christlike, and *Doctor Who* is one of my all-time-favorite shows, but its anti-Christian messaging is hard to miss.[6] "Weeping angels" feed on human lifespans. "Headless monks" are ruled by faith: decapitation has rendered them

---

4. Colleen Gilliard, "Why the British Tell Better Children's Stories," *The Atlantic*, January 6, 2016, https://www.theatlantic.com/entertainment/archive/2016/01/why-the-british-tell-better-childrens-stories/422859/.

5. See Jonathan Petre, "J. K. Rowling: 'Christianity Inspired Harry Potter,'" *The Telegraph*, October 20, 2007, http://www.telegraph.co.uk/culture/books/fictionreviews/3668658/J-K-Rowling-Christianity-inspired-Harry-Potter.html.

6. See Rebecca McLaughlin, "How the Hero of 'Doctor Who' Is—and Is Not—Like Jesus," The Gospel Coalition, January 12, 2018, https://www.thegospelcoalition.org/article/hero-doctor-not-like-jesus/.

literally thoughtless. The fifty-first century church is a military opera-
tion. The list of compelling stories, shows, and songs that invite us to
reject religion is long, and we forget how much of the cultural capital
we see as universal was sculpted by Christianity.

To some extent, of course, we Christians have dug our own grave.
The entrenchment of the culture wars has led many believers to lose
touch with their heritage, while Christians and atheists alike assume
that *secular* means normative. Christians invented the university and
founded most of the world's top schools to glorify God. And yet studying is seen as a threat to faith. Christians invented science, yet science
is seen as antithetical to Christianity.[7] Christians have told some of the
best stories in history. But if the tales are too good, too entrancing, too
magical, we assume that the authors cannot espouse this supposedly
story-killing faith.

What fruit has this borne for today's students?

The Rising Generation of "Nones"

In 2016, the largest survey of incoming freshmen to US universities
found that 30.9 percent claimed no religious affiliation—a dramatic 10
percent rise since 2006.[8] This group broke down into freshmen who
selected "none" (16 percent), those who identified as agnostic (8.5 percent), and those who claimed atheism (6.4 percent). While the growth of
the nonreligious population has been rapid, this is no license to cede the
university to secularism. Sixty-nine percent of US college students still
identify as religious, and 60.2 percent identify as Christian. To be sure,
checking the box on a survey is not proof of active faith. But when more
students identify as Baptist than atheist, we need to be careful about
exaggerated claims of secularization. Nor is the decline in religious affiliation a by-product of diversity: atheism in America is overrepresented
by white men, while women and students of color are more likely to be
religious.[9] Indeed, at historically black universities, 85.2 percent of stu-

---

7. We will unearth the Christian origins of science in chap. 7, "Hasn't Science Disproved
Christianity?"

8. See Kevin Eagan et al., *The American Freshman: National Norms 2016* (Los Angeles: Co-
operative Institutional Research Program at the Higher Education Research Institute at UCLA,
2017), 38, https://heri.ucla.edu/monographs/TheAmericanFreshman2016.pdf.

9. Sixty-eight percent of self-identified atheists in the US are men, and 78 percent are white,
compared with 66 percent of the general population. See Michael Lipka, "10 Facts about Athe-

dents identify as Christian, and only 11.2 percent as agnostic, atheist, or none.[10] Nevertheless, the proportion of religiously unaffiliated students in the US is growing—fast. So, are today's students simply waking up to the fact that we do not need religion anymore?

At an empirical level, the answer seems to be no.

Religion: A Miracle Drug

In 2016, Harvard School of Public Health professor Tyler Vander-Weele and journalist John Siniff wrote a *USA Today* op-ed entitled "Religion May Be a Miracle Drug."[11] The piece begins, "If one could conceive of a single elixir to improve the physical and mental health of millions of Americans—at no personal cost—what value would our society place on it?" The authors go on to outline the mental and physical health benefits that are correlated with regular religious participation—for most Americans, going to church—even to the extent of reducing mortality rates by 20–30 percent over a fifteen-year period. Research suggests that those who regularly attend services are more optimistic, have lower rates of depression, are less likely to commit suicide, have a greater purpose in life, are less likely to divorce, and are more self-controlled.[12]

Of course, we need only open a newspaper to see that religious beliefs can cause harm. But to say that religion is bad for you is like saying, "Drugs are bad for you," without distinguishing cocaine from life-saving medication. In general, religious participation appears to be good for your health and happiness. Turn this data on its head and the trend toward secularization in America is a public-health crisis.[13]

What makes religious participation so powerful?

---

ists," Pew Research Center, June 1, 2016, http://www.pewresearch.org/fact-tank/2016/06/01/10 -facts-about-atheists/.

10. See Eagan et al., *American Freshman*, 38.

11. Tyler VanderWeele and John Siniff, "Religion May Be a Miracle Drug," *USA Today*, October 28, 2016, https://www.usatoday.com/story/opinion/2016/10/28/religion-church-attendance -mortality-column/92676964/.

12. For a detailed literature review on the effect of religious participation on health and well-being, see Tyler VanderWeele, "Religion and Health: A Synthesis." in *Spirituality and Religion within the Culture of Medicine: From Evidence to Practice*, ed. Michael J. Balboni and John R. Peteet (New York: Oxford University Press, 2017).

13. VanderWeele summarizes his research thus: "Public health relevance is often described as a function of the prevalence of the exposure and the size of the effect. On these grounds, religious participation, as will be argued in this review, is a powerful social determinant of health." Vander-Weele, "Religion and Health," 357.

The Power of Relationships

Part of the answer is relationships. Religion fosters relationships, and relationships matter. The director of the Harvard Study of Adult Development, a seventy-five-year study of well-being, summarizes its findings like this: "Good relationships keep us happier and healthier. Period."[14] Throughout the study, the subjects expected their happiness would depend on fame, wealth, and high achievement. But, in reality, the happiest and healthiest people prioritized relationships with family, friends, and community.

Perhaps we do not need a seventy-five-year study to convince us that loneliness is lethal. Our single-portion society teaches us to prioritize choice over commitment. We resist being tied down because we fear missing out, and in doing so, we miss out on the things that matter most. But does the power of community account for the impact of religion? Would going to the local golf club once a week and enjoying a shared interest with a consistent group yield similar results? It seems not. Community support alone seems to account for less than 30 percent of the positive effect of religious participation.[15] So, what else is in play?

The Benefits of Seven Biblical Principles

I want to explore seven counterintuitive biblical commands and how they relate to the findings of modern psychology. This is not an exhaustive list, and I make no claim that Christianity holds a monopoly on these principles or that a positive effect on health and happiness is the litmus test for truth. But as this chapter is entitled "Aren't We Better Off without Religion?," it seems logical to examine some of the principles of the world's largest religion and see how they impact our ability to thrive.

It Really Is More Blessed to Give Than to Receive

In our acquisitive culture, the biblical demand that Christians serve and give to others feels out of joint. The claim that "it is more blessed to give than to receive" (Acts 20:35) cuts against the grain of our individualized, success-focused mind-set. But a growing body of research

---

14. Robert Waldinger, "What Makes a Good Life? Lessons from the Longest Study on Happiness," TEDxBeaconStreet (video), November 2015, https://www.ted.com/talks/robert_waldinger_what_makes_a_good_life_lessons_from_the_longest_study_on_happiness.
15. See, for example, Shanshan Li et al., "Association of Religious Service Attendance with Mortality among Women," *JAMA Internal Medicine* 176, no. 6 (2016): 777–85.

suggests that giving is good for us. Volunteering has a positive impact on our mental and physical health.[16] Actively caring for others often yields greater physical and psychological benefits than being cared for.[17] Helping others in the workplace seems to improve career satisfaction.[18] And financial generosity has psychological payoffs.[19]

Many nonreligious people are passionately engaged in serving and giving, while many Christians live self-centered lives. But as atheist social psychologist Jonathan Haidt observes:

> Surveys have long shown that religious believers in the United States are happier, healthier, longer-lived, and more generous to charity and to each other than are secular people. . . . Religious believers give more money than secular folk to secular charities, and to their neighbors. They give more of their time, too, and of their blood.[20]

No Christian lives up to the radical example of Jesus, who gave his life to save his enemies. Too many churches enable a self-focused Christianity that ignores New Testament ethics. But the faint echoes of Christ in the lives of Christians seem to pay dividends—both for society and for individuals.

Love of Money Disappoints

For those of us raised on a steady diet of capitalism, the Bible's critique of wealth is tough to swallow. Jesus taught that it was harder for a rich

---

16. For a summary of this research, see Caroline E. Jenkinson et al., "Is Volunteering a Public Health Intervention? A Systematic Review and Meta-Analysis of the Health and Survival of Volunteers," *BMC Public Health* 13 (2013): 773. See also Donald P. Moynihan, Thomas DeLeire, and Kohei Enami, "Volunteering Makes You Happier, but Why You Volunteer Also Matters: Other-Oriented Motivations and Cumulative Life-Satisfaction," Robert M. La Follette School of Public Affairs (website), November 2017, https://www.lafollette.wisc.edu/images/publications/working papers/Moynihan-2017-004-volunteering.pdf.

17. See, for example, Susan Brown et al., "Providing Social Support May Be More Beneficial Than Receiving It: Results from a Prospective Study of Mortality," *Psychological Science* 14, no. 4 (2003): 320–27.

18. Donald P. Moynihan, Thomas DeLeire, and Kohei Enami, "A Life Worth Living: Evidence on the Relationship between Prosocial Motivation, Career Choice, and Happiness," *American Review of Public Administration* 4, no. 3 (2015): 311–26.

19. See, for example, Lara B. Aknin et al., "Prosocial Spending and Well-Being: Cross-Cultural Evidence for a Psychological Universal," *Journal of Personality and Social Psychology* 104, no. 4 (April 2013): 635–52.

20. Jonathan Haidt, "Moral Psychology and the Misunderstanding of Religion," *Edge*, September 21, 2007, https://www.edge.org/conversation/jonathan_haidt-moral-psychology-and-the-misunderstanding-of-religion. Haidt warns, "You can't use the New Atheists as your guide to these lessons. The New Atheists conduct biased reviews of the literature and conclude that there is no good evidence on any benefits except the health benefits of religion."

man to enter the kingdom of God than for a camel to go through the eye of a needle (Matt. 19:23–24; Mark 10:25; Luke 18:24–25). The apostle Paul called the love of money "a root of all kinds of evil" (1 Tim. 6:10). But in the US at least, the love of money is still holding sway. In the 2016 survey *The American Freshman*, 82.3 percent of freshmen checked "becoming very well off financially" as an "essential" or "very important" life objective.[21] This represents an increase of nearly 10 percent in the last decade and has overtaken "raising a family" as a top priority.[22] Beyond our student years, many of us live as if money will buy us happiness, sacrificing family and friendship on the altar of career. But as Haidt comments, "Wealth itself has only a small direct effect on happiness because it so effectively speeds up the hedonic treadmill."[23]

A little money can make a big difference to the truly poor—a reality reflected in the Bible's unrelenting demand that those with extra share with those without. But while the literature is complex, there is evidence to suggest that beyond a basic level of security, increased wealth is only slightly correlated with an increased sense of well-being.[24] As economist Jeffrey Sachs notes in the *World Happiness Report 2018*, in the US, "income per capita has more than doubled since 1972 while happiness (or subjective well-being, SWB) has remained roughly unchanged or has even declined."[25] The biblical warnings against the love of money turn out to be more true than we realized: invest your life in money over relationships, and the returns will not satisfy.

Work Works When It's a Calling

While the Bible eviscerates the love of money, it does not call us to a leisurely life. Rather, it tells a story in which humans are made to be in

---

21. Eagan et al., *American Freshman*, 47.

22. The same survey in 2006 reported that 75.5 percent of students indicated that "raising a family" was an "essential" or "very important" life objective, while 73.4 percent of students indicated that "being very well off financially" was an "essential" or "very important" life objective.

23. Jonathan Haidt, *The Happiness Hypothesis: Finding Modern Truth in Ancient Wisdom* (New York: Basic Books, 2006), 89.

24. See, for example, Daniel Kahneman and Angus Deaton et al., "High Income Improves Evaluation of Life but Not Emotional Well-Being," *Proceedings of the National Academy of Sciences* 287, no. 38 (2010); and E. Diener et al., "Wealth and Happiness across the World: Material Prosperity Predicts Life Evaluation, Whereas Psychosocial Prosperity Predicts Positive Feeling," *Journal of Personality and Social Psychology* 99, no. 1 (2010): 52–61.

25. John F. Helliwell, Richard Layard, and Jeffrey D. Sachs, *World Happiness Report 2018* (New York: Sustainable Development Solutions Network, 2018), 146.

relationship with God and with each other, and to pour themselves into meaningful work. In the first century, few people had our freedom to choose their profession. If your father was a carpenter, you had better be into woodworking! But regardless of their situation or status, people could choose *how* they worked. The apostle Paul encouraged Christian slaves (a significant proportion of the early church) that even *their* work could be a calling, and exhorted them to put their hearts into it, seeing themselves as working for the Lord, not any human master (Col. 3:23–24).[26] So Christians are called to see work as part of their *worship*—whether they are designing a building or sweeping its floors.

Again, this proves to be good advice. Psychological research suggests that we need meaningful work to thrive. If we work just for money, we tend to find it unsatisfying; but if we put our hearts into our work and see it as a calling that resonates with our values, connects us to people, and fits within a larger vision, we experience joy. University of Pennsylvania psychology professor Angela Duckworth tells a parable to illustrate this: "Three bricklayers are asked, 'What are you doing?' The first says, 'I am laying bricks.' The second says, 'I am building a church.' The third says, 'I am building the house of God.' The first bricklayer has a job. The second has a career. The third has a calling."[27]

We can apply this to the least glamorous jobs. One study observed the attitudes of janitors emptying bedpans and cleaning up vomit in a hospital. Those who saw themselves as part of a team caring for the sick, and who went above and beyond to do their job with excellence, saw their work as a calling and enjoyed it far more than those who worked just for a paycheck.[28] So, whether we are performing brain surgery or cleaning up vomit, we can put our hearts into our work, connect it with a larger purpose, and gain satisfaction.

We Really Can Be Happy in All Circumstances

This view of work ties into a yet more counterintuitive biblical claim. After multiple experiences of physical and psychological

---

26. We will explore the biblical texts on slavery and whether the Bible justifies slaveholding in chap. 10.

27. Angela Duckworth, *Grit: The Power of Passion and Perseverance* (New York: Scribner, 2016), 149.

28. Haidt, *Happiness Hypothesis*, 222.

trauma, the apostle Paul wrote this from prison: "I have learned the secret of being content in any and every situation, whether well fed or hungry, whether living in plenty or in want. I can do all this through him who gives me strength" (Phil. 4:12–13 NIV). This sounds like wishful thinking. But modern psychology suggests that we have a highly developed ability to synthesize happiness. Harvard psychology professor Daniel Gilbert calls this our "psychological immune system." To illustrate the point, he quotes the seventeenth-century polymath Thomas Browne: "I am the happiest man alive. I have that in me that can convert poverty to riches, adversity to prosperity. I am more invulnerable than Achilles; fortune hath not one place to hit me."[29]

Gilbert asks, "What kind of remarkable machinery does this guy have in his head? Well, it turns out it's precisely the same remarkable machinery that all of us have." Gilbert (a self-declared atheist) does not note that Browne was drawing on his Christian faith to immunize himself against suffering. Indeed, Browne's *Religio Medici*, from which Gilbert quotes, is a theological memoir structured around the Christian virtues of faith, hope, and love.

Gilbert highlights other individuals who have found joy in adversity, including Moreese Bickham, an African American man who was dubiously convicted of murdering two white police officers and spent thirty-seven years in prison. On his release, Bickham declared: "I don't have one minute's regret. It was a glorious experience."[30] Again, Gilbert does not mention that Bickham was sustained by his Christian faith, or that he thanked God for the injury he suffered prior to his imprisonment: "I never had a personal relationship with [God]," Bickham reflected, "until I was laying at the point of death with a bullet shot [through the] top of my heart."[31]

---

29. Dan Gilbert, "The Surprising Science of Happiness," TED2004 (video), February 2004, https://www.ted.com/talks/dan_gilbert_asks_why_are_we_happy. The quotation comes from Simon Wilken, ed. *The Works of Sir Thomas Browne: Pseudodoxia Epidemica*, bks. 5–7, *Religio Medici* (London: Henry G. Bowen, 1852), 444.

30. Quoted in Kevin Sack, "After 37 Years, Inmate Tastes Freedom," *New York Times*, January 11, 1996, http://www.nytimes.com/1996/01/11/us/after-37-years-in-prison-inmate-tastes-freedom.html.

31. Quoted in "Former Death Row Prisoner Moreese Bickham Dies at 98: He Served 37 Years for Killing Klansmen Cops," *Democracy Now*, May 5, 2016, https://www.democracynow.org/2016/5/5/former_death_row_prisoner_moreese_bickham.

The ability to synthesize happiness is not limited to followers of Jesus. Buddhism devotes much attention to helping people maintain internal peace in the face of adversity. Jewish and Muslim practices also anchor to inner well-being. But there is a remarkable correspondence between the psychological immune system Gilbert describes and the biblical call to contentment.

Gratitude Is Good for Us

The possibility of contentment in all circumstances relates to another counterintuitive biblical ethic. Paul commands Christians to "rejoice always, pray without ceasing, give thanks in all circumstances" (1 Thess. 5:16). This seems unrealistic, even insensitive. But Paul was writing not from an armchair but from profound experiences of suffering: beatings, shipwreck, rejection, sickness, and the prospect of execution. And psychologists today have discovered that conscious, daily gratitude is quite literally good for you. In experimental comparisons, those who kept gratitude journals on a weekly basis exercised more, reported fewer physical symptoms, felt better about their lives, and were more optimistic about the upcoming week than those who recorded hassles or neutral life events.[32] Psychology professor Robert Emmons calls gratitude "the forgotten factor in happiness research."[33]

Gratitude is buried at the heart of Christianity. Christians believe not only that God created us and every good thing we have, but also that he offers us salvation as a free gift, won for us by Jesus's death in our place. For the Christian, therefore, thankfulness is not just a positivity technique: it is a deep disposition toward a life-giving and life-saving God.

Self-Control and Perseverance Help Us Thrive

Much contemporary culture revolves around instant gratification. But Christians are called to live lives characterized by long-term endurance

---

32. See, for example, Robert A. Emmons and Michael E. McCullough, "Counting Blessings versus Burdens: An Experimental Investigation of Gratitude and Subjective Well-Being in Daily Life," *Journal of Personality and Social Psychology* 84, no. 2 (February 2003): 377–89.

33. For a scholarly introduction to the field, see Robert A. Emmons and Michael E. McCullough, eds., *The Psychology of Gratitude*, Studies in Affective Science (Oxford: Oxford University Press, 2014).

and costly self-control. For example, the apostle Peter urged his readers, "Make every effort to add to your faith goodness; and to goodness, knowledge; and to knowledge, self-control; and to self-control,
perseverance; and to perseverance, godliness; and to godliness, mutual
affection; and to mutual affection, love" (2 Pet. 1:5–7 NIV). Jesus
called the Christian life a "hard" road (Matt. 7:14), and multiple biblical texts describe a race that we must run with endurance and passion.
For example, the writer to the Hebrews urges, "Let us run with endurance the race that is set before us, looking to Jesus, the founder and
perfecter of our faith, who for the joy that was set before him endured
the cross" (Heb. 12:1–2).

Once more, the Bible judges the human condition well. Unglamor-
ous as they are, perseverance and self-control appear to be key predic-
tors of flourishing across a range of indexes.[34] Indeed, psychologist
Angela Duckworth suggests that the quality of *grit*, which she defines
as "passion and perseverance for very long-term goals," can be more
predictive of a person's success than social intelligence, good looks,
health, or IQ.[35]

Forgiveness Is Foundational

When one of Jesus's disciples suggested an upper limit for forgiveness—
"as many as seven times?"—Jesus replied, "Not . . . seven times, but
seventy-seven times" (Matt. 18:21–22). He taught his followers to pray,

> Forgive us our sins,
>> for we ourselves forgive everyone who is indebted to us.
>> (Luke 11:4)

And as he was being nailed to the cross, Jesus prayed for the soldiers
who were executing him, "Father, forgive them, for they know not
what they do" (Luke 23:34). Jesus grounded human forgiveness in the
radical forgiveness of God, arguing that forgiven people *must* forgive.
Again, this turns out to be for our good. Forgiveness—particularly

---

34. See, for example, Angela Duckworth and James J. Gross, "Self-Control and Grit," *Current
Directions in Psychological Science* 23, no. 5 (2014): 319. For more on the importance of self-
regulation, see, for example, Laurence D. Steinberg, *Age of Opportunity: Lessons from the New
Science of Adolescence* (Boston: Mariner, 2015), 16.
35. Duckworth, *Grit*, 149.

forgiveness not dependent on the actions of the offender—has been linked to multiple positive mental and physical health outcomes.[36]

In the New Testament, the forgiveness ethic is coupled with the command not to take revenge. But this is not ultimately an abandonment of justice. Rather, it is an acknowledgment that final justice lies in the hands of God. Christians are commanded to protect the weak and vulnerable, but not to seek their own revenge or vindication. Instead, Christians must forgive as they have been forgiven.

How do these counterintuitive strands of biblical wisdom weave together in the fabric of a life?

Would You Rather Be Bob or Mary?

In 2006, the same year that Richard Dawkins published *The God Delusion*, atheist psychologist Jonathan Haidt published *The Happiness Hypothesis: Finding Modern Truth in Ancient Wisdom*. In one of the book's most striking moments, Haidt sketches two profiles. First, we meet Bob: "Bob is 35 years old, single, white, attractive, and athletic. He earns $100,000 a year and lives in sunny Southern California. He is highly intellectual, and he spends his free time reading and going to museums."[37]

Next, we meet Mary:

> Mary and her husband live in snowy Buffalo, New York, where they earn a combined income of $40,000. Mary is sixty-five years old, black, overweight, and plain in appearance. She is highly sociable, and she spends her free time mostly in activities related to her church. She is on dialysis for kidney problems.

Mary has health problems, lives in relative poverty, and has doubtless endured a lifetime of discrimination. But Haidt throws us a curveball: "Bob seems to have it all, and few readers of this book would prefer Mary's life to his. Yet if you had to bet on it, you should bet that Mary is happier than Bob." Haidt bases his diagnosis on a range of

---

36. For surveys of research, see Loren L. Toussaint, Amy D. Owen, and Alyssa Cheadle, "Forgive to Live: Forgiveness, Health, and Longevity," *Journal of Behavioral Medicine* 35, no. 4 (2012): 375–86; Loren L. Toussaint, Everett L. Worthington, and David R. Williams, eds., *Forgiveness and Health: Scientific Evidence and Theories Relating Forgiveness to Better Health* (Dordrecht: Springer, 2015).

37. Haidt, *Happiness Hypothesis*, 87.

factors, the first of which are Mary's advantages of stable marriage and religion—and the two are not unrelated. While simply identifying as a Christian does not reduce your likelihood of divorce, regular church attendance seems to have a significant protective effect on marriage.[38] Frequent church participation and the battery of psychological goods that comes with it enable Mary to beat out her more privileged counterpart.

What should we make of this data indicating that religious people have a happiness advantage? Harvard psychology professor Steven Pinker dismisses it with a quip from George Bernard Shaw: "The fact that a believer is happier than a skeptic is no more to the point than the fact that a drunken man is happier than a sober one."[39] But this is too easy an out. Drunk people are not more self-controlled, more likely to care for others, more deeply engaged with their work, more likely to be healthy and long-lived, or less likely to divorce than are sober people. The metaphor of religious participation as an elixir to improve mental and physical well-being is far more apt.

We Need Something Larger Than Ourselves

Haidt summarizes our basic psychological needs like this: "Just as plants need sun, water, and good soil to thrive, people need love, work, and a connection to something larger."[40] That "something larger" might take various forms, but a sense of connection to God is its most visceral incarnation. And that kind of connectivity is hard to replicate. We can commit ourselves to a political ideology, or to an ethical cause, like pursuing racial justice or campaigning against human rights abuses. These are good in themselves and will certainly bring meaning to our lives. But, as we will explore in chapter 4, when we examine the historical and philosophical foundations of many of our deepest ethical commitments, we find ourselves stumbling upon Christianity again.

So What?

We began this chapter wondering if we are simply better off without religion. My classmates at Cambridge certainly thought so. But while

---

38. For a summary of this research, see VanderWeele, "Religion and Health," 368.
39. Steven Pinker, *Enlightenment Now: The Case for Reason, Science, Humanism, and Progress* (New York: Penguin, 2018), 287.
40. Haidt, *Happiness Hypothesis*, 222.

it is impossible to explore all the relevant data, there is compelling evidence that many individual and social goods arise from religious participation, and that Christianity in particular is well aligned with the findings of modern psychology.

Does this alignment prove that Christianity is true? Certainly not! Rather, it should raise a hundred questions in our minds—questions the chapters following will explore. But the positive effects of religious participation on our mental and physical health should give us pause before we buy the claim that religion poisons everything. Tyler VanderWeele, Harvard professor and world expert on the mental and physical benefits of religious participation, believes that Christianity provides the best framework for understanding different aspects of reality.[41] He suggests that "any educated person should, at some point, have critically examined the claims for Christianity and should be able to explain why he or she does, or does not, believe them."

No matter what we currently believe, we must all confront Christianity: the most widespread belief system in the world, with the most far-reaching intellectual footprint, and a wealth of counterintuitive wisdom concerning how humans should thrive. So let's begin.

---

41. For more thoughts from Professor VanderWeele, see Tyler VanderWeele, "Evidence, Knowledge and Science: How Does Christianity Measure Up?," The Veritas Forum, February 12, 2016, http://www.veritas.org/how-does-christianity-measure-up/.

2

Doesn't Christianity Crush Diversity?

Senganglu Thaimei (Sengmei to her friends) is a *New York Times* feature waiting to be written. Born to the Rongmei tribe in the extreme northeast of India, she is a professor of English literature at Delhi University and writes short stories that reimagine the tales of her tribe from the perspective of their marginal women. Alongside this subversive retelling of tribal narratives, Professor Thaimei is keenly engaged in preserving tribal culture. And preservation is necessary. Like the other Naga tribes, the Rongmei were reached by Western missionaries in the early nineteenth century. Today, the tribe is over 80 percent Christian, and tribal traditions are declining.

For many, the idea that Christianity is a white, Western religion, intrinsically tied to cultural imperialism, stands as a major ethical barrier to considering Christ. We celebrate diversity and lament the ways religion has been used by Westerners to destroy indigenous cultures. When I met Sengmei in June 2016, my white guilt complex went into overdrive. I knew the history of British imperialism in India, but I knew nothing of the Naga tribes, and if you are looking for a cliché of missionary activity, it doesn't get much more painful than white American Baptists preaching to remote tribal communities with a tradition of headhunting!

But Sengmei's personal narrative complicates the picture. Raised by nonreligious parents, she started following Jesus when she was a teenager, after a Rongmei friend brought her to church. Today, Seng-mei is married to a man from a kindred tribe (the Liangmai), who pastors a multiethnic, multicultural church in New Delhi, and her passion for literature is surpassed only by her passion for sharing her faith.

Sengmei's story illustrates an uncomfortable truth: some of the people most affected by the wrongs of Western Christians are also some of biblical Christianity's most ardent advocates. Indeed, Seng-mei warned me not give Western missionaries too much credit for the Christianization of the Naga tribes. Westerners saw only a handful of converts, who then effectively evangelized their tribes. (The Rongmei people were reached later than the other Naga tribes, by Kuki missionaries.) And while Sengmei deplores the ways Western culture was packaged with Christianity, she is equally clear about the positive effects of Christianization, particularly on the status of tribal women.

I visited India to meet with twelve Christian academics. Ten came from Naga tribes and represented seven different indigenous languages. Tribal Indians, though not counted in the caste system, often face racial discrimination, and the fact that most are Christians adds to their alienation in a country dominated by Hinduism. But my new friends were keen to explode the misconception that Christianity is innately Western. As cultural anthropology professor and proud Naga tribe member Kanato Chophi put it, "We must abandon this absurd idea that Christianity is a Western religion."

Is Literacy Western?

Perhaps an analogy will help. It's not that there is no connection between Christianity and Western culture. Christianity dominated Europe for centuries. Many cultural artifacts produced in the West—paintings, plays, poems, and palaces—are infused with Christian ideas. But while Christianity held a monopoly on Western culture, Western culture never held a monopoly on Christianity. Indeed, calling Christianity "Western" is like calling literacy "Western." Western culture has undoubtedly been shaped by literacy, and Westerners have sought to impose literacy on others—often to the detriment of traditional living. But there are at least three reasons why no one in his or her right mind would claim that literacy is innately Western: first, literacy did not originate in the West; second, most literate people today are not Westerners; and third, it is frankly offensive to the majority world to suggest that they are literate only by appropriation. The same reasons make the claim that Christianity is a Western religion indefensible. What's more, the Bible itself rejects that claim.

The Bible's Diversity Ethics

Contrary to popular conceptions, the Christian movement was multicultural and multiethnic from the outset. Jesus scandalized his fellow Jews by tearing through racial and cultural boundaries. For instance, his famous parable of the good Samaritan was shocking to its first hearers because it cast a Samaritan—a member of a hated ethnoreligious group—as a moral example. Today's equivalent would be telling a white Christian who had been raised with unbiblical, racist assumptions a story in which the hero was a black Muslim. Likewise, John's Gospel records Jesus's life-changing conversation with a Samaritan woman at a well. Jews did not associate with Samaritans—much less a Jewish rabbi with a morally compromised Samaritan woman! But Jesus didn't care. Or rather, he cared deeply about this marginalized, religiously and sexually suspect female foreigner.

The diversity of the Christian movement kindled by Jesus caught fire after his resurrection. Before leaving them to return to his Father, Jesus commanded his Jewish disciples to "go . . . and make disciples of all nations" (Matt. 28:19), and in the book of Acts, which records the first wave of Christianity, God's Spirit enabled them to proclaim Jesus's message in different languages. Those who heard were "from every nation under heaven," including people from modern-day Iran, Iraq, Turkey, Egypt, and Italy (Acts 2:5–11).[1] Moreover, the hyper-Jewish apostle Paul, whose mission was to reach the non-Jewish world, ripped up the social barriers of his day. He wrote to the church in Colossae, "Here there is not Greek and Jew, circumcised and uncircumcised, barbarian, Scythian, slave, free; but Christ is all, and in all" (Col. 3:11);[2] and to the Galatians, "There is neither Jew nor Greek,

---

1. Parthians (Persians), Medes (Iranians), and Elamites (Iranians); residents of Mesopotamia (Iraq), Cappadocia (Turkey), Pontus (Turkey), Asia, and Phrygia (Turkey); Egyptians and Romans.
2. Scythians were a people group from a region in what is modern-day Iran.

there is neither slave nor free, there is no male and female, for you are all one in Christ Jesus" (Gal. 3:28).

Socioeconomic diversity was likewise a core ethic from the start. Jesus made loving the poor central to his teaching and ministry, and his brother James commanded Christians not to treat rich people better than poor people in their gatherings. "If you show partiality," he warned, "you are committing sin and are convicted by the law as transgressors" (James 2:8–9). In chapter 9, we will explore the radical intimacy of the language used to describe the church, binding people of different races, statuses, and backgrounds in deep fellowship. The idea that Christianity is a diversity-resistant, white Western religion of privilege is utterly irreconcilable with the New Testament.

The First African Christian

It is a common misconception that Christianity first came to Africa via white missionaries in the colonial era. But in the New Testament, we meet a highly educated African man who became a follower of Jesus centuries before Christianity penetrated Britain or America. In Acts 8, God directs the apostle Philip to the chariot of an Ethiopian eunuch. The man was "a court official of Candace, queen of the Ethiopians, who was in charge of all her treasure" (Acts 8:27). Philip hears the Ethiopian reading from the book of Isaiah and explains that Isaiah was prophesying about Jesus. The Ethiopian immediately embraces Christ and asks to be baptized (Acts 8:26–40). This story is sandwiched between the first mention of the apostle Paul and Paul's trainwreck conversion on the road to Damascus. Both stories stand out as being obviously orchestrated by God.

We have no records of how people back home responded when this Ethiopian official brought the message of Jesus to Queen Candace's court. But we do know that in the fourth century, two slave brothers precipitated the Christianization of Ethiopia and Eritrea, which led to the founding of the second officially Christian state in the world, half a century before the Christianization of Rome.[3] We also know

---

3. See Semere T. Habtemariam, "Two Slave Brothers Birthed Africa's Oldest State Church," *Christianity Today*, May 17, 2018, https://www.christianitytoday.com/history/2018/may/africa-christianity-axum-empire-ethiopian-orthodox-tewahedo.html.

that Christianity took root in Egypt in the first century and spread by the second century to Tunisia, the Sudan, and other parts of Africa. Furthermore, Africa spawned several of the early church fathers, including one of the most influential theologians in Christian history: the fourth-century scholar Augustine of Hippo. Today, while most of Northern Africa is dominated by Islam, over 60 percent of the population of sub-Saharan Africa identifies as Christian. By 2050, this part of the world could be home to 40 percent of the world's self-identifying Christians.[4] I get a foretaste of this in my own community: nearly half of the children in the Christian club at my daughters' public elementary school are first-generation African immigrants, most of them from Ethiopia and Eritrea.

My Flight Companion

I am flying as I write. My neighbor is a twelve-year-old Ghanaian boy wearing three wristbands. One identifies him as an unaccompanied minor. One reads, "Commitment to Kindness." The third says, "Walking with Jesus." My new friend has lived in the United States for a year and worships at a Ghanaian Presbyterian church. He tells me there are *lots* of Christians in Africa, but fewer in America because Americans believe in diversity. I point out that—contrary to popular belief—Christianity is the most ethnically, culturally, socioeconomically, and racially diverse belief system in all of history. The fact that it unites him and me across age, sex, race, culture, and country of origin is a case in point!

The Middle East: Home to the World's Oldest, Fastest-Growing, and Most Persecuted Churches

Centuries of Western art depicting a fair-skinned Jesus incline us to forget that Christianity came from the Middle East. Jesus's followers were first called "Christians" in Antioch, the ruins of which lie in modern-day Turkey. Today, this region has one of the smallest proportions of Christians. But what Middle Eastern Christians lack in quantity, they make up in history.

---

4. See "The Future of World Religions: Population Growth Projections, 2015–2050," Pew Research Center, April 2, 2015, http://www.pewforum.org/2015/04/02/religious-projections-2010-2050/.

Iraq is home to one of the oldest continuous Christian communities in the world—churches begun centuries before the foundation of Islam. The rapid decimation of these ancient faith communities is tragic. In 1987, the Christian population of Iraq was estimated at 1.4 million (about 8 percent of the population). After the Gulf War, that number dropped dramatically. And since the rise of ISIS, some of the oldest Christian settlements have been entirely depopulated by persecution. If we continue to believe that Christianity is a Western religion, we will have no conceptual category for what is happening today, as some of the world's oldest Christian communities are being stamped out.[5]

But the story of the Middle Eastern church is not only one of retreat. In 1979, there were an estimated five hundred Christians from a Muslim background in Iran. A year later, the Islamic Revolution transformed a relatively tolerant Muslim-majority country into an oppressive regime. Women were deprived of rights they had previously enjoyed. Extreme imams grasped power. Public executions became commonplace. This led to much religious disillusionment among Iranians. Unprecedented numbers sought refuge in Christianity, and today there are hundreds of thousands of Christians in Iran. Sprouting from a tiny seed, the Iranian church is the fastest-growing Christian movement in the world.[6]

Does Christianity Belong in India?

If Christianity is the most ethnically dispersed major world religion, Hinduism is the least.[7] India is home or ancestral home to the vast majority of Hindus.[8] Muslims form the largest religious minority, representing 14 percent of Indians, while the twenty-seven million Christians in India are slightly more than 2 percent.[9] So, does Christianity really belong in India?

---

5. See Peter Feaver and Will Inboden, "We Are Witnessing the Elimination of Christian Communities in Iraq and Syria," *Foreign Policy*, September 6, 2017, https://foreignpolicy.com/2017/09/06/we-are-witnessing-the-elimination-of-christian-communities-in-iraq-and-syria/.

6. Mark Howard, "The Story of Iran's Church in Two Sentences," The Gospel Coalition, July 30, 2016, https://www.thegospelcoalition.org/article/the-story-of-the-irans-church-in-two-sentences/.

7. See "The Global Religious Landscape," Pew Research Center, December 18, 2012, http://www.pewforum.org/2012/12/18/global-religious-landscape-exec/.

8. The other majority-Hindu countries in the world are Nepal, which borders India, and the tiny island nation of Mauritius, in the Indian Ocean.

9. "Census of India—India at a Glance: Religious Compositions," Office of the Registrar General and Census Commissioner, India, accessed September 14, 2018, http://www.censusindia.gov.in/2011census/C-01.html.

The current Hindu-nationalist government would say no. Partly in reaction to the history of colonization by Christians and Muslims, the government is seeking to equate being Indian with being Hindu. The history of British imperial rule has led many to see Christianity as synonymous with Western culture.

But India's Christian heritage is ancient. The church in South India claims a lineage going back to the first century, when the apostle Thomas is believed to have brought the gospel to India. While this is impossible to verify, historian Robert Eric Frykenberg concludes, "It seems certain that there were well-established communities of Christians in South India no later than the third and fourth centuries, and perhaps much earlier."[10] Thus, Christianity took root in India centuries before the Christianization of Britain.

One of the areas of tension between Hinduism and Christianity is precisely the question of diversity. The traditional Hindu caste system categorizes people according to prescribed social status and ties this to beliefs about Brahma, the Hindu god of creation. Brahmans (mainly priests and intellectuals) are believed to have come from Brahma's head; Kshatriyas (the warrior class), from his arms; Vaishyas (traders), from his thighs; and Sudras (menial workers), from Brahma's feet. But there was also a group below the Sudras: the Dalits, or untouchables.

In *Ants among Elephants: An Untouchable Family and the Making of Modern India*, Sujatha Gidla explains:

> The untouchables, whose special role . . . is to labor in the fields of others or to do the work that Hindu society considers filthy, are not allowed to live in the village at all. . . . They are not allowed to enter temples. Not allowed to come near sources of drinking water used by other castes. Not allowed to eat sitting next to a caste Hindu or to use the same utensils.

Gidla references thousands of other "restrictions and indignities." The caste system is no longer officially endorsed, and India's current president comes from a Dalit family. But its vestiges remain.

---

10. Robert Eric Frykenberg, *Christianity in India: From Beginnings to the Present* (Oxford: Oxford University Press, 2010), 115.

"Every day in an Indian newspaper," writes Gidla, "you can read of an untouchable beaten or killed for wearing sandals [or] riding a bicycle."[11]

The Bible, by contrast, insists on the equal value and dignity of all humans. The first churches united high and low classes, rich and poor, slaves and masters, and people of different racial backgrounds in uncomfortable, boundary-crushing fellowship. Tragically, many majority-Christian societies have failed to deliver on this promise and have created stratification that demeans some and exalts others. The treatment of untouchables in India is painfully reminiscent of black American history. But as we will explore later in this book, racial segregation and stratification have no foundation in Christianity: indeed, they are specifically condemned.

Given this context, it is perhaps not surprising that a disproportionate number of India's Christians come from the untouchable class. If the dominant belief system places little value on your life, a faith that elevates you to being a worth-dying-for child of God becomes attractive. Mother Teresa exemplified this in her care for the castaways of Indian society. She described her ministry in Calcutta as meeting Jesus "in the distressing disguise of the poor," a reference to Jesus's hard-hitting parable of the sheep and the goats.[12] But while her work is generally celebrated in India, the impact of colonial rule and the insensitivity of many Western missionaries have left deep scars. Gandhi is supposed to have said: "I like your Christ. I do not like your Christians. Your Christians are so unlike your Christ." The mind-set that melds Christianity with Western cultural dominance does not belong in India. But biblical Christianity, which lays a foundation for human equality and love across differences, certainly does.

Beautiful Cows!

While following Christ in a majority-Hindu country presents challenges, connection to such an ancient culture can aid understanding of biblical texts.

11. Sujatha Gidla, *Ants among Elephants: An Untouchable Family and the Making of Modern India* (New York: Farrar, Straus and Giroux, 2017), 4.

12. Mother Teresa, *In the Heart of the World: Thoughts, Stories and Prayers*, ed. Becky Benenate (Novato, CA: New World Library, 1997), 23.

This came home to me in a conversation with a Hindu-background Nepalese friend at church. I asked her what her name—Deepa—means. She answered, "Light," and returned the question. I gave her my usual line, which always gets a laugh: "Rebecca has three meanings: a good wife, one of enchanting beauty, and a cow." But Deepa's response caught me off guard: "A cow! How lovely!" I explained that in the West calling a woman a cow is not a compliment! She explained that in Nepal cows are revered. Even when it came to understanding my own biblical name, I had a cultural disadvantage.

If I want to appreciate the texture of the Scriptures, I need to listen to brothers and sisters who grew up in cultures closer to those of the ancient Near East than my own. Every culture has its blind spots. Diversity helps us all to see.

China: The Largest Christian Country in the World?

While the church in China likely does not reach back as far as in Egypt, India, or Iraq, there is evidence of Christianity from as early as the eighth century AD.[13] For most of the twelve hundred years since, however, Christianity had not truly gained a foothold. Until quite recently, that is. Today, despite frequent government crackdowns, the church in China is growing in a way that almost no one could have predicted. I say *almost* no one, because there is a sense in which one Western missionary to China did predict it.

James Hudson Taylor died in Changsha in 1905, fifty years after he first set foot in Shanghai. Unlike many other missionaries of his day, Taylor refused to package Christianity with Western culture. He wore Chinese clothes, grew a pigtail (as was the custom for Chinese men), and renounced Western comforts. Taylor had a deep love for the people he served. He undertook medical training and regularly tended two hundred patients a day. He reflected, "I have found that there are three stages in every great work of God: first, it is impossible, then it is difficult, then it is done."[14]

---

13. A Nestorian monument inscribed with the date 781 was discovered near Xi'an, Shaanxi, in 1623. See Kathleen L. Lodwick, *How Christianity Came to China: A Brief History* (Minneapolis: Fortress, 2016), 2.

14. Quoted in Leslie T. Lyall, *A Passion for the Impossible: The Continuing Story of the Mission Hudson Taylor Began* (London: OMF, 1965), 5.

Taylor lived between stages one and two in the conversion of the country he loved. We appear today to be living between stages two and three. It is hard to get accurate data on the number of Christians in China. Due to government persecution, many worship in unofficial "house churches." But, as noted in my introduction, conservative estimates in 2010 put China's Christian population at over sixty-eight million, and the number of Chinese Protestants has grown by an average of 10 percent annually since 1979. Experts like Fenggang Yang predict that there will be more Christians in China than in the United States by 2030, and that China could be a majority-Christian country by 2050.[15] Of course, there is much uncertainty. Government resistance to Christianity seems to be surging. But if China does swing from Communist to Christian in the next thirty years, the consequences for global politics could be immense.

The Park Incident

When my first daughter was four, we were playing in the sand at a local park. An older, Chinese-speaking woman was there with her grandson. My daughter asked her name and where she came from— then whether she trusted in Jesus. I cringed. The woman replied, "I'm sorry?" My daughter repeated the question: "Do you trust in Jesus?" I prayed that the ground would swallow me up. Then, in a barely audible voice, I explained that we were Christians, and that my daughter sometimes liked to ask if other people trust in Jesus too. The woman replied: "Oh, do I trust in Jesus? Yes! I do trust in Jesus! It's the most important thing in the world! I'm so glad you do too!"

I had looked at an older, Chinese-speaking woman and assumed she was not a Christian. She had looked at a younger, white-British woman and assumed the same. We were both wrong.

Reverse Traffic

The missionary zeal of many Asian Christians can be disconcerting for Westerners. When a high school friend of mine moved to South

---

15. Antonia Blumberg, "China on Track to Become World's Largest Christian Country by 2025, Experts Say," *Huffpost*, April 22, 2014, http://www.huffingtonpost.com/2014/04/22/china-largest-christian-country_n_5191910.html. For commentary on this, see Jamil Anderlini, "The Rise of Christianity in China," *Financial Times*, November 7, 2014. https://www.ft.com/content/a6d2a690-6545-11e4-91b1-00144feabdc0.

Korea to teach, her Facebook posts were sprinkled with good-natured complaints about locals trying to convert her. Friends invited her to church. Strangers accosted her in the street to tell her about Jesus. And (my favorite) her personal space was invaded on a train, when someone shoved an earphone into her ear so she could listen to a sermon. She wanted to sleep in on Sunday mornings. Couldn't they let a nice white, Western, post-Christian girl be?

My friend's experience illustrates our need for an image upgrade rooted in a genuine mind-set change. Many of us associate Christianity with white, Western imperialism. There are reasons for this—some quite ugly, regrettable reasons. But most of the world's Christians are neither white nor Western, and Christianity is getting less white Western by the day. This is partly thanks to the missionary activities of non-Westerners. For instance, despite its small population and Christian minority (29 percent), South Korea exports the second largest number of missionaries of any country in the world.[16] As Yale law professor and leading black public intellectual Stephen Carter has observed, there is "a difficulty endemic to today's secular left: an all-too-frequent weird refusal to acknowledge the demographics of Christianity." Carter points out that in the US, black women are by far the most Christian demographic, while "around the globe, the people most likely to be Christians are women of color." He warns, "When you mock Christians, you're not mocking who you think you are."[17] Those of us who grew up in the West must adjust to the fact that our culture does not own Christianity. In fact, quite the reverse.

I got my first taste of reverse traffic when I was sixteen. I had gone with my youth group to serve in an orphanage in Romania. On Sunday, we worshiped with a small house church. The girl leading worship was my age. I had been raised in London. She had been raised under Communism on a farm in rural Romania. When she entered the room, her guitar slung over her shoulder, she threw her arms around me and shouted: "Sister! I am so happy there are Christians even in England!"

---

16. See "Over 27,000 Korean Missionaries Ministering Worldwide, according to Study," *Christianity Daily*, June 8, 2016, http://www.christianitydaily.com/articles/8179/20160608/over-27-000-korean-missionaries-ministering-worldwide-according-study.htm.
17. Stephen L. Carter, "The Ugly Coded Critique of Chick-fil-A's Christianity," *Bloomberg*, April 21, 2018, https://www.bloomberg.com/view/articles/2018-04-21/criticism-of-christians-and-chick-fil-a-has-troubling-roots.

What about America?

When I first moved to the US and discovered that many people associate evangelical Christianity with racism, I was bewildered. The New Testament is one of the most emphatically anti-racist texts ever written. Fellowship across racial and ethnic differences is as intrinsic to the message of Jesus as care for the poor. And yet there is a painful association between racism and the breed of American Christianity that stops its ears to the Scriptures and conflates white-centered nationalism with biblical faith.

In a 1960 interview, Martin Luther King lamented, "I think it is one of the tragedies of our nation—one of the shameful tragedies—that 11 o'clock on Sunday morning is one of the most segregated hours."[18] In the same interview, King declared, "Any church that stands against integration and that has a segregated body is standing against the spirit and the teachings of Jesus Christ." Read the New Testament, and you will find that trying to marry biblical Christianity to white-centric nationalism is like trying to marry a cat to a mouse: one is designed to hunt the other, not mate with it.

Today, American churches often fail to live up to the ideals of biblical diversity, both via lack of integration between black and white Americans and by portraying immigration as an erosion of America's Christian identity. In fact, the opposite is true: most immigrants to the US are Christians, and the racial demographic that is eroding Christianity in America is white. We must not let an unbiblical white-centrism define our view of Christianity. In a 2017 *New Yorker* article on the future of evangelicalism, New York pastor and best-selling author Tim Keller writes:

> The enormous energy of the churches in the global South and East has begun to spill over into the cities of North America, where a new, multiethnic evangelicalism is growing steadily. Non-Western missionaries have started thousands of new urban churches there since the nineteen-seventies. Here in New York City, even within Manhattan, I have seen scores of churches begun over the last fifteen years that are fully evangelical by our definition, only a minority of which are white.[19]

---

18. Martin Luther King Jr., "Meet the Press" interview, April 17, 1960.
19. Timothy Keller, "Can Evangelicalism Survive Donald Trump and Roy Moore?," *The New Yorker*, December 19, 2017, https://www.newyorker.com/news/news-desk/can-evangelicalism-survive-donald-trump-and-roy-moore.

American churches have far to go in living up to the biblical promise. And yet my Sunday mornings involve a rich experience of diversity. To my left is a Chinese grad student from MIT. To my right, a Harvard PhD student from Nigeria. Behind me sits an African American woman with her teenage son. In front, is a white manual laborer in his sixties. Our pastor is blue eyed and white; his wife is Native American. Last night, my Bible study group comprised fourteen people who had been raised in eight countries across four continents. Forming bonds across differences is often hard. But it is as intrinsic to Christian community as singing.

The Most Diverse Movement in All of History

The fact that Christianity has been a multicultural, multiracial, multiethnic movement since its inception does not excuse the ways Westerners have abused Christian identity to crush other cultures. After the conversion of the Roman emperor Constantine in the fourth century, Western Christianity went from being the faith of a persecuted minority to being linked with the political power of an empire, and power is perhaps humanity's most dangerous drug.

But, ironically, our habit of equating Christianity with Western culture is itself an act of Western bias. The last book of the Bible paints a picture of the end of time, when "a great multitude that no one could number, from every nation, from all tribes and peoples and languages" will worship Jesus (Rev. 7:9). This was the multicultural vision of Christianity from the beginning. For all the wrong turns made by Western Christians in the last two thousand years, when we look at church growth globally today, it is not crazy to think that this vision could ultimately be realized. So, if you care about diversity, don't dismiss Christianity: it is the most diverse, multiethnic, and multicultural movement in all of history.

3

How Can You Say There's
Only One True Faith?

In 2015, I met an Iranian science professor from a world-class university. I asked him how he came to be a Christian.[1] He replied, "Through the ministry of J. S. Bach!" My new friend had been raised in a Muslim family. But when the Islamic revolution swept through Iran in 1980, he abandoned his familial faith. Alongside his scientific studies, my friend was a semiprofessional flutist. Classical music was banned by the new government, so music lovers crowded into private houses to savor illicit sonatas. Before one secret concert, my friend rehearsed a Bach flute sonata with his musical mentor but was stopped a few bars in: "I cannot hear the cross of Christ in what you are playing," his mentor complained. My friend was bewildered: with little knowledge of Christianity, he had no idea what his mentor meant. But the challenge stuck with him. Gradually, he began to apprehend the profoundly Christian fabric of Bach's works; and when he first walked into a church a few years later, he sensed the same reality.

At the conference where we met, I led a session exploring how Christian professors might grow in their ability to persuade skeptical audiences to consider Jesus. My friend was troubled. In Iran, he had witnessed the full force of religious coercion. He had converted from

---

1. My friend travels back to Iran regularly and could face repercussions if he was publicly known to have converted to Christianity. For this reason, I will not mention his name.

Islam to Christianity partly as a reaction *against* that force. Now a Christian, he longed for others to come to know Jesus. But he was wrestling: was it wrong to try to persuade someone to change his or her beliefs?

My friend is an expert in breast cancer diagnostics, so I asked him to imagine a scene. He is sitting across from a middle-aged woman from a poor educational background. She has just told him that she believes she's *not* at risk of breast cancer and has refused a mammogram. How should he respond?

The Universal Offense

When questions of truth carry life-and-death consequences, we see persuasion as an act of love. But what species of truth is religious truth? Are the various world religions making competing claims on reality, or are they simply different voicings of one truth? And, if they are making competing claims, does disagreement entail hostility, or can people of conflicting beliefs live peacefully together?

To our modern ears, the idea of one religion claiming to be *the* truth is anathema. Most religious claims cannot be proved beyond reasonable doubt (at least not until one dies or the world ends), so the idea that they are objective and universal seems like a category confusion. It is one thing to say that Christianity is true for you, but to claim that Jesus rightly demands the allegiance of every human being—regardless of one's cultural background or current beliefs— seems offensive and absurd. As one bumper sticker puts it, "My God is too big for any one religion."

The Elephant in the Room

The view that all religions are equal paths to truth is often illustrated by a parable from an ancient Hindu text. The story tells of a group of blind men describing an elephant. One man touches its trunk and compares it to a snake. Another feels its ear and compares it to a fan. The third man places his hand on the elephant's leg and says it is like a tree trunk. A fourth pushes on the elephant's side and insists it is like a wall. The fifth man holds the tail and finds it rope-like. The last man feels a tusk and declares that the elephant is like a spear.

This story paints a vivid picture of our individual limitations. It is a corrective to our natural arrogance and seems to be a humble approach, offering a framework for respecting all religions equally. But on closer inspection, the elephant paradigm creates more problems than it solves. Here are seven.

The Problem of Respect

The story of the elephant seems respectful: religions are not right or wrong; each holds an aspect of the truth. But the tale works only because the narrator is *not* blind. He or she sees the whole picture and smiles indulgently at the blind believers arguing over their seemingly contradictory faiths. To say that Christianity and Islam or Islam and Hinduism are just two sides of the same truth coin reduces pluralism to a patronizing posture by which we don't respect others enough to take their beliefs seriously. Boil the elephant paradigm down, and it recalls physicist Wolfgang Pauli's reported critique of a junior scientist's paper: "It's not even wrong!"

Conversely, to say "I think you are wrong about this" need not be disrespectful or unkind. For Christians, who are commanded to love even their enemies—let alone people with whom they merely disagree—it must not be. One of my wisest and gentlest seminary professors put it like this: "It's often said that you should respect other people's beliefs. But that's wrong: what's vital is that you respect other *people*." Indeed, when examined more closely, attempting to persuade others to change their beliefs is a sign of respect. You are treating them as thinking agents with the ability to decide what they believe, not just products of their cultural environment. We should not be offended when people challenge our beliefs: we should be flattered!

Take a conversation I had with a Jewish-atheist friend after an event we had both attended at Harvard, in which the chair of the philosophy department had discussed the Bible with a leading New Testament scholar. This friend and I have been debating faith questions on and off for years. On this occasion I said to him, "I know you think that what I believe is crazy." His then-girlfriend (a gentler soul than either of us) interjected, "I'm sure he doesn't think your beliefs are *crazy*!" But I persisted, "Yes, he does! I believe the entire universe revolves around a first-century Palestinian Jew who died on a cross and was supposedly raised from the dead. That's crazy, right?" My atheist friend agreed. I pointed out that his scientific atheism, particularly when coupled with his belief in universal human equality, required him to believe some crazy things too. This friend is one of the smartest guys I know: he might well win a Nobel Prize someday. But I believe that he is wrong on the most important questions that can be asked—and he thinks I am wrong too! Not just slightly wrong, but completely and profoundly wrong.

Such directness would not fly in most relationships. We are all more governed by our feelings than by our rationality, and emotions run high in debates about beliefs. But disagreement is not evidence of disrespect. Indeed, I debate hardest with the people I respect the most, because I take their ideas seriously. But our society seems to be losing the art of debate within friendships, and we instead surround ourselves with people who think like us.

This happens across the political spectrum. In a *New York Times* op-ed entitled "The Dangers of Echo Chambers on Campus," Pulitzer Prize–winning journalist Nicholas Kristof confessed, "We [liberals] champion tolerance, except for conservatives and evangelical Christians. We want to be inclusive of people who don't look like us—so long as they think like us."[2] This is a risk for us all. If our commitment to diversity is more than skin deep, we must cultivate deep friendships with smart people with whom we fundamentally disagree.

To be sure, it is possible to hide bullying under the banner of free speech and open disagreement. In conversations with people who are less educated than we are, or who are living as religious minorities, we must be sensitive to the power dynamics at play. We must not steamroll others, whether we are advocating for Christianity, atheism, or any other belief. But for all the risks associated with taking people's beliefs seriously enough to disagree, there is a greater risk in not doing so. We start believing that our friends are not even wrong, we fail to test our own beliefs, and—where beliefs carry life-and-death consequences—we fail to love our friends.

---

2. https://www.nytimes.com/2016/12/10/opinion/sunday/the-dangers-of-echo-chambers-on -campus.html.

But are there real consequences to disagreements about religious truth, or does religious truth simply boil down to cultural preference? If I say, "Christianity is true, and Hinduism, Islam, and Buddhism are not," is that like saying, "Stop smoking; it could kill you," or is it more like saying, "My grandmother's cooking is better than yours"?

The Problem of Truth

In 2016, the Oxford English Dictionary's word of the year was *post-truth*: "relating to or denoting circumstances in which objective facts are less influential in shaping public opinion than appeals to emotion and personal belief."[3] In the same year, Americans on all sides lamented and watched with horror as unsubstantiated stories gained political mileage. And yet the post-truth mentality has been central to our view of religion for decades. Have we been seeing the consequences of this in public life? Or is religious belief in a different category, because it is personal?

In 2017, the #MeToo movement hit. Thousands of women stepped out of silence to reveal the abuse and harassment they had endured at the wandering hands of powerful men. Oprah Winfrey made an impassioned speech at the Golden Globe Awards commending the women who had spoken out: "What I know for sure," she declared, "is that speaking your truth is the most powerful tool we all have."[4]

The truth of a sexual assault is undoubtedly personal: it is in an important sense "your truth." But if that truth is not also objective, it is a lie. The women who have spoken out are ultimately commended not for telling *their* truth but for telling *the* truth. The truth is often hard to prove—which is why, tragically, so many women do not speak out, fearing their testimony will not be believed against that of a more powerful man. But no one doubts that there is truth to be discovered here—truth that is personal *and* objective.

Of course, in some ways, our religious convictions are different from our beliefs about our personal histories. We are eyewitnesses to

---

3. https://en.oxforddictionaries.com/definition/post-truth.
4. CNN Entertainment, January 10, 2018, https://www.cnn.com/2018/01/08/entertainment/oprah-globes-speech-transcript/index.html.

our own lives in a way that we cannot be to the ancient history on which faith often rests. And yet sometimes we find that our beliefs about our own narratives are wrong. Imagine a woman discovering that her husband has been cheating on her for years. She is suddenly forced to change her beliefs about her own life as she reinterprets data in the light of this new information. In this sense, our beliefs about our own lives and our religious beliefs are cut from the same cloth. Both are personal. Both are grounded in the best evidence we have. Both make claims on truth. But both are also subject to error.

It is my personal belief that Jesus is God in the flesh, my only hope in life or death. This belief shapes me deeply, and I have had many experiences that have seemed to support it. But if my atheist friends are right, then my trust in Jesus is mistaken. However deeply I believe, when I die, my life will end. Jesus will not return and call me back to life. I will simply rot. We cannot categorize religious beliefs as purely subjective simply because they are personal. Physicist Neil deGrasse Tyson famously quipped to Stephen Colbert, "The good thing about science" is that "it's true whether or not you believe in it."[5] But this is not limited to science: it's the good thing about truth. Period.

In fact, the existence of scientific truth exposes another fault line within the mind-set that claims religious truth cannot be right or wrong. What happens when religious belief clashes with scientific evidence? My scientist friends are the first to acknowledge that science does not *prove* hypotheses but rather seeks to develop hypotheses to fit the available data. The more science advances, the more we are confronted with counterintuitive data—particularly on the macro and micro scales. For instance, things we perceive as solid (like the chair on which I am sitting right now) turn out to be 99.9999 percent empty space. But while most of us would defend the right of a religious person to hold unscientific beliefs (for example, the belief that the sun rotates around the earth), we would not think this discredited the reality of objective truth in science, and on important points, we would want to persuade that person to change his or her mind.

---

5. https://www.salon.com/2014/03/11/neil_degrasse_tyson_science_is_true_whether_or_not _you_believe_in_it/.

The Problem of History

The incompatibility of different religions comes into sharp focus when we examine history. Historical truth is challenging: we all bring our individual and cultural biases to questions of history, and sources have often been distorted or selectively destroyed. But we cannot abandon the search for objective truth in history. There is just too much at stake.

We feel this most keenly when people deny vital historical facts. For instance, while the evidence that Hitler's regime systematically exterminated six million Jews is overwhelming, many attempts have been made to deny this truth. These attempts must be rejected. Likewise, the history of slavery in America, which we will return to in chapter 10, or the assassination of Martin Luther King. These things happened. They are jagged, historical facts and must be acknowledged, irrespective of perspective. But what about questions of ancient history?

The further we rewind the historical clock, the harder it is to be sure. For example, we have persuasive evidence that Julius Caesar was assassinated on March 15, 44 BC. It is possible that our sources are unreliable and that Julius Caesar was assassinated on February 15, or that he was not assassinated at all. But even if we have less certainty about this historical happening than more recent or larger-scale events, this does not move the assassination of Julius Caesar into the realm of subjective reality. Julius Caesar was either assassinated on March 15, 44 BC, or he was not.

What light does this shed on religious truth?

The central truth claim on which Christianity stands or falls is that Jesus was physically raised from the dead. There is historical evidence for this claim, outrageous as it may seem. Alternative theories (as we will see in chap. 6) are surprisingly unpersuasive, and the extraordinary phenomenon of the early church erupting from a small group of dispirited and cowardly followers of a crucified rabbi cries out for an ignition spark.[6] But whether we think the evidence is strong or weak, it is still a historical claim. Just as Julius Caesar either was assassinated

---

6. For a serious historical treatment of the resurrection, see N. T. Wright, *The Resurrection of the Son of God* (Minneapolis: Fortress, 2003). For a short article by an MIT professor, see Ian Hutchinson, "Can a Scientist Believe in the Resurrection?," The Veritas Forum, March 25, 2016, http://www.veritas.org/can-scientist-believe-resurrection-three-hypotheses/.

on March 15, 44 BC, or was not, so Jesus either was raised from the dead in ca. AD 33 or was not. Our believing or not believing in the resurrection may change *us*, but it does not change the objective reality of what took place two thousand years ago. And this is a question on which the three great monotheistic religions disagree. Christians believe that Jesus rose from the dead. Muslims believe that Jesus did not die, but that he was instead taken up into heaven. Jews (and atheists and agnostics, for that matter) believe that Jesus died and remained dead. These claims are mutually exclusive. At this foundational level, religious truth cannot be untangled from historical truth. Even when we narrow our scope to monotheistic faiths, to say that all religions are equally true is to lose our grip on history.

The Problem of Conversion

My friend Praveen Sethupathy is a professor of genetics at Cornell University. When he was a freshman (also at Cornell), a classmate asked him what he believed, and he said he was a Hindu; but the question unsettled him. Praveen's parents had immigrated from India. He had grown up with Hindu culture but had little knowledge of Hindu beliefs. So he started to explore. Praveen dug into ancient Hindu texts and appreciated their richness. But the process sensitized him to the fact that other world religions made different truth claims. With the mind-set of a budding scientist, he did not want to assume that the religion he had inherited was right, so he explored other beliefs and read other religious texts. In the Gospels, Praveen found something that surprised him: Jesus was the supposed hero of the story, but at the climax of the tale, he hung naked, disfigured, and pathetic on a cross—quite unlike the Hindu superhero, Krishna. But somehow the power inversion of this crucified man attracted Praveen. After months of reading, questioning, and sifting through evidence, he started following Jesus.

This change was disturbing for Praveen's family. Living as members of a racial and religious minority in America, they feared Praveen was rejecting his Indian heritage and wondered whether he would change his name (which is steeped in Hindu lore) to a Western-sounding name like Peter or John. But Praveen reassured them that following Jesus did not entail rejecting the culture he loved: "Becoming Christian had nothing to do with rejecting my Indian heritage, or being called by a different name. Rather, it was about embracing God's interwoven presence in the history of mankind, Christ's love and sacrifice for us, and our desperate need for him."[7] There were certainly aspects of his Hindu heritage that he would need to leave to follow Christ. But Praveen was proud to be Indian, and proud of the rich culture from which he came and which he planned to pass on to his children.

Praveen came to Christianity after a period of careful reflection. Now a professor of genetics, he is used to evaluating evidence and forming hypotheses to fit the data. It remains his firm belief that Jesus is the Son of God and the Savior of the world. Much as he appreciates his Hindu heritage, he does not believe the fundamental claims of Hinduism to be true. Ask Praveen how he can say that there is only one true faith, and he will tell you that he has no choice: to claim that Hinduism and Christianity are ultimately compatible is to do violence to both.

At the other end of the spectrum, I have friends who were raised Christian but no longer believe. Some have been hurt by experiences in church. Others have lost faith in Christianity's claims. Some are now agnostic; others atheist. I care about these friends, and I long for them to turn back to Jesus. But I would not dream of telling them that Christianity and atheism are two paths to the same truth. When they say they do not trust in Jesus, I respect them enough to believe them.

The Problem of Ethics

My secular friends celebrate religious diversity and uphold the rights of religious minorities to practice their faith. This is a beautiful instinct. But what happens when religious beliefs clash with core secular ethics? Many who believe that all religions are equally true, or at least that no one should claim his or her own religion is *the* truth, also affirm universal ethical beliefs: for example, that racism is wrong, that people should have freedom of sexual expression, or that men and women should be valued equally. Few think these beliefs are contingent on cultural context. But if we say to our traditional Muslim

---

7. Praveen Sethupathy, "My Name Means 'Skillful,'" *The Curator Magazine*, March 4, 2013, http://www.curatormagazine.com/author/praveensethupathy/.

friends, "We uphold your right to be a Muslim, so long as you embrace equal roles for men and women, the legitimacy of same-sex marriage, and the freedom of your teenagers to experiment sexually," are we truly upholding their right to practice their faith? Even if we chose to give some religious people a pass to believe things we find ethically problematic, particularly if they are living as ethnic minorities and wield no political power, few of us will consign our deepest ethical beliefs to the "true-for-me-but-not-for-you" bucket. Again, there is too much at stake.

The Problem of Monotheism

It is tempting in our melting-pot societies to think that living alongside people of different faiths is a purely modern phenomenon. But people of different religious beliefs have been coexisting for millennia, sometimes in conflict and sometimes in peace. One way in which religious difference was negotiated was through polytheism. This allowed different tribes to worship their own local gods, and regional gods to be integrated with a larger set. Polytheism certainly did not prevent interreligious violence or desire for conquest, as evidenced by the Greek and Roman Empires. But there was the possibility of accommodation: everyone's gods could be gods without necessarily hurting anyone's dignity.

This potential for accommodation was compromised, however, when a fiercely monotheistic faith emerged. Judaism introduced a fundamental belief that Israel's covenant God had created the heavens and the earth, a fearless assertion that this God is the only true God, and a foundational command to worship him alone. Christianity and, later, Islam built upon these foundations, asserting that there was one true, universal God, who had uniquely revealed himself, and that other so-called gods are idols.

Judaism, Christianity, and Islam have been asserting that there is only one true faith among a panoply of other "gods" for millennia. The early Jews made this claim among the pagan, polytheistic religions of the ancient Near East. The early Christians made this claim among the pagan, polytheistic religions of the Roman Empire. Monotheism is at its heart exclusive and universal. It proclaims that there is only one true God, who made the universe and demands the allegiance of every human. Claiming that monotheism fits with an all-religions-are-one approach is like claiming someone can be in two places at one time: it's possible, but only if you kill the person first and dismember the body!

The Problem of Jesus

The final problem with the elephant approach is the problem of Jesus. While it might be possible to square some religions with each other, particularly those with multiple gods, Christianity is like a puzzle piece drawn from the wrong set: however hard we try to bend the edges, it won't fit. This problem stems both from Jesus's direct statements—for example, his famous assertion "I am the way, and the truth, and the life. No one comes to the Father except through me" (John 14:6)—and from the actions by which he claimed to be God in the flesh, a claim that both Jews and Muslims hold to be blasphemous.

One of my favorite examples of this distinctiveness of Jesus comes early in his ministry. Jesus was teaching in a house so packed that no one else could squeeze in. Determined to get their paralyzed comrade in front of this healer, a group of friends dug a hole in the roof and lowered him down. Jesus looked at the man and said, "Son, your sins are forgiven" (Mark 2:5). The crowd must have been confused: Why was Jesus talking about forgiveness, when what the man clearly needed was healing? The religious leaders were outraged: "Why does this man speak like that? He is blaspheming! Who can forgive sins but God alone?" (Mark 2:7).

Jesus asked, "Which is easier, to say to the paralytic, 'Your sins are forgiven,' or to say, 'Rise, take up your bed and walk'?" (Mark 2:9). He then proved his authority to forgive sins by telling the paralyzed man to get up. Notice that he did not deny the premise of the religious leaders' complaint: only God has the right to forgive sins. But he demonstrated that their conclusion was wrong: Jesus had that right, because he was God in the flesh.

Later, Jesus looked into the eyes of a bereaved woman and said: "I am the resurrection and the life. Whoever believes in me, though he die, yet shall he live, and everyone who lives and believes in me shall never die" (John 11:25–26). This is not the teaching of a good man. As

Oxford professor and author C. S. Lewis argued, this is the teaching of an egotistical maniac or an evil manipulator, or God in the flesh.

Time and again, the Gospels record Jesus doing outrageous things only God can do: commanding the wind, forgiving sins, feeding multitudes, raising the dead. His universal claim is finally rammed home in his parting words to his disciples: "All authority in heaven and on earth has been given to me. Go therefore and make disciples of all nations, baptizing them in the name of the Father and of the Son and of the Holy Spirit, teaching them to observe all that I have commanded you" (Matt. 28:18–20).

Jesus claims rule over all of heaven and earth. He presents himself not as one possible path to God, but as God himself. We may choose to disbelieve him. But he cannot be one truth among many. He has not left us that option.

4

Doesn't Religion Hinder Morality?

In 2014, ISIS attacked a village of Kurdish-speaking Yazidis in Iraq. Nadia Murad, aged twenty-one, was taken to a slave market in Mosul and bought by a judge, whose job involved condemning people to death for minor offenses. The judge raped Nadia daily. He beat her when she displeased him. When she tried to escape, he let his guards gang-rape her. "You're my fourth sabiyya [slave]," the judge told Nadia. "The other three are Muslim now. I did that for them. Yazidis are infidels—that's why we are doing this. It's to help you."[1]

We read this account with horror and disgust. But the judge's actions were not unjust according to his moral code. ISIS's "Research and Fatwa Department" had studied the Yazidis and concluded that they were nonbelievers, whose enslavement was justified under Shariah law. An informational booklet, *Questions and Answers on Taking Captives and Slaves*, gave their fighters guidelines. Examples included:

> *Question*: Is it permissible to have intercourse with a female slave who has not reached puberty?
> *Answer*: It is permissible to have intercourse with a female slave who hasn't reached puberty if she is fit for intercourse.

---

1. "Nadia Murad's Tale of Captivity with Islamic State," *The Economist*, November 30, 2017, https://www.economist.com/news/books-and-arts/21731804-young-yazidi-iraqi-was-raped-daily -her-abuse-blessed-jihadist-groups-twisted.

> *Question*: Is it permissible to sell a female captive?
>
> *Answer*: It is permissible to buy, sell, or gift female captives or slaves, for they are merely property.[2]

The plan to eradicate the Yazidis was two-pronged: kill the men and older women, rape and enslave the young women. The men of ISIS were fulfilling not just their desires but also their religious duty.

Problems with the Claim That Religion Hurts Morality

In 1999, Nobel Prize–winning physicist Steven Weinberg made this claim: "Religion is an insult to human dignity. With or without it you would have good people doing good things and evil people doing evil things. But for good people to do evil things, that takes religion."[3]

At first, this logic seems compelling. While we may doubt that the judge who abused Nadia Murad was in any meaningful sense a "good person," we cannot deny the litany of evils perpetrated by people of all faiths. And sometimes we can see underlying virtue in religiously motivated acts of violence: for example, the suicide bomber who shows great courage in service of his cause and genuinely believes that he is acting for good by destroying himself and others. But while religion has certainly motivated people to harm others in self-sacrificing ways, there are three problems with the claim that religion hinders morality.

The first problem is its lack of specificity. Religion is an all-encompassing term, stretching from ISIS to the Amish, and from pagan child sacrifice to Buddhist meditation. Saying that religion hinders morality is like saying philosophy hinders morality: we must evaluate each religious tradition and differentiate between them as we would between Marxism and Libertarianism. No one would look at Stalin's genocides and say, "Philosophy hinders morality," or even, "Socialism hinders morality," though there is clear connective tissue between socialism and the Marxist philosophy that motivated Stalin's evil acts. To make any meaningful statement about religion and morality, we must be more specific.

---

2. Nadia Murad, *The Last Girl: My Story of Captivity, and My Fight against the Islamic State* (New York: Duggan, 2017), ix–x.

3. This widely reprinted remark about religion made at a science conference in April 1999 in Washington, DC, won Weinberg the Freedom from Religion Foundation's "Emperor Has No Clothes Award." Freedom from Religion Foundation, accessed September 14, 2018, https://ffrf.org/outreach/awards/emperor-has-no-clothes-award/item/11907-steven-weinberg.

The second problem with the claim that religion hinders morality is that it does not fit the data. Of course, there are millions of instances every day of religious people acting immorally—sometimes in dramatic, headline-grabbing ways. But there is also substantial evidence that religious practice correlates with a range of moral goods. In his 2018 book *The Character Gap: How Good Are We?*, philosopher Christian Miller observes that "literally *hundreds* of studies" link religious participation with better moral outcomes.[4] For example, sociologists Christopher Ellison and Kristen Anderson discovered that levels of domestic violence in a US sample were almost twice as high for men who did not attend church versus those who attended once a week or more.[5] Religious participation has also been linked to lower rates for forty-three other crimes.[6] In North America, regular service attenders donate 3.5 times the money given by their nonreligious counterparts per year and volunteer more than twice as much.[7]

Such studies seldom make the news: "Christian donates to charity" is hardly headline material! And as atheist social psychologist Jonathan Haidt warns, "You can't use the New Atheists as your guide" on these matters, as "the new atheists conduct biased reviews of the literature and conclude that there is no good evidence on any benefits except the health benefits of religion." But the weight of evidence, as Haidt observes, is not in favor of the "religion hinders morality" hypothesis: "Even if you excuse secular liberals from charity because they vote for government welfare programs," he notes, "it is awfully hard to explain why secular liberals give so little blood."[8]

---

4. Christian B. Miller, *The Character Gap: How Good Are We?* (Oxford: Oxford University Press, 2018), 239.

5. Christopher Ellison and Kristen Anderson, "Religious Involvement and Domestic Violence among U.S. Couples," *Journal for the Scientific Study of Religion* 40, no. 2 (2001): 269–86. For similar results, see D. M. Fergusson et al., "Factors Associated with Reports of Wife Assault in New Zealand," *Journal of Marriage and the Family* 48, no. 2 (1986): 407–12; and C. G. Ellison, J. P. Bartkowski, and K. L. Anderson, "Are There Religious Variations in Domestic Violence?," *Journal of Family Issues* 20, no. 1 (1999): 87–113.

6. See T. D. Evans et al., "Religion and Crime Reexamined: The Impact of Religion, Secular Controls, and Social Ecology on Adult Criminality," *Criminology* 33, no. 2 (1995): 195–217.

7. For a summary of this research, see Arthur Brooks, *Who Really Cares* (New York: Basic Books, 2006).

8. Jonathan Haidt, "Moral Psychology and the Misunderstanding of Religion," *Edge*, September 21, 2007, https://www.edge.org/conversation/jonathan_haidt-moral-psychology-and-the-misunderstanding-of-religion.

The third problem with the claim that religion hinders morality cuts deeper still. It assumes there is a universal measuring stick of morality, sized by self-evident truths to which all of us (Christian, atheist, Muslim, Hindu, Buddhist, Jew) can assent. But as Nadia Murad's story reminds us with terrible poignancy, there is not.

What about the Universal Declaration of Human Rights?

Belief in a freestanding universal morality arises partly from a common misunderstanding of the Universal Declaration of Human Rights. The composition and widespread adoption of that document was an extraordinary achievement, but not one accomplished without theological foundation. Eleanor Roosevelt, who chaired the committee, was a devout Christian strongly motivated by her faith.[9] Charles Malik, who represented majority-Muslim Lebanon and became a key framer of the declaration, was a Greek Orthodox theologian. Despite Chinese representative Peng-chung Chang's insistence that all direct references to God be removed from the agreement, it has subsequently been critiqued precisely because of its Judeo-Christian influence.

While most Muslim-majority countries signed the declaration in 1948, influential Saudi Arabia did not. The Saudi representative argued that the declaration violated Islamic law and failed to accommodate the cultural and religious contexts of non-Western countries. Likewise, in 1982, Iran's representative Said Raja'i Khorasani deemed the declaration a "secular understanding of the Judeo-Christian tradition" that "could not be implemented by Muslims" and "did not accord with the system of values recognized by the Islamic Republic of Iran."[10] While Khorasani by no means represents the views of all Muslims, this tension is no small challenge, given that Islam is the second most widespread belief system in the world.

And the problem of universalizing human rights is not limited to traditionalist Islam. Officially atheist North Korea tops the list

---

9. For more on the often overlooked importance of Eleanor Roosevelt's Christian faith, see Harvard law professor Mary Anne Glendon, "God and Mrs. Roosevelt," *First Things*, May 2010, https://www.firstthings.com/article/2010/05/god-and-mrs-roosevelt.

10. Quoted in Sohrab Behdad and Farhad Nomani, eds., *Islam and the Everyday World: Public Policy Dilemmas*, Routledge Political Economy of the Middle East and North Africa (London: Routledge: 2006), 75.

for human rights abuses, while officially atheist China and majority-Hindu India rank high on the watch list.[11] Many of the ideals enshrined in the declaration are not universally recognized. So why do they seem self-evident to us? To answer that question, we need to widen our historical lens.

The Origins of Human Rights

The idea that all human beings should be valued equally was far from normative in the ancient world. In Greek and Roman thought, free men had more inherent dignity and worth than women, slaves, or children, and disabled infants were routinely disposed of. Plato and Aristotle supported direct eugenics, the latter declaring, "Let there be a law that no deformed child shall live."[12] Into this world stepped a first-century Jewish rabbi who elevated women, valued children, loved the poor, and embraced the sick. The early Christian insistence on brotherhood across racial and ethnic boundaries, even across the dichotomy of slave and free, became a spark to ignite a new moral imagination.[13] Values that many of us in the West today consider to be universal and independent of religious thought turn out not to have sprung from the ground during the Enlightenment but to have grown from the gradual spread and influence of Christian beliefs.[14]

To be sure, many secular scholars have attempted to establish a basis for human rights that is untethered to religious moorings. In *Humanism and the Death of God*, philosopher Ronald Osborn surveys some recent forays into this territory. But he concludes, "Core, humanistic values of inviolable human dignity, inalienable human rights, and intrinsic human equality" cannot be upheld by a scientific naturalism that will ultimately always crumble into nihilism. Rather,

11. See Human Rights Risk Index 2016-Q4, Reliefweb, December 2016, https://reliefweb.int/report/world/human-rights-risk-index-2016-q4.

12. Aristotle, *The Politics*, ed. Stephen Everson (Cambridge: Cambridge University Press, 1988), 192. See also Plato, *The Republic*, trans. Allan Bloom (New York: Basic Books, 1968), 140.

13. For a detailed exposition of this, see Ronald E. Osborn, "The Great Subversion: The Scandalous Origins of Human Rights, or Human Rights and the Slave Revolt of Morals," *The Hedgehog Review* (University of Virginia) 17, no. 2 (Summer 2015): 91–100.

14. For an exploration of the Christian roots of human rights, see Kyle Harper, "Christianity and the Roots of Human Dignity," in *Christianity and Freedom*, vol. 1, *Historical Perspectives*, ed. Timothy Samuel Shah and Allen D. Hertzke, Cambridge Studies in Law and Christianity (Cambridge: Cambridge University Press, 2016), 123–48.

they must be sustained by "a vision of personhood *such as* the one found in an historically unprecedented way" in Christianity.[15] Osborn locates this view not just in the belief that humans are made "in the image of God" (a belief common to the Abrahamic faiths) but also in the specifically Christian belief that God became human in the person of "a poor manual laborer from a defeated backwater of the Empire who was tortured to death by the political and religious authorities of his day."[16]

British political scientist Stephen Hopgood expresses pessimism about the future of human rights in today's climate: "The world in which global rules were assumed to be secular, universal and non-negotiable," he argues, "rested on the presumption of a deep world-wide consensus about human rights—but this consensus is illusory."[17] Hopgood asserts, "The ground of human rights is crumbling beneath us," and he predicts that as American global influence wanes and China emerges as the most powerful country in the world, concern for human rights will decline. This news seems dire. But if human rights came to us from our Christian heritage, perhaps we can be more optimistic about a world in which China plays a larger role just at the time when Christianity is gaining influence there.

To be clear, many nonreligious people are passionately committed to human rights, and many secular philosophers argue for human rights and equality as the most efficacious way for human societies to organize themselves. But when it comes to a robust philosophical foundation for human rights from a secular perspective, building materials are hard to come by. We can invoke sociological and economic data to argue that societies seem to thrive when higher value is placed on human life, and when human equality is upheld. But this is a pragmatic foundation rather than a moral one. Rejecting a Christian foundation for human rights, the late atheist intellectual Christopher Hitchens declared: "How do I know there are such things as human rights? I don't. I don't know there are such things. . . . Our [grounding

---

15. Ronald Osborn, *Humanism and the Death of God* (Oxford: Oxford University Press, 2017), 1–5.
16. Osborn, *Humanism and the Death of God*, 6.
17. Stephen Hopgood, *The Endtimes of Human Rights* (Ithaca, NY: Cornell University Press, 2013), x.

for human rights] is about as tenuous as our position as a primate species on a rather dodgy planet."[18]

Peter Singer's Accidental Convert

The realization that human equality has no firm secular foundation
dawned gradually for one of the few people who knew both me and
my husband before we knew each other. Sarah, Bryan, and I were all
PhD students at Cambridge. Sarah was a brilliant historian: smart,
kind, attractive, cool, and, like many of our grad-school friends, po-
litely hostile to the Christian faith. Postgraduation, we drifted into
Facebook-only friendship, and I was surprised a few years ago when I
noticed that Sarah had married an outspokenly Christian man. I mes-
saged her to ask what had happened. This is her story.

Sarah grew up in Australia in a loving, nonreligious home. By the
time she went to Sydney University, she was a critic of Christianity, and
when she showed up for grad school at King's College, Cambridge,
she fit right in. King's is the California of Cambridge colleges, known
for its party culture and liberal politics: the smattering of Christians
(including my Oklahoma-grown husband) made no dent in the anti-
religious armor of the student body, and Sarah remained comfortable
in her atheism. But, in a bizarre twist of events, it was moving from
Cambridge to Oxford and attending a series of lectures by atheist
philosopher and fellow Australian Peter Singer that changed her life.

Singer, a Princeton professor, is one of the rare secular philosophers
who face atheism's lack of grounding for human equality head-on.
Rather than basing human worth on the unique status of *Homo sapi-
ens*, he argues that beings should be valued according to their capacities: self-awareness, ability to suffer, and so on. By Singer's calculation,
"A week-old baby is not a rational and self-conscious being, and there
are many nonhuman animals whose rationality, self-consciousness,
awareness, capacity, and so on, exceed that of a human baby a week
or a month old." Therefore, "the life of a newborn baby is of less value
. . . than the life of a pig, a dog, or a chimpanzee."[19]

---

18. "Hitchens and Haldane—Why Human Rights?," The Veritas Forum (video), February 17,
2011, https://www.youtube.com/watch?v=yo_JJGcx-Ks.

19. Peter Singer, *Practical Ethics*, 2nd ed. (Cambridge: Cambridge University Press, 1999), 169.

Singer does not lack compassion. In *The Life You Can Save: How to Do Your Part to End World Poverty* (2010), he lays a radical challenge on the world's rich to act on behalf of the world's poor, and he puts much of his own money where his mouth is. But as Sarah listened to Singer's lectures, she experienced a "strange intellectual vertigo":

> I was committed to believing that universal human value was more than just a well-meaning conceit of liberalism. But I knew from my own research . . . that societies have always had different conceptions of human worth, or lack thereof. The premise of human equality is not a self-evident truth: it is profoundly historically contingent. I began to realise that the implications of my atheism were incompatible with almost every value I held dear.[20]

One afternoon, Sarah noticed that her library desk stood in the theology section. She picked up a book of sermons and was surprised to discover how intellectually compelling, complex, and profound Christianity could be.

The next blow came at a faculty dinner. Sarah sat next to a science professor, Andrew Briggs, who asked if she believed in God.[21] Unsure how to respond, Sarah said she was agnostic. He replied, "Do you really want to sit on the fence forever?" That question made her realize that if the question of human equality mattered, she needed to think more about the question of God: "I don't know" was no longer good enough.

After Oxford, Sarah took up an assistant professorship at Florida State University. There she met Christians whose lives were deeply shaped by Jesus: they fed the homeless, ran community centers, and housed migrant farm laborers. Finally, shortly before her twenty-eighth birthday, she walked into a church for the first time earnestly seeking God. She soon felt overwhelmed: at last she felt fully known and unconditionally loved. Sarah describes her new understanding like this:

---

20. Sarah Irving-Stonebraker, "How Oxford and Peter Singer Drove Me from Atheism to Jesus," The Veritas Forum, May 22, 2017, http://www.veritas.org/oxford-atheism-to-jesus/.

21. Professor Briggs is the coauthor of a fascinating book on science and Christianity entitled *The Penultimate Curiosity: How Science Swims in the Slipstream of Ultimate Questions* (Oxford: Oxford University Press, 2016).

Christianity, it turned out, looked nothing like the caricature I once held. . . . God wants broken people, not self-righteous ones. And salvation is not about us earning our way to some place in the clouds through good works. On the contrary; there is nothing we can do to reconcile ourselves to God. As a historian, this made profound sense to me. I was too aware of the cycles of poverty, violence and injustice in human history to think that some utopian design of our own, scientific or otherwise, might save us.[22]

Sarah discovered that the longing for justice that had drawn her to "radical, leftist ideologies" was ultimately more satisfied by the radical message of Jesus, who abandoned his rights and embraced suffering, humiliation, and death to save others. "To live as a Christian," she writes, "is a call to be part of this new, radical, creation. I am not passively awaiting a place in the clouds. I am redeemed by Christ, so now I have work to do." Sarah's deep-seated belief in human equality and her desire for justice left her unsatisfied with atheism. She was morally homesick for a place she had never known.

Bad Faith

Paul Offit, a professor of pediatrics and vaccinology at the University of Pennsylvania, made a parallel discovery. Dr. Offit had good reason to think religion hindered morality. In 1991, a measles epidemic had swept through Philadelphia. Hundreds of children got sick. Nine died. Offit was an attending physician at the Children's Hospital of Philadelphia. But what differentiated these measles-stricken patients from other sick kids was how unnecessary their suffering was. Two Philadelphia churches, whose adjoining schools educated hundreds of children, had refused vaccination and medical care. Thus, the disease took hold and spread.

This incident was one among many that prompted Offit to write a book entitled *Bad Faith: How Religious Belief Undermines Modern Medicine*. Being nonreligious, he assumed he would "sound the same themes that have been sounded by militant atheists like Richard Dawkins, Christopher Hitchens, and Sam Harris: that religion is

---

22. Irving-Stonebraker, "Singer Drove Me from Atheism."

illogical and potentially harmful."[23] But as Offit read the Bible and explored the history of medicine, he changed his mind. Jesus's advocacy for children moved him to tears. He concluded:

> Independent of whether you believe in the existence of God . . . you have to be impressed with the man described as Jesus of Nazareth. At the time of Jesus' life, around 4 B.C. to 30 A.D., child abuse, as noted by one historian, was "the crying vice of the Roman Empire." Infanticide was common. Abandonment was common. Hippocrates, who lived about 400 years before Jesus, often wrote about how physicians should ethically interact with patients. But Hippocrates never mentioned children. That's because children were property, no different than slaves. But Jesus stood up for children, cared about them, when those around him typically didn't.[24]

Offit now calls Christianity "the single greatest breakthrough against child abuse" in history, observing, among other things, that the first Christian emperor of Rome outlawed infanticide in 315 and provided a nascent form of welfare in 321 so poor families would not have to sell their kids.[25] Ultimately, Offit changed the subtitle of his book from *How Religious Belief Undermines Modern Medicine* to *When Religious Belief Undermines Modern Medicine*, acknowledging the massive impact Christianity has had on medicine and ethics.

Atheism Can't Ground Morality

Despite the historical handprints of Christianity on everything from human rights to pediatric medicine, would we not be better off in today's world with a common morality grounded on secular beliefs? There are two problems with this aspiration. First, the population of the world is overwhelmingly religious. If the world were a single democracy in which every human being had a vote and we asked this electorate to nominate a belief system on which to ground morality,

---

23. Paul A. Offit, "Why I Wrote This Book: Paul A. Offit, M.D., *Bad Faith: When Religious Belief Undermines Modern Medicine*," Hamilton and Griffin on Rights (blog), March 17, 2015, http://www.hamilton-griffin.com/2015/03/17/why-i-wrote-this-book-paul-a-offit-m-d-bad-faith -when-religious-belief-undermines-modern-medicine/.

24. Offit, "Why I Wrote This Book."

25. Paul Offit, *Bad Faith: When Religious Belief Undermines Modern Medicine* (New York: Basic Books, 2015), 127.

Christianity would win. It would also represent the most diverse coalition. Why would we seek to build global morality on atheism, when it represents a relatively small proportion of the world's population, concentrated primarily in people living under Communist regimes?

But the second problem runs even deeper.

In 2012, Duke philosophy professor Alex Rosenberg addressed a series of questions from an atheist perspective in *The Atheist's Guide to Reality: Enjoying Life without Illusions*:

- *Is there a God?* No.
- *What is the nature of reality?* What physics says it is.
- *What is the purpose of the universe?* There is none.
- *What is the meaning of life?* Ditto.
- *Why am I here?* Just dumb luck.
- *Does prayer work?* Of course not.
- *Is there a soul? Is it immortal?* Are you kidding?
- *Is there free will?* Not a chance!
- *What happens when I die?* Everything pretty much goes on as before, except us.
- *What is the difference between right and wrong, good and bad?* There is no moral difference between them.
- *Why should I be moral?* Because it makes you feel better than being immoral.
- *Is abortion, euthanasia, suicide, paying taxes, foreign aid, or anything else you don't like forbidden, permissible, or sometimes obligatory?* Anything goes.[26]

While I do not know professor Rosenberg personally, I'm sure he would be as appalled by the Q&A in the ISIS booklet at the beginning of this chapter as you and I are (see p. 59). But according to the moral answers he derives simply from atheism, there is a straightforward answer to the question, "Is it permissible to have intercourse with a female slave who has not reached puberty?" Anything goes.

To be clear, this does not mean that atheists cannot construct and live by moral frameworks grounded on human equality. Many do. But this is not the logical outworking of atheism. As atheist MIT

---

26. Alex Rosenberg, *The Atheist's Guide to Reality: Enjoying Life without Illusions* (New York: Norton, 2011), 2–3.

philosophy professor Alex Byrne observes, "You can consistently hold atheism together with the idea that science tells you virtually nothing about the nature of reality, any view you like about morality or human nature or anything else."[27] Not only does atheism *per se* not yield a moral framework, but a scientific atheist must paper over a crack in his or her worldview between its take on humanity from a scientific versus an ethical perspective. Alan Lightman, another MIT professor and popular science writer, articulates his agnosticism like this:

> Our consciousness and our self-awareness create an illusion that we are made out of some special substance, that we have some kind of special ego-power, some "I-ness," some unique existence. But in fact, we are nothing but bones, tissues, gelatinous membranes, neurons, electrical impulses and chemicals.[28]

This may seem refreshingly honest. But if science is all we have, our sense of self is just an illusion, and we have no moral agency; morality is no more than preference. "We are a bunch of atoms, like trees, and like donuts," Lightman continues. So, eat a donut, or eat a child. Anything goes.

Lightman is not a lone voice crying out in the wilderness for the abandonment of a concept of self. Popular New Atheist Sam Harris argues in his 2012 book *Free Will* that free will is no more than a delusion, and that "the idea that we, as conscious beings, are deeply responsible for the character of our mental lives and subsequent behavior is simply impossible to map onto reality."[29] Neither Lightman nor Harris draws the moral conclusion that "anything goes." But given their beliefs about what human beings are, we are left with the lingering question *Why not?* Purely pragmatic answers will not do.

Is this understanding of humanity the inevitable outworking of science? Not at all. Another MIT professor, world-class plasma physicist Ian Hutchinson, explains his view like this:

27. Alex Byrne, "Is Atheism a Worldview?," The Veritas Forum (video), September 19, 2016, https://www.youtube.com/watch?v=oeynhmPHqB4.

28. "Alan Lightman Shares His Worldview," The Veritas Forum (video), September 16, 2011, https://www.youtube.com/watch?v=6Ny30CgaRmU.

29. Sam Harris, *Free Will* (New York: Free Press, 2012), 13.

I am an assembly of electrons and quarks interacting though quantum chromodynamics and the electroweak forces; I am a heterogeneous mixture of chemical elements. . . . I am a system of biochemical processes guided by genetic codes; but I am also a vast and astoundingly complex organism of cooperating cells; I am a mammal, with hair and warm blood; I am a person, husband, lover, father; and I am a sinner saved by grace.[30]

Hutchinson started following Jesus when he was an undergraduate at King's College, Cambridge. His Christian beliefs offer a worldview within which human beings cannot be reduced to their scientific components but are made in God's image, given moral agency, and loved by their Maker to the point of sacrificial death.

What about Evolutionary Altruism?

At this point, Christians traditionally invoke evolution to ram home the point. They observe that competition, violence, and the eradication of the weak fuel the engine that drives evolution; therefore, if you reduce human beings down to their scientific components and exclude other levels of meaning, evolution is incompatible with a belief system that values humans equally. But a new frontier of evolutionary science has emerged in recent years that has given some atheists hope that science can ground our morality after all. Martin Nowak, who directs Harvard's Program for Evolutionary Dynamics, is a pioneer of the field of evolutionary altruism. He argues that humans are fitted by evolution not just to compete but to cooperate—even, at times, to sacrifice their own interests for the good of others.

Nowak describes five mechanisms for cooperation: direct reciprocity ("I scratch your back, you scratch mine"), indirect reciprocity ("I scratch your back, and someone will scratch mine"), spatial selection ("I cooperate within my network"), multilevel selection ("If most people in my tribe cooperate, we'll out-compete other tribes"), and kin selection ("I'll sacrifice for members of my clan").[31] These mechanisms

---

30. Ian Hutchinson, *Can a Scientist Believe in Miracles? An MIT Professor Answers Questions on God and Science* (Downers Grove, IL: InterVarsity Press, 2018), 32.

31. These mechanisms are summarized in Martin A. Nowak with Roger Highfield, *Super-Cooperators: Altruism, Evolution, and Why We Need Each Other to Succeed* (New York: Free Press, 2012), 270–71.

elevate human behavior beyond straightforward selfishness. But can they ground our moral beliefs?

Atheist psychologist Steven Pinker uncovers one of the inherent fault lines in that conclusion. He points out that if virtue is equated with "sacrifices that benefit one's own group in competition with other groups . . . then fascism would be the ultimate virtuous ideology."[32] Pinker describes our innate moral sense like this: "Whatever sense of empathy nature bequeathed us by default applies to a very narrow circle of individuals: pretty much, our family and close allies within the clan or village."[33]

A convinced secular humanist, Pinker believes that universal human rights can be grounded in reason, without appeal to God, by progressively expanding this circle. He recognizes that science cannot do that work for us, but he compares the discovery of objective moral principles to the discovery of mathematical principles. Nature gave us concepts of one, two, three, and many. We figured out the rest. Perhaps universal, objective ethical principles are similarly within our grasp.

Pinker acknowledges the challenge for atheists of believing in *objective* morality: that right and wrong exist, irrespective of personal or cultural preference. But he echoes Plato to argue that invoking God does not help:

> Does God have good reason for designating certain acts as moral and others as immoral? If not—his dictates are divine whims—why should we take them seriously? . . . And if, on the other hand, God was forced by moral reasons to issue some dictates and not others—if a command to torture a child was never an option—then why not appeal to those reasons directly?[34]

But this misses the point of theism. Unlike us, the God of the Bible is not a late arrival to the universal crime scene, trying to make moral sense of the world. He is the Creator. From a theistic perspective, there

32. Steven Pinker, "The False Allure of Group Selection," *Edge*, June 18, 2012, https://www.edge.org/conversation/steven_pinker-the-false-allure-of-group-selection.

33. "What Is the Source of Morality," The Veritas Forum (video), December 28, 2010, https://www.youtube.com/watch?v=TDkJku5s5jY.

34. Steven Pinker, "The Moral Instinct," *New York Times*, January 13, 2008, https://www.nytimes.com/2008/01/13/magazine/13Psychology-t.html.

is such a thing as a child—who might make moral demands on us— only because God created children. To borrow from Pinker's scientific analogy, just as God freely devised the physical principles that govern the universe, so he freely ordained the moral laws that govern us. Ethical principles are no more divine whims than the laws of gravity. With a theistic worldview, morality and reality spring from the same source.

In an article on evolution and cooperation, Nowak (himself a Catholic) points to God's love as foundational to the universe in every sense: "God's creative power and love is needed to will every moment into existence. . . . An atemporal Creator and Sustainer lifts the entire trajectory of the world into existence."[35]

Far from undermining the possibility of a loving Creator, the glimmerings of a moral instinct in our biological past fit well with belief in a God who wants us to love as he loves.[36]

Science, Ethics, and Coherence

The question of coherence is central to the challenge of atheist morality. The point is not that nonreligious people cannot construct and live by frameworks that uphold human equality. They can. But today's secular humanism offers a worldview in which morality and reality are at odds: Human beings are a collection of atoms laboring under a false belief that they are even moral agents. And yet humans are of immense, equal, and inalienable worth.

Christianity, by contrast, claims that the God who created the stars and galaxies also created us for special relationship with him, and calls us to the kind of radical, self-giving love that overflows from his own heart. Faith in a loving, rational God, who created humans in his image and calls us to love both our neighbor and our enemy, is not only the historical source of our beliefs about human equality but also their best justification. And yet Christians can make no claim to innate moral superiority. To be a Christian is to acknowledge your

---

35. Martin Nowak, "How Might Cooperation Play a Role in Evolution?," Big Questions Online, January 13, 2014, https://www.bigquestionsonline.com/2014/01/13/how-might-cooperation-play-role-evolution/.

36. Nowak has explored the theological implications of his research on cooperation. See Martin A. Nowak and Sarah Coakley, eds., *Evolution, Games, and God: The Principle of Cooperation* (Cambridge, MA: Harvard University Press, 2013).

utter moral failure and to throw yourself on the mercy of the only truly good man who ever lived. But as my friend Sarah discovered, the Christian worldview offers a grounding for altruism and a reason to dare to believe that ultimate justice is more than a delusionary longing in the illusionary mind of the collection of atoms you mistakenly call "me."

5

Doesn't Religion Cause Violence?

In 1930, between the two world wars, the famous British philosopher Bertrand Russell made this claim:

> Religion prevents us from removing the fundamental causes of war; religion prevents us from teaching the ethic of scientific co-operation in place of the old fierce doctrines of sin and punishment. It is possible that mankind is on the threshold of a golden age; but, if so, it will first be necessary to slay the dragon that guards the door, and this dragon is religion.[1]

Looking at the broad sweep of human history, we cannot but see Russell's point. People of every major religion have engaged in horrifically violent acts, often appealing to divine mandates for their violence. Maybe religion itself is the problem. Perhaps if we just slay that dragon, humans will lay down their swords.

This chapter will confront famous and forgotten instances of religiously motivated violence. It will also examine instances of widespread violence that stand outside religion, and suggest an alternative cause of violence that cuts across people of all beliefs. Finally, it will consider the violence that stands at the heart of the Christian faith.

But first, the dragon religion.

---

1. Bertrand Russell, *Has Religion Made Useful Contributions to Civilization? An Examination and a Criticism* (Chicago: Watts, 1930). Republished in Russell, *Why I Am Not a Christian: And Other Essays on Religion and Related Subjects* (n.p.: Touchstone, 1967), 47.

"I Couldn't Be a Christian because of the Crusades"

Last night, I had a conversation with a thoughtful homeless person about faith. We were chatting after a weekly meal our church provides for those struggling to get by. At one point in our conversation, he cited the Crusades as a reason not to consider Christianity. I've often heard the same sentiment from friends with PhDs. What should we make of this famous bloodstain on the Christian record?

Rejection of violence dripped from Jesus's lips. "If anyone slaps you on the right cheek," he instructed his disciples, "turn to him the other also" (Matt. 5:39). And when those same disciples tried to resist his arrest with swords, Jesus rebuked them and healed their victim (Luke 22:50–51). His radical commandment "Love your enemies and pray for those who persecute you" (Matt. 5:44) flipped the script that flows from human nature and has shaped most ethical systems in human history: morality applies to my in-group; outsiders can be virtuously destroyed. And Jesus's words sprang to life as Roman soldiers nailed him to the cross and he prayed for their forgiveness (Luke 23:34). His first followers continued this path of love in the face of violence, and many went to their deaths for proclaiming Jesus as Lord. But how does all this square with the last two thousand years of Christian history? Were Jesus's words just a muzzle on a dragon that could easily be shaken off?

The Crusades, depicted as the violent, unprovoked imposition of Western religion on peaceful Eastern Muslims, are typically the first example we reach for when invoking acts of Christian violence and when seeking paradigms for Muslim-Christian conflict. While the Crusades took place almost a thousand years ago, crusading language was deployed on both sides in the wake of 9/11. George W. Bush warned, "This crusade, this war on terrorism. It's gonna take a while";[2] and Osama Bin Laden wrote, "We hope that these brothers will be the first martyrs in the battle of Islam in this era against the new Jewish and Christian crusader campaign that is led by the Chief Crusader Bush under the banner of the cross."[3] So, what, if

---

2. "Remarks by the President upon Arrival," The White House (website), September 16, 2001, https://georgewbush-whitehouse.archives.gov/news/releases/2001/09/20010916-2.html.

3. Quoted in a statement released to Arabic news network Al-Jazeera calling on Pakistanis to resist an American attack on Afghanistan, published by *The Guardian*, May 24, 2001, https://www.theguardian.com/world/2001/sep/24/afghanistan.terrorism22.

anything, did the medieval Crusades have to do with present-day conflicts?

To begin to answer this question, we must uncover some common misconceptions. Historian Thomas Madden calls the Crusades "one of the most misunderstood events in western history" and notes that recent popular histories of the Crusades have recycled "myths long ago dispelled by historians."[4] Central to this mythology is the afore-mentioned idea that the Crusades were an unprovoked attempt by Western Christians to force their faith on peace-loving Eastern Mus-lims. The truth is almost opposite. The Crusades were, in historian Robert Louis Wilken's words, "a Christian counter offensive against the occupation of lands that had been Christian for centuries before the arrival of Islam."[5]

While the Christian movement began with emphatic nonviolence, Muhammad himself led the first Muslim armies. Madden describes the period between the foundation of Islam and the first Crusade like this:

> With enormous energy, the warriors of Islam struck out against the Christians shortly after Mohammed's death. They were extremely successful. Palestine, Syria, and Egypt—once the most heavily Christian areas in the world—quickly succumbed. By the eighth century, Muslim armies had conquered all of Christian North Africa and Spain. In the eleventh century, the Seljuk Turks conquered Asia Minor (modern Turkey), which had been Christian since the time of St. Paul.[6]

Jerusalem was first taken by Muslim forces in 637, five years after Muhammad's death. But their leader, Caliph Omar, continued to allow Christian pilgrims to visit their holy places, on payment of a fee. When the city was recaptured by Turkish Muslims in 1076, however, the atmosphere changed. Pilgrims were attacked. The city's patriarch was kidnapped. Holy places were desecrated. Cries for help from Eastern Christians prompted Pope Urban II to call a conference of European

---

4. Thomas F. Madden, *The New Concise History of the Crusades*, rev. ed. (Oxford: Roman and Littlefield, 2006), viii.
5. Robert Louis Wilken, "Christianity Face to Face with Islam," *First Things*, January 2009, https://www.firstthings.com/article/2009/01/christianity-face-to-face-with-islam.
6. Thomas F. Madden, "The Real History of the Crusades," *Crisis*, March 19, 2011, https://www.crisismagazine.com/2011/the-real-history-of-the-crusades.

leaders in France in 1095, and after eight days of deliberation, Western Christians resolved to intervene. This conference launched the first Crusade. Its aim was to retake Jerusalem.

The first Crusade achieved its goal: Jerusalem fell. But in many other ways it was disastrous. There was massive loss of life even before the Crusaders reached Jerusalem. When the remnant of the army finally arrived, they were exhausted and starving. Jerusalem itself was well stocked, so the siege did more harm to those outside the city walls than to those within. But when Jerusalem was taken, the brutality extended even beyond the norms of medieval warfare. Tens of thousands of Muslims were killed, including women and children.

While we must understand the desire to retake Jerusalem in its historical context and the centuries of conquest by Muslim armies that Eastern Christians had sustained, this needless slaughter of women and children represented a stunning failure of Christian ethics. Some attempted to parallel the fall of Jerusalem with Joshua's defeat of Jericho in the Old Testament, when only Rahab the prostitute and her family were spared because she had helped Joshua's spies. But although in the Old Testament God's people were at times directed to exact God's judgment on other nations (and vice versa), the New Testament shifts the paradigm. Jesus consistently taught nonviolence, and on the cross he took the full force of God's judgment on the nations on himself. It is possible to make a Christian argument for military intervention to protect the vulnerable: defending a persecuted religious minority (whether Christians in eleventh-century Jerusalem or Jews in twentieth-century Germany) would certainly fall within this scope. But the repeated New Testament directives against violence make the indiscriminate slaughter of civilians unjustifiable from any recognizably Christian perspective.

The stain of cruelty is made more vivid by Crusader violence against Jews along the way. As Madden points out, these were "isolated incidents in direct violation of Church law and condemned by churchmen and secular leaders alike."[7] But the bouts of anti-Semitic violence nonetheless illustrate an appetite for murder. Furthermore, in

---

7. Thomas F. Madden, "Crusaders and Historians," *First Things*, June 2005, https://www.first things.com/article/2005/06/crusaders-and-historians.

a move shocking to contemporaries, the fourth Crusade involved the sacking of Constantinople, the largest Christian city in the world. This was partly a revenge attack against the Eastern Orthodox Christian majority for an earlier massacre of Latin Christians. But it exposes a tragic reality of Christian history: despite the biblical bonds of brotherhood across differences, despite Jesus's command to his followers to love even their enemies, despite Jesus's own repudiation of violence and the way the early Christians gladly faced martyrdom, the last two thousand years have seen Christians repeatedly embroiled in violence against each other.

This continued through the Reformation period and into our more recent past, from the conflict between Catholics and Protestants in Northern Ireland to the Rwandan genocide in 1994, when hundreds of thousands of Tutsis were slaughtered by the majority-Hutu government in a country with one of the highest rates of professed Christianity in Africa.[8]

Without question, many acts of violence have been perpetrated by Christians through the centuries. In some cases—when committed in defense of the vulnerable—they may have been justifiable according to Christian ethics. In others, they have been utterly irreconcilable with the teachings of Jesus.[9] But to this day, the ethical standards by which we judge episodes of violence like the Crusades (in all their complexity) are those given to us by Christianity, which breaks down the "them and us" of tribal ethics and insists on the humanity and worth of one's enemies.

But in spite of this, can we not turn to a more peaceful religion than Christianity? For many of my friends who have abandoned monotheism but want to retain a spiritual identity, there is an obvious answer.

What about Buddhism?

Many of us see Buddhism as the outlier on the global religious scene. If Islam and Christianity conjure up visions of jihads and Crusades,

---

8. For details of Christian complicity in the genocide, see Timothy Longman, *Christianity and Genocide in Rwanda* (Cambridge: Cambridge University Press, 2011).

9. In the early phase of Christians wielding political power, the fourth-century theologian Augustine of Hippo formulated criteria for a "just war" and specifically disqualified acts of violence aimed at conversion.

Buddhism evokes peaceful meditation. No dragon here. But if we are shocked by the tactics of ISIS, we must also be appalled by the violence against Rohingya Muslims in Buddhist-majority Myanmar.

When the soldiers reached Hasina's village, they held her and the other women at gunpoint while they executed the men and boys. Then they led the women and girls, five at a time, toward a hut. "I was trying to hide my baby under my scarf, but they saw her leg," Hasina recalled. "They grabbed my baby by the leg and threw her onto the fire."[10] After beating and raping the women, the soldiers shut the door and set fire to the hut. Doctors Without Borders estimated that nine thousand Rohingya, including a thousand children, died after attacks like this. The genocide continues as I write.

A 2018 *New York Times* op-ed entitled "Why Are We Surprised When Buddhists Are Violent?" reminded us that there is "no shortage of historical examples of violence in Buddhist societies." The article cites Sri Lanka's civil war from 1983 to 2009, which was fueled by "specifically Buddhist nationalism"; violence in modern Thailand; violence within the Dalai Lama's own sect; and "a growing body of scholarly literature on the martial complicity of Buddhist institutions in World War II–era Japanese nationalism."[11] The point is not that Buddhism is particularly violence inducing. Millions of Buddhists lead peaceful lives. But if we think of Buddhism as a religion free of blood, we deceive ourselves, and we will overlook Buddhist-perpetrated violence—particularly when targeted against Muslims. The mindful dragon can breathe fire too.

The 2016 Martin Scorsese film *Silence* drew our attention to another counterintuitive rearing of the dragon's head. We tend to romanticize traditional Eastern religions. But *Silence* gave voice to the persecution of Christians (European-origin and Japanese) at the hands of the Shinto-Buddhist government in seventeenth-century Japan. Tens of thousands of Christians were executed in ways so atrocious that martyr accounts struggled to describe them. Violence of this scale and

10. Quoted in Nicholas Kristof, "Is This Genocide?," *New York Times*, December 15, 2017, https://www.nytimes.com/2017/12/15/opinion/sunday/genocide-myanmar-rohingya-bangladesh.html.

11. Dan Arnold and Alicia Turner, "Why Are We Surprised When Buddhists Are Violent?," *New York Times*, March 5, 2018, https://www.nytimes.com/2018/03/05/opinion/buddhists-violence-tolerance.html.

brutality should be branded on our consciousness. And yet we have forgotten. Indeed, our collective amnesia regarding the massacre of Christians in seventeenth-century Japan contrasts sharply with our vivid memory of the Crusades, five hundred years earlier. The persecution of Christians in Japan is another square peg in the round hole of our stereotypes.

The rest of this book could excavate the mound of violence by religious people and barely scratch its surface. To be sure, some dragons would breath more fire per capita than others: violence perpetrated in the name of Islam is hard to miss, both in the fourteen hundred years since its founding and in the contemporary world. But in an analysis of violent history, no major world religion emerges without blood on its hands. While Jews have lived for centuries as a persecuted Diaspora, enduing oppression and violence at the hands of majorities, the ongoing Israeli-Palestinian conflict will give most of us pause before we declare the Jewish record violence-free. So, was Bertrand Russell right? Can we safely conclude that slaying the dragon of religion would usher in the golden age of peace?

Communist Dream, Communist Nightmare

Jesus's championing of the poor and oppressed has rung loud through the centuries. He claimed he had come "to proclaim good news to the poor" (Luke 4:18), and the first Christians took this very seriously. Goods were held in common. Those who owned land and houses sold them, and the money was distributed to those in need (Acts 4:32–35). By the fourth century, Christians had invented hospitals, established welfare systems, and cared for the needy.[12] Indeed, fourth-century theologian John Chrysostom argued from Scripture that failing to give charitably amounted to robbing the poor, and as Christianity spread, so did concern for the least.[13]

But as Karl Marx surveyed Europe in the mid-nineteenth century, he saw how far supposedly Christian countries had fallen short of the biblical promise. He concluded that Christianity was not a key

---

12. The first known hospital was founded in 370, by Basil, Bishop of Caesarea, who used his own fortune to set up a hospital for the care of the sick.

13. See John Chrysostom, *Four Discourses, Chiefly on the Parable of the Rich Man and Lazarus*, discourse 2, chap. 4.

to release the poor but a drug to tranquilize them. "Religion," he wrote, "is the sigh of the oppressed creature, the heart of a heartless world, and the soul of soulless conditions. It is the *opium* of the people. The abolition of religion as the *illusory* happiness of the people is the demand for their *real* happiness."[14] The removal of religion was, therefore, a step on the road to justice.

But Marx's dream looks like a tattered rag when held up against the violent and oppressive nightmare of Communism. Sixty-one million people killed in the former Soviet Union. Thirty-five million slaughtered in the People's Republic of China. Combine these with the horrific democides and human rights abuses perpetrated by smaller Communist states (North Korea, Cambodia, Vietnam, and so on), and influential political scientist R. J. Rummel concludes:

> Of all religions, secular and otherwise, that of Marxism has been by far the bloodiest. . . . Marxism has meant bloody terrorism, deadly purges, lethal prison camps and murderous forced labor, fatal deportations, man-made famines, extrajudicial executions and fraudulent show trials, outright mass murder and genocide.[15]

Rummel calls the sheer numbers killed in Soviet Russia and Communist China "almost impossible to digest" and attributes them to "the working out of Marxism."[16] Before concluding that religion is the problem, we must recognize that a specifically anti-religious ideology has led millions to commit atrocious acts. Unlike Fascism, this ideology was founded not on clearly pernicious beliefs but on a desire for universal justice. The slaughters of Communism suggest that—sometimes at least—slaying that dragon of religion can unleash a more terrible beast.

Hitler's Religion

No discussion of religion and violence is complete without accounting for the Holocaust. This genocide emanated from a country that had

---

14. Karl Marx, *Early Writings*, trans. Rodney Livingstone and Gregor Benton (London: Penguin, 1992), 244.

15. R. J. Rummel, "The Killing Machine That Is Marxism," WND (website), December 15, 2004, https://www.wnd.com/2004/12/28036/.

16. R. J. Rummel, *Death by Government* , rev. ed. (New York: Transaction, 1997), 101.

been majority Christian for centuries, and to the extent that Christians were complicit, it is to our everlasting shame. Therefore, we must ask ourselves, from which ideological dragon did the Holocaust emerge? If the evils of Communism are a blot on atheism, were the evils of the Nazis a Christian stain?

Hitler was devilishly aware of religion's power. Claiming to guard Germany from atheistic Communism, he invoked God in his earliest speeches and declared in *Mein Kampf*, "I believe to-day that my conduct is in accordance with the will of the Almighty Creator."[17] In 1933, shortly after assuming power, he oversaw the signing of a Concordat between the Vatican and the German Reich that ostensibly protected church freedoms and interests. If Marx saw the elimination of religion as a flagstone on the path to justice, Hitler worked rather to harness the power of religion for his own ends. But for all the ways in which Christians failed to oppose Hitler's devastating rise, the religion he harnessed was not Christianity. Indeed, according to Baldur von Schirach, head of the Hitler Youth movement, "the destruction of Christianity was explicitly recognized as a purpose of the National Socialist movement."[18]

Rather than rejecting Christianity outright, the Nazis endorsed what they called "Positive Christianity," changing the Bible to fit their ends. First, Jesus was rebranded as Aryan. While the New Testament is emphatic about Jesus's Jewish identity, Hitler declared, "I can imagine Christ as nothing other than blond and with blue eyes, the devil however only with a Jewish grimace."[19] Nazi-era Bibles removed the Old Testament and edited the Gospels to purge references to Jesus's Jewishness, his missional prioritization of the Israelites, and his fulfillment of Hebrew Scripture. This required extraordinary editorial gymnastics. The New Testament is a profoundly Jewish text, and trying to unhitch Jesus from the Old Testament is like trying to unhitch Shakespeare from the English language. Indeed, a major question for

---

17. Adolf Hitler, *Mein Kampf—My Struggle*, ed. Rudolf Hess, trans. James Murphy (n.p.: Haole Library, 2015), 38.

18. Quoted in Joe Sharkey, "Word for Word/The Case against the Nazis; How Hitler's Forces Planned to Destroy German Christianity," *New York Times*, January 13, 2002, https://www.nytimes.com/2002/01/13/weekinreview/word-for-word-case-against-nazis-hitler-s-forces-planned-destroy-german.html.

19. *Völkischer Beobachter*, April 28, 1921, quoted in Richard Steigmann-Gall, *The Holy Reich: Nazi Conceptions of Christianity, 1919–1945* (Cambridge: Cambridge University Press, 2004), 37.

the first Christians was whether it was even possible to be a Christian without first *becoming* Jewish. And while the answer was a clear no, that answer was given by the apostle Paul: a self-declared "Hebrew of Hebrews" (Phil. 3:5).

Beyond their anti-Jewish hatchet job, Nazis edited New Testament texts in other ways to align with their ideology. For instance, Jesus's world-changing Sermon on the Mount was purged of deep compassion for the weak and made militaristic.[20] Finally, and most stunningly of all, the Nazis replaced Jesus with Hitler himself.

Joseph Goebbels, minister for public enlightenment and propaganda, said of Hitler: "We are witnessing the greatest miracle in history. A genius is building a new world!"[21] The Nazi version of the Ten Commandments proclaimed, "Honor your Führer and Master." Hitler Youth were taught prayers resembling the Lord's Prayer, but addressed to the Führer:

> Adolf Hitler, you are our great Führer.
>   Thy name makes the enemy tremble.
>   Thy Third Reich comes, thy will alone is law upon the earth.
>   Let us hear daily thy voice and order us by thy leadership, for
> we will obey to the end and even with our lives.
>   We praise thee! Hail Hitler![22]

Hitler Youth were called to nothing short of worship: "Your name, my Führer, is the happiness of youth, your name, my Führer, is for us everlasting life."[23] Thus, Nazi Germany was founded on a new religion, with a new messiah and an ideology that could not have been further from Christian belief.

Tragically—by conviction or coercion—many German pastors bought the lie. Worse still, many sold it. The spirit of the German people had been crushed by the First World War, and Hitler's promise of reestablishing national pride was all too seductive. Moreover, an ugly strain of anti-Semitism that had dogged European Christianity for

---

20. For an overview of Nazi-era Bibles, see Susannah Heschel, *The Aryan Jesus: Christian Theologians and the Bible in Nazi Germany* (Princeton, NJ: Princeton University Press, 2010), 106–10.

21. Quoted in Jean-Denis G. G. Lepage, *Hitler Youth, 1922–1945: An Illustrated History* (Jefferson, NC: McFarland.: 2008), 87.

22. Quoted in Lepage, *Hitler Youth*, 87.

23. Quoted in Lepage, *Hitler Youth*, 87.

centuries, and been stoked by Martin Luther's intense disappointment that the Protestant Reformation had not brought about the massive turning to Jesus of the Jews that he had hoped for, made the increasing victimization of Jews all too easy for some German Christians to swallow. An appeal by certain Christian leaders claimed, "The eternal God created for our nation a law that is peculiar to its own kind. It took shape in the Leader Adolf Hitler, and in the National Socialist state created by him."[24] The price for nonconformity was high. Churches that failed to support the regime were stormed by Nazi mobs, accompanied by gestapo, the secret police. But the departure from true Christianity was undeniable.

In 1937, two years before the outbreak of World War II, the pope penned an encyclical to German Catholics in which he accused Hitler of "a war of extermination" against the church. "Beware, Venerable Brethren," he wrote, "of that growing abuse, in speech as in writing, of the name of God as though it were a meaningless label, to be affixed to any creation . . . of human speculation."[25] Exposing the conflict between Christianity and nationalism, he wrote, "None but superficial minds could stumble into concepts of a national God, of a national religion; or attempt to lock within the frontiers of a single people, within the narrow limits of a single race, God, the Creator of the universe." Objecting to the removal of the Old Testament, which was, "exclusively the word of God," the pope declared, "Nothing but ignorance and pride could blind one to the treasures hoarded in the Old Testament." He further decried the rewriting of the Gospels: "The peak of the revelation as reached in the Gospel of Christ is final and permanent. It knows no retouches by human hand; it admits no substitutes or arbitrary alternatives such as certain leaders pretend to draw from the so-called myth of race and blood." Moreover, the pope emphatically denounced Hitler's messiah cult:

> Should any man dare, in sacrilegious disregard of the essential differences between God and His creature, between the God-man and

---

24. "Directives of the Church Movement German Christians (Movement for a National Church) in Thuringia," in *The Nazi Years: A Documentary History*, ed. Joachim Remak (Long Grove, IL: Waveland, 1990), 95–96.

25. Pope Pius XI, "Mit Brennender Sorge: On the Church and the German Reich," Papal Encyclicals Online, February 20, 2017, http://www.papalencyclicals.net/pius11/p11brenn.htm.

the children of man, to place a mortal, were he the greatest of all times, by the side of, or over, or against, Christ, he would deserve to be called prophet of nothingness.

Much ink has been spilled on the question of how complicit the pope had been in Hitler's advancement. But the message of this letter is unequivocal: the Nazis mangled Christianity beyond recognition.

In the same year, thousands of Protestants protested Nazi tactics. Seven hundred pastors were arrested. Many were executed or sent to concentration camps. The most famous leader was pastor and theologian Dietrich Bonhoeffer, who was among the first to identify the abhorrent nature of the Nazi's stance toward Jews. He challenged Christians to regard the Jews as the "neighbor fallen among thieves" of Jesus' parable of the good Samaritan: that is, one whom Christ commands us to rescue whatever the cost. And the cost was great. In 1939, Bonhoeffer wrote, "When Christ calls a man, he bids him come and die."[26] And in 1945, he was executed in a concentration camp at Flossenbürg, days before its liberation by Allied forces.

Two students, Hans and Sophie Scholl, were also among many other Christians who died opposing Hitler. They started a resistance movement called the White Rose and published pamphlets denouncing the mass deportation and execution of Jews as "the most frightful crime against human dignity, a crime that is unparalleled in the whole of history"; and boldly proclaimed, "Every word that comes from Hitler's mouth is a lie."[27] "We fight with our words," said Sophie. The siblings paid for their defiance. On February 18, 1943, Sophie stood at the top of the stairs overlooking a university atrium and flung leaflets into the air, watching them flutter down the stairwell. A janitor saw her and reported her to the gestapo. Sophie and Hans were arrested, interrogated, and beheaded.

Too few Christians showed this kind of courage. Too many submitted, like proverbial frogs, to the slow boil of Nazi propaganda. But the radical contrast between Nazi-endorsed "Positive Christianity" and

---

26. Dietrich Bonhoeffer, *Life Together*, trans. John W. Doberstein (New York: HarperCollins, 1954), 8.

27. Quoted in Richard Hurowitz, "Remembering the White Rose," *New York Times*, February 21, 2018, https://www.nytimes.com/2018/02/21/opinion/white-rose-hitler-protest.html.

any recognizably biblical faith stunned many into action, despite the price tag for resistance. As Bonhoeffer observed to a friend when led to execution, "This is the end, but for me it is the beginning of life."[28]

Hitler's Science

Hitler came to power three years after Russell had declared that "religion prevents us from teaching the ethic of scientific co-operation in place of the old fierce doctrines of sin and punishment." But if Hitler spawned a new religion to support his racist ideology, he also sought to justify it by science. He argued in *Mein Kampf*:

> If Nature does not wish that weaker individuals should mate with the stronger, she wishes even less that a superior race should intermingle with an inferior one; because in such a case all her efforts, throughout hundreds of thousands of years, to establish an evolutionary higher stage of being, may thus be rendered futile.[29]

In Hitler's view, the Aryan race was simply superior, and maintaining racial purity was an evolutionary ethic:

> The stronger must dominate and not mate with the weaker, which would signify the sacrifice of its own higher nature. Only the born weakling can look upon this principle as cruel, and if he does so it is merely because he is of a feebler nature and narrower mind; for if such a law did not direct the process of evolution then the higher development of organic life would not be conceivable at all.[30]

As we will see in chapter 7, evolution had been claimed as a scientific foundation for frameworks as divergent as Communism, capitalism, and Calvinism. Moreover, Hitler's grasp of evolution was as much the product of intermediary thinkers as any direct derivation from Darwin himself.[31] But we can see the horrifying logic: if evolution depends on the survival of the fittest, perhaps one race can claim to

---

28. Bonhoeffer, *Life Together*, 13.
29. Hitler, *Mein Kampf*, 125.
30. Hitler, *Mein Kampf*, 125.
31. While Darwin did believe that evolution entailed a hierarchy of races, he made only passing reference to Jews and noted similarities between Jews and Aryans, which Hitler strongly opposed. See Robert J. Richards, *Was Hitler a Darwinian? Disputed Questions in the History of Evolutionary Theory* (Chicago: University of Chicago Press, 2013), 202.

be more fit and out-compete others. Indeed, to recall Steven Pinker's observation once more, under many current construals of the ethics bequeathed to us by evolution, virtue equals "sacrifices that benefit one's own group in competition with other groups," and on these terms, Hitler's fascism was "the ultimate virtuous ideology."[32]

Hitler's Philosopher

One of Hitler's strongest intellectual influences was nineteenth-century German philosopher Friedrich Nietzsche. Nietzsche saw that, while God had been declared functionally dead by a certain species of Enlightenment rationalism, Europe was still trading on Christian ethics. In *Twilight of the Idols*, he wrote, "When one gives up the Christian faith, one pulls the right to Christian morality out from under one's feet. This morality is by no means self-evident. . . . By breaking one main concept out of [Christianity], the faith in God, one breaks the whole: nothing necessary remains in one's hands."[33] Nietzsche recognized the ideology later espoused by Hitler as antithetical to Christianity, both in its origins and in its values.

> Christianity, sprung from Jewish roots, and comprehensible only as a growth on this soil, represents the counter-movement to any morality of breeding, of race, privilege: it is the *anti-Aryan* religion par excellence. Christianity—the revaluation of all Aryan values . . . the gospel preached to the poor and base, the general revolt of all the downtrodden, the wretched, the failures, the less-favored, against "race."[34]

In *Thus Spoke Zarathustra*, Nietzsche imagined an *Übermensch*, or "Superman," who would rise above good and evil and throw off this "slave morality." Zarathustra compared the evolutionary relationship between apes and humans to the relationship between

---

32. Steven Pinker, "The False Allure of Group Selection," *Edge*, June 18, 2012, https://www.edge.org/conversation/steven_pinker-the-false-allure-of-group-selectionhttps://www.edge.org/conversation/steven_pinker-the-false-allure-of-group-selection.

33. Friedrich Nietzsche, "Skirmishes of an Untimely Man," chap. 8 of *The Twilight of the Idols*, in *The Portable Nietzsche*, ed. and trans, Walter Kaufmann (New York: Penguin, 1976), 515–16.

34. Friedrich Nietzsche, "The 'Improvers' of Mankind," chap. 6 of *The Twilight of the Idols*, in *The Portable Nietzsche*, 504–5.

humans and the *Übermensch*.[35] Hitler mapped this idea onto Aryan Germans and rejected the morality of weakness offered by Christianity.[36]

Reckoning with Nazism

Hitler's philosophy was based on poor science and went beyond its scope. The idea that there is an evolutionary hierarchy of races is scientifically unsustainable. But Hitler's belief in racial hierarchy was supported by many scientists of the day, both in Germany and abroad. This must make us cautious when people suggest that we can replace religion with science and expect a better world to emerge. Science is not designed to give us morals. It can help us build chemical weapons and chemotherapy drugs, but it cannot tell us whether and when to use them. As we saw in the last chapter, science cannot ground the belief that human beings should be valued equally.

If we lay Nazism at the feet of the dragon religion (of whatever breed), then we must also lay it at the feet of contemporary science. Hitler invoked both. Furthermore, as Nietzsche pointed out, we cannot cling to supposedly self-evident moral truths of human equality and repudiation of violence and racism without any philosophical foundation: "When one gives up the Christian faith, one pulls the right to Christian morality out from under one's feet."[37]

What about Democracy?

What if we have been asking the wrong question? Perhaps religion is largely irrelevant to the problem of violence, and the answer is simply the establishment of liberal democracy. Hitler himself gained power in a supposed democracy, so democracy is no sure prophylactic against genocidal dictators. But liberal democracy has proved to be correlated with a range of goods. As Pinker remarks, democracies

---

35. "Man is a rope stretched between the animal and the Superman—a rope over an abyss." Friedrich Nietzsche, *Thus Spake Zarathustra*, trans. Thomas Common (1909), prologue, sec. 4.

36. For an excellent treatment of Hitler's relationship with Nietzschean philosophy, see Ronald Osborn, *Humanism and the Death of God: Searching for the Good after Darwin, Marx, and Nietzsche* (Oxford: Oxford University Press, 2017), 128–75.

37. Nietzsche, *The Portable Nietzsche*, 515.

"have higher rates of growth, fewer wars and genocides, healthier and better-educated citizens, and virtually no famines."[38]

Democracy first sprang up in Athens in the fifth century BC. But Athenian democracy was not grounded in universal claims about freedom and equality. Suffrage was limited to adult male citizens and "depended on the homogeneity of male house owners who spoke the same language, worshipped the same deities, and were willing to serve in the army in defense of the city state."[39] Philosophers were skeptical. Plato argued against democracy on the grounds that it was foolish to share power beyond gifted elites. Aristotle saw democracy as an improvement on monarchy only if the monarch was a tyrant rather than a benevolent king.[40] Since then, democracy has spread in fits and starts, with many false springs. But to us in the West today, democracy seems to be a self-evident good, as native to modernity as science or the Internet. There are two problems with this view.

First, we forget Christianity's relationship with the growth and spread of democracy. This road has been neither straight nor smooth. Christians have both helped to cultivate democratic ideals of equality and perpetuated repressive ideas of statism and elitism.[41] We must not romanticize a complex past. And yet the biblical ethic of human equality regardless of status, its insistence that leaders are servants, and its realism about human nature have enabled countries whose public soil has been tilled by Christianity to embrace the distribution of power that democracy represents. The complex unity we call America is a case in point.

Moreover, the link between Christianity and democracy is evident beyond the West. Political scientist Robert Woodberry has shown that the historic prevalence of Protestant missionaries "explains about half the variation in democracy in Africa, Asia, Latin America and Oceania and removes the impact of most variables that dominate current

---

38. Steven Pinker, *Enlightenment Now: The Case for Reason, Science, Humanism, and Progress* (New York: Penguin, 2018), 200.

39. John W. de Gruchy, *Christianity and Democracy: A Theology for a Just World Order* (Cambridge: Cambridge University Press, 1995), 16.

40. De Gruchy, *Christianity and Democracy*, 17.

41. See John Witte, ed. *Christianity and Democracy in Global Context* (Boulder, CO: Westview, 1993).

statistical research."[42] Missionaries have been "a crucial catalyst initiating the development and spread of religious liberty, mass education, mass printing, newspapers, voluntary organizations, and colonial reforms, thereby creating the conditions that made stable democracy more likely."[43] This correlation is one example of the positive effects that have sprung from missionary activity.

The second factor we forget when we perceive liberal democracy as the natural form of government is its questionable compatibility with the second most widespread belief system. Unlike Christianity, Islam prescribes a political structure and set of laws that are hard to wed to democracy. In 2017, only six of the fifty-seven member states of the Organization of Islamic Cooperation were deemed democracies by the Economist Intelligence Unit *Democracy Index 2017*—all of them substantially "flawed." This tension underlies the Western misreading of the so-called Arab Spring of 2010–2012. Westerners watched eagerly, expecting that the protests taking place across six majority-Muslim countries would give birth to liberal democracies. In Tunisia (where the protests started) they did. But Libya, Syria, Yemen, and Iraq devolved into civil wars—involving thousands of civilian deaths and the harrowing rise of ISIS—while the protests in Bahrain were quashed. There are multiple reasons for this outcome. But one was that many of the protesting factions were led by conservative Islamists seeking to overthrow secular regimes and implement Sharia law rather than establish liberal democracies.

Democracy does not just happen, nor is its spread inevitable. The Economist's *Democracy Index 2017* white paper reported that the average democracy score fell from 5.52 in 2016 to 5.48 in 2017 (on a scale of 0 to 10).[44] As Islam continues to spread in the coming decades, we cannot assume that democracy will not see further decline. To hatch and survive, democracy must be nested in the right

---

42. Robert D. Woodberry, "The Missionary Roots of Liberal Democracy," *American Political Science Review* 106, no. 2 (2012): 244.

43. Woodberry, "Missionary Roots of Liberal Democracy," 244. This result is consistent across different continents and subsamples, and robust to more than fifty controls and to instrumental variable analyses.

44. See also "Democracy Continues Its Disturbing Retreat," *The Economist*, January 31, 2018, https://www.economist.com/graphic-detail/2018/01/31/democracy-continues-its-disturbing -retreat.

philosophical foundations. To be sure, many democratic countries in the West have seen substantial secularization. But countries where Christian belief and practice have declined still cling to a Christian philosophical heritage that demands equal human value, religious liberty, and care for the poor. Even in India, the world's largest democracy, with a proportionally small Christian population, the democratic model was drawn from a tradition of British liberalism and American models, which in turn rested on their Christian heritage.[45] Whatever our beliefs about Jesus, if we long for the global spread of democracy, the spread of Christianity—not least its ascendency in China—may be our best hope.

The Deeper Problem

But this brings us back to the problem diagnosed by Marx: the failure of Christians to deliver on the New Testament promise. To be sure, Christianity has had a huge impact for peace and justice, unparalleled by any other worldview. But the record of Christian failure is also long. Why did the Crusaders indulge in unnecessary slaughter? Why did so many German pastors support Hitler? How did majority-Christian America embrace slavery? The list goes on. I believe there are two primary reasons for the failure of supposedly Christian countries to live up to Jesus's teaching. Both were articulated by Jesus himself.

First, we cannot assume that everyone who identifies as a Christian authentically is one—particularly in societies where claiming to follow Jesus is not a ticket to martyrdom but a path to power. Describing the final judgment, Jesus spoke of many who will be surprised by their condemnation, when their failure to care for the poor and oppressed will reveal their failure to follow him.[46] Second, the Bible teaches us to expect moral failure from Christians. We are not naturally good people who behave badly only if we have been deprived of the proper upbringing, education, or circumstances. Rather, we are innately sinful, veering toward selfishness like a car with a misaligned steering wheel. I see this in my own heart, day after day. While Christians are

---

45. See Sumit Ganguly, "The Story of Indian Democracy," *Foreign Policy Research Institute* (website), June 1, 2011, https://www.fpri.org/article/2011/06/the-story-of-indian-democracy/.
46. See, e.g., Matt. 25:41–45.

released by Jesus's death from the punishment due for their sin, the Bible is clear that Christians will not be free from the plague of sin until Jesus returns. I can expect to see signs of growth in my life. But I must steel myself for an ongoing, lifelong struggle with sin. As the apostle John declared, "If we say we have no sin, we deceive ourselves, and the truth is not in us" (1 John 1:8).

For many of us in the West today, our selfishness is not served by violence. My life would not improve if I committed murder. But put me in a situation where violence is to my advantage, and who knows what I might be capable of. I would like to think I would have given my life to resist the Nazis. But my moral courage has never been tested in that way, and the older I get, the less confident I am of my own virtue. We saw in the last chapter good evidence to suggest that the Christian worldview generally helps people to be more loving and less violent. But even in the microcosm of a church, Christians are confronted by moral failure. As Bonhoeffer put it, "Just as surely as God desires to lead us to a knowledge of genuine Christian fellowship, so surely must we be overwhelmed by a great sense of disillusionment with others, with Christians in general, and, if we are fortunate, with ourselves."[47] Disillusionment is not the end of the Christian life. It's the beginning.

The Central Violence of the Christian Faith

Staked at the heart of Christianity is a symbol of extreme violence—the brutal, torturous, state-sponsored execution of an innocent man. Christians believe that this execution was orchestrated by God himself. Some argue from this that Christianity glorifies violence. But the meaning of the cross is precisely the opposite. Violence is the use of power by the strong to hurt the weak. At the cross, the most powerful man who ever lived submitted to the most brutal death ever died, to save the powerless. Christianity does not glorify violence. It humiliates it.

The skewering of violence at the cross speaks to our most fundamental problem, which is not lack of education or democracy or

---

47. Bonhoeffer, *Life Together*, 27.

opportunity but the gruesome reality the Bible calls sin. And the strange claim of Jesus's resurrection offers us hope that evil will not ultimately triumph, and that anyone who gives up his or her life to follow Christ will find it. This belief, when drunk of deeply, motivates action. It motivated Christians in the fourth century to create places where the sick and poor could be cared for—places we now call hospitals. It motivated Martin Luther King to believe that nonviolent resistance could overcome violent oppression. And it motivates Christians today to sacrifice themselves across the world in the service of others. In a *New York Times* op-ed entitled "Evangelicals without the Blowhards," Pulitzer Prize–winning journalist and human rights activist Nicholas Kristof writes: "Go to the front lines, at home or abroad, in the battles against hunger, malaria, prison rape, obstetric fistula, human trafficking or genocide, and some of the bravest people you meet are evangelical Christians (or conservative Catholics, similar in many ways) who truly live their faith."[48]

Does religion cause violence? It certainly can. But millions of people are driven by their faith to love and serve others. And Christianity, in particular, has served as a fertilizer for democracy, a motivation for justice, and a mandate for healing. If we think the world would be less violent without it, we may need to check our facts.

---

48. Nicholas Kristof, "Evangelicals without Blowhards," *New York Times*, June 31, 2017, http://www.nytimes.com/2011/07/31/opinion/sunday/kristof-evangelicals-without-blowhards.html.

6

How Can You Take the Bible Literally?

Have you ever had your heart broken? I have. I could tell you what happened. But instead I'm going to tell you what didn't happen. No one called an ambulance. No one checked my blood pressure. No one attempted CPR.

If you have ever been broken-hearted, you know that the pain can feel as real as a cardiac arrest. But what if I had a heart attack, my husband dialed 911, and the operator said: "I'm so sorry to hear about your wife's heart; don't try to do anything; just hold her, listen to her, and let her know you love her"?

Our lives can depend on distinguishing literal truth from metaphor. If a friend told you she was going to murder her husband, you would probably infer that she was annoyed with him and planning to express that in strong language! If your brother told you he literally died of embarrassment when the girl he liked read his Valentine's Day card, you would not marvel at his resurrection. But if he told you he was contemplating suicide because he was so heartbroken at her rejection, you would do well to take him literally. Both literal and figurative language can describe reality. We can tell lies with literal words and speak the truth through metaphor. Indeed, when it comes to the Bible, some of the deepest truths are metaphorically expressed.

In this chapter, we will explore the misconception that it is inconsistent to read some biblical passages literally and others not, the assumption that not always "taking the Bible literally" licenses us to dodge its miraculous claims, the question of contradictions in the Gospels, and the idea that the New Testament is not a trustworthy source regarding the first-century Jew known as Jesus of Nazareth.

Is It Inconsistent to Read Some Texts Literally and Others Not?

Our lives are littered with metaphors. We bust our gut working. We love with our whole heart. Recent research in communication studies has verified what poets have known for millennia: we humans find metaphors memorable, persuasive, and moving. Our brains are wired for word pictures that liken one thing or experience to another. They ignite our imagination and connect us to their author, drawn together by the shared experience that makes the metaphor work. Like a private joke or a common language, metaphors build relationship. It's why lovers write poetry.

We somehow forget this when it comes to the Bible. In a 2014 survey, US pastors were asked which of the following most accurately reflected their view of the Bible.

- "The Bible is the actual word of God and is to be taken literally, word for word" (28 percent).
- "The Bible is the inspired word of God but not everything in it should be taken literally" (47 percent).
- "The Bible is an ancient book of fables, legends, history, and moral precepts recorded by man" (21 percent).[1]

Instinctively, we expect that these statements categorize pastors in descending order of how seriously they take the Bible. But if you read the words of Jesus himself, you will soon realize that to "take the Bible literally, word for word" is often to miss the point.

When Jesus says, "I am the good shepherd," he is not claiming to be a farmer. He is inhabiting the metaphor of God as shepherd: "The LORD is my shepherd," declared the Old Testament shepherd-turned-

---

1. Lydia Saad, "Three in Four in U.S. Still See the Bible as Word of God," Gallup, June 4, 2014, http://news.gallup.com/poll/170834/three-four-bible-word-god.aspx.

king David (Ps. 23:1). When Jesus says, "I am the true vine" (John 15:1), he is not claiming planthood. Rather, he is inviting us to recall the Old Testament metaphor of Israel as God's vine. Indeed, people often misunderstood Jesus because they took him literally.

In John's Gospel, Jesus chases money changers out of the temple and challenges the shocked bystanders, "Destroy this temple, and in three days I will raise it up." "It has taken forty-six years to build this temple," they respond, "and will you raise it up in three days?" But John explains that Jesus is talking about his body—the true temple, where God meets with his people and the real sacrifice is made (John 2:19–21). Later, a Jewish leader named Nicodemus visits Jesus at night. Jesus says he should be born again. "How can a man be born when he is old?" asks Nicodemus. "Can he enter a second time into his mother's womb and be born?" (John 3:4). Later still, Jesus breaks racial, religious, and gender barriers by asking a Samaritan woman for a drink, before claiming he can provide living water (John 4:10). Again, she takes him literally and misses his point.

The truths expressed metaphorically in these and other Scriptures are startlingly real. Indeed, if the message of the Bible is true, the literal realities of our own lives are embodied metaphors to point us to the transcendent God.

We make metaphors by noticing connections: love is a sickness; life is a marathon; parents are like helicopters. But God did not notice fatherly love and decide to call himself our Father. God created fatherhood, so that the best human fathers could give us a glimpse of his paternal care. God did not notice the intimacy of sex and marriage and decide to call Jesus the Bridegroom and the church his bride.[2] Rather, God created sex and marriage so that marriage at its best might give us a taste of his passionate, sacrificial, unconditional love. John's Gospel starts with a metaphor: "In the beginning was the Word" (John 1:1). This conjures up the Bible's opening lines, when God creates by speaking. John identifies that Word as Jesus himself and floods our understanding with metaphors: Jesus is the Light of the World, the Lamb of God, the temple, the true Vine, the Good Shepherd, the living water, the way, and the door.

---

2. See chap. 8 for an extended discussion of this metaphor.

Metaphors and Miracles

Does this mean the Bible is *not* intended to be taken literally, or that we can navigate around any challenging text by calling it metaphorical? Not at all. As with any conversation, some parts are intended literally, others not. Usually it is easy to tell. For example, the New Testament writers emphasize that Jesus was literally raised from the dead—bones, wounds, and all. Attending to the powerful metaphors that circulate throughout the Scriptures does not for a moment reduce the radical claims that the Bible makes: claims of miracles, everlasting truth, and a life-and-death decision we must make. Indeed, some of Jesus's hardest teachings are expressed metaphorically. "Enter by the narrow gate," he warns. "For the gate is wide and the way is easy that leads to destruction, and those who enter by it are many" (Matt. 7:13). The use of metaphor here is obvious. But there are times when people who take the Bible seriously disagree on whether a statement is literal or metaphorical, history or parable.

Much blood was spilled during the Protestant Reformation over how we should understand Jesus when he says to his disciples, "This is my body," as he breaks bread, and, "This is my blood," as he pours out wine. Are these metaphors? Or is Jesus miraculously turning himself into the bread and wine that Christians eat and drink when they remember his death? Catholics and Protestants disagree. Moreover, Jesus's miracles often double as metaphors. By forgiving a paralytic before healing his legs, Jesus invites us to see parallels between the physical and spiritual healings. When he calls his first fisherman-disciples to follow him, he directs a miraculous catch and then tells them to leave their nets to become "fishers of men" (Luke 5:1–11).

But when Jesus's miracles are invested with metaphorical meaning, this does not mean they did not literally happen. Jesus's ability to do what only God can do points to who he is. "What sort of man is this," his terrified disciples wonder, "that even winds and sea obey him?" (Matt. 8:27).

Parables and Poetry

The true-while-nonliteral complexity is further exposed by Jesus's parables. To take one example, the famous parable of the good Samaritan is not prefaced by, "Then Jesus told a parable." And the events he describes are realistic. Jesus tells of a man who is robbed, assaulted, and left for dead while walking from Jerusalem to Jericho—a notoriously danger-ous route. Jesus describes two religious men walking past the victim and giving him a wide berth—again, quite plausible for men who would be made ceremonially unclean by touching a dead body. The most surprising element of the story is its hero: the person who finally takes pity on the injured man is a Samaritan. Yet there is no obvious clue within the text that Jesus is not recounting actual events. But if we are familiar with his teaching style, we understand instinctively that this is not a crime scene report, but a parable told for its meaning. Once again, we must be careful to distinguish between true and literal, and we must be attentive to the genre of any biblical text in order to grasp its meaning.

If parables are one example, poetry—a major literary feature, par-ticularly in the Old Testament—is another. We find a whole book of biblical poetry in the Psalms, which functioned as the songbook of the Israelites. We also find substantial poetic tracts in the writings of the Old Testament prophets, and we find poetic features in the first five books of the Bible, known as the Pentateuch. Poetic writing is not an embarrassment to the Bible but part of its power. And yet we must recognize its character and read it on its own terms. At times, failing to recognize the figurative features with the biblical text is like taking a love poem to the grocery store and wondering why you can't find all the items on its shelves.

Isn't the Bible Full of Contradictions?

After a talk on Christianity and rationality, math professor Satyan Devadoss was challenged about the seeming problem of contradic-tions. His response was disarming. Rather than immediately denying that the Bible is "full of contradictions," as we might expect from someone who believes that it is the Word of God, Devadoss gave the audience an example—in case they didn't have one in mind—citing the different orders of creation in Genesis 1 and 2. He then explained that these seemingly contradictory accounts were theologically rather than chronologically ordered, and that they are juxtaposed to give us bifocal vision. We tend to assume that we are the first generation to notice such differences. But we are not. In fact, the accounts were clearly placed side by side for theological reasons.

An analogy with Jesus's teaching may be helpful. Jesus called himself "the good shepherd" (John 10:11). But he is also called "the Lamb of God" (John 1:29). How can you be both a shepherd and a lamb? Well, Jesus is both the Shepherd-King and the Passover-lamb sacrifice. He is the Priest and the sacrifice, the Prophet and the Word, the Alpha and the Omega. You can dismiss these as contradictions, or you can experience them as paradoxes describing a man who transcends our understanding. Indeed, as New Testament scholar Peter Williams points out, Jesus frequently *taught* through paradoxes. "The presence of such deliberate formal contradictions," he argues, "does not mean that the contradictory statements are not both true in some way at a deeper level."[3]

The sophistication of biblical writing is evident in the early chapters of Genesis. For instance, in Genesis 2, God forbids Adam to eat fruit from the tree of the knowledge of good and evil, warning "in the day that you eat of it you shall surely die" (Gen. 2:17). Adam eats the fruit. But he lives on to father three sons. There are three possible ways to interpret this warning in its context. First, God was speaking not of a physical death but of a spiritual one. This aligns with the New Testament, where the apostle Paul routinely uses life and death as spiritual categories.[4] Indeed, just like Jesus's decision to forgive a paralyzed man before healing him, it highlights the primary importance of our spiritual condition. The second possibility is that God did not mean a literal same day but was warning that once Adam ate of the forbidden fruit, his physical death would become inevitable. This aligns with a God-sized perspective on time. "Do not overlook this one fact," writes Peter, "that with the Lord one day is as a thousand years, and a thousand years as one day" (2 Pet. 3:8). A final though biblically untenable approach to Genesis 2:17 is to say that God meant both *day* and *die* literally, but that he lied or changed his mind.

Christians take a range of views on the exact genre of the early chapters of Genesis, but the language of Genesis 2:17 reminds us that (scientific questions aside) those who take a purely literal approach to Genesis 1–3 are still left with puzzles within the text: puzzles that would have been evident to the first readers and must therefore be

---

3. Peter J. Williams, *Can We Trust the Gospels?* (Wheaton, IL: Crossway, 2018), 127.
4. See, e.g., Col. 2:13: "You, who were dead in your trespasses and the uncircumcision of your flesh, God made alive together with [Christ]."

intentional. Indeed, the fact that Genesis 2 and 3 force us to consider whether God is talking about physical death or spiritual death, and wonder if even the devastation of physical death might be less disastrous than alienation from God, is part of its persuasive power. We are inclined to assume that we are more sophisticated than a text written thousands of years ago. But the more we read the Bible, the more we will find we are not. MIT professor Rosalind Picard discovered this when she was a teenager and a "proud atheist." She thought the Bible would be "full of fantastical crazy stuff," but she was surprised: "I started reading the Bible," she recalls, "and it started to change me."[5]

But what about seeming contradictions in the accounts of Jesus's life? I argued in chapter 3 that Christianity stands or falls on the literal, historical reality of Jesus's death and resurrection. Does the presence of apparent contradictions in the Gospels not undermine this case?

What about Contradictions in the Gospels?

The four Gospels speak with one voice about Jesus's identity, mission, and message, but there are many differences between them in terms of ordering and detail. New Testament professor Bart Ehrman has written extensively about these differences and concluded that the Bible is irreconcilably contradictory. Some of his examples, however, betray observer bias and lead him to draw unnecessary conclusions. For instance, Ehrman notes that in Matthew's Gospel Jesus declares, "Whoever is not with me is against me" (Matt. 12:30), while in Mark he says, "The one who is not against us is for us" (Mark 9:40). Ehrman asks: "Did he say both things? Could he mean both things? How can both be true at once? Or is it possible that one of the Gospel writers got things switched around?"[6] But you have only to watch a football game to understand: when there are two sides, you cannot be on both. And as we noted earlier, Jesus frequently taught through paradox. That is not so strange. Peter Williams cites the opening lines of *A Tale of Two Cities* ("It was the best of times, it was the worst of times")

5. Rosalind Picard, in response to an interview question from *New York Times* columnist Ross Douthat about her path from atheism to faith, The Veritas Forum (video), January 12, 2016, thehttps://www.youtube.com/watch?v=3ScEV1IbL5A.

6. Bart D. Ehrman, *Jesus, Interrupted: Revealing the Hidden Contradictions in the Bible (And Why We Don't Know about Them)* (New York: HarperOne: 2010), 41.

as a familiar literary example to help us understand.[7] Nonetheless, apparent contradictions in the Gospels take a variety of forms and warrant careful study.

Some puzzles arise from the assumption that Jesus did things only once. When we see him saying or doing similar things in different places or at different times, we might conclude that the Gospel writers got mixed up. But like itinerant preachers, politicians, and activists today, first-century rabbis routinely repeated their teachings to spread their message. Sometimes even miracles are repeated for a reason. For example, Matthew's Gospel records Jesus feeding five thousand men (plus women and children) with five loaves and two fish (Matt. 14:13–21). In the next chapter, he feeds over four thousand with seven loaves and a few small fish (Matt. 15:32–39). Jesus has similar conversations with his disciples in both episodes. At first, it seems extraordinary that the disciples could have forgotten the first miracle so quickly. We wonder if this is just a retelling of the same event, with some of the details (location, number of loaves, and so on) mixed up. But in the following chapter, Jesus recalls these two events. He warns his disciples to beware of the yeast of the Pharisees and Sadducees, and they think he is complaining that they have forgotten to bring bread. "Do you not remember the five loves for the five thousand, and how many baskets you gathered?" Jesus replies, "Or the seven loaves for the four thousand, and how many baskets you gathered? How is it that you fail to understand that I did not speak about bread?" (Matt. 16:9–11).

When we notice the locations of the two miracles, we spot their significance: the second feeding occurs in an area with a high proportion of Gentiles. If Jesus's first miracle recalls the provision of bread from heaven via Moses for the starving Israelites, the second extends this provision to non-Jews. Jesus may have fed large crowds dozens of times during his ministry. As John says, if everything Jesus said or did were written down, "the world itself could not contain the books that would be written" (John 21:25). But Matthew records these two miracles back-to-back to make a theological point.

Some apparent differences between the Gospels arise from our modern sense of time and the norms of a historical account. Ehrman

---

7. Williams, *Can We Trust the Gospels?*, 127.

gives an example: Luke's Gospel records Jesus's ascension into heaven directly after the account of Jesus's first resurrection appearances to his disciples (Luke 24). Acts (also believed to be written by Luke) tells us that Jesus's post-resurrection appearances lasted forty days before his ascension. Is this a contradiction? No. The Gospels frequently telescope events together in a seemingly hectic rush ("and then . . . and then . . . and then"), when in fact there were significant periods between. Again, there are modern parallels. If a friend told me her boss had changed his mind, she might say, "One minute he's telling me to do this, and the next minute he's telling me to do that instead." The two conversations could be a week apart, but the "one minute" formulation makes a point.

Our modern sensibilities make us less inclined to change the order in which events took place. But the genre of historical writing was different in the first century than it is today. Particularly in John's Gospel, events are often recorded in an order that emphasizes theology over chronology. The best modern analogy here is perhaps in film. We are used to experiencing parts of the story in a nonchronological order. For example, right after a character meets a grown woman, we may see a flashback to their childhood relationship. My husband's impeccable engineer's brain often struggles to spot these transitions. When I explain that we just jumped back twenty years to show the characters' back-story, he says, "How did you know?" Often I can't explain: I just know! We expect this from films that narrate actual historical events as much as from fiction. Sometimes, the Gospel writers take a similar approach.

Our sense of location can also be more rigid than that of our forebears. The Gospel writers are not always as precise with their settings as we would be, though they are often *more* precise, and puzzles can arise from our ignorance. For example, Luke's Gospel situates Jesus's ascension at Bethany (Luke 24:50), while Acts has the disciples returning "from the Mount of Olives" (Acts 1:12). This appears contradictory, until you realize that Bethany is traditionally associated with the West Bank city of al-Elzariya, which lies on the southeast slope of the Mount of Olives.

Even today, we sometimes use technically contradictory labels for the same place. For example, I live in Cambridge, Massachusetts.

Boston is on the other side of the Charles River and is an entirely separate city, with a different government, school system, and identity. But I routinely tell people that I live in Boston, because Cambridge is in the greater Boston area. It's also less confusing for my British friends than saying Cambridge and having to explain which one I mean!

What about the Other Gospels?

Dan Brown's historical novel *The Da Vinci Code* popularized the idea that the four Gospels included in the Bible were selected at the expense of other accounts that painted a more authentic picture of Jesus. But, critical as he is of the Bible, Bart Ehrman acknowledges that the New Testament Gospels are "the oldest and best sources we have for knowing about the life of Jesus," observing that this is "the view of all serious historians of antiquity of every kind, from committed evangelical Christians to hardcore atheists."[8]

Some suggest that the excluded "gospels" represent a more feminist version of Christianity that was squeezed out by the early church.[9] For example, some Gnostic texts gave a primary role to Mary among Jesus's disciples. But if you read the actual texts, you will discover that they are far from consistently feminist. The so-called Gospel of Thomas ends like this: "Simon Peter said to him, 'Let Mary leave us, for women are not worthy of life.' Jesus said, 'I myself shall lead her in order to make her male, so that she too may become a living spirit resembling you males. For every woman who will make herself male will enter the kingdom of heaven.'"[10]

This misogynistic perspective would have jibed with much ancient philosophy. But the contrast between this statement and Jesus's high view of women in the canonical Gospels is stark. Regardless of their theological content, however, is it true that the "gospels" that did not make it into our Bibles were excluded for political reasons and have as much right to be included as those that did?

---

8. Bart D. Ehrman, *Truth and Fiction in* The Da Vinci Code (Oxford: Oxford University Press, 2004), 102.

9. For a concise treatment of the noncanonical gospels and the views popularized by Dan Brown, see Garry Williams, *The Da Vinci Code: From Dan Brown's Fiction to Mary Magdalene's Faith* (Fearn, Ross-shire, UK: Christian Focus, 2006).

10. The Gospel of Thomas, saying 114, *The Nag Hammadi Library*, ed. James M. Robinson (San Francisco: Harper, 1990), 138.

While other writings about Jesus were circulating in the early centuries of the church, there is good evidence that the four New Testament Gospels were closer to the life, death, and resurrection of Jesus, in terms of both date of composition and connection to the apostles who witnessed these events. From extant manuscripts, it seems that the New Testament Gospels were far more widely read than the other writings, even before the formal establishment of the canon, and that they were being bound together as a collection as early as the late second century.[11] In many instances, the other "gospels" are also different in genre. The Gospel of Thomas, for instance, is a collection of sayings, rather than a record of events and teachings.[12] But how confident can we be that the Gospels included in our Bibles today are close enough to the events of Jesus's life to be reliable sources?

Jesus and the Eyewitnesses

Ehrman stands in a long line of academics who have argued that the Gospels are internally inconsistent and poorly aligned with known history, because they are products of extended oral traditions that were theologically manipulated by later generations. For some time, this view prevailed in the academy. In recent decades, however, multiple scholars have risen to great academic heights presenting fresh arguments for the historicity of the Gospels. For an excellent, accessible summary of the various kinds of evidence we can examine to evaluate the authenticity of the Gospels, I commend Peter Williams's recent book *Can We Trust the Gospels?*, which makes the case that, were it not for the extraordinary claims of the Gospels that lead many to presuppose their falsity—they would pass historical tests with flying colors. Far from wondering whether a barely historical figure may or may not have existed, we have far more manuscript evidence for the life of Jesus from copies of the Gospels than we do for the lives of some other important historical figures of his time, even including Tiberius, the Roman emperor who ruled during Jesus's public ministry.[13] We

---

11. Charles E. Hill, *Who Chose the Gospels? Probing the Great Gospel Conspiracy* (Oxford: Oxford University Press, 2010).

12. For evidence of the dependence of the Gospel of Thomas on New Testament writings, see S. J. Gathercole, *The Composition of the Gospel of Thomas: Original Language and Influences* (Cambridge: Cambridge University Press, 2012).

13. Williams, *Can We Trust the Gospels?*, 39–41.

also have the witness of multiple hostile, non-Christian sources, attesting to the basic facts of Jesus's life, death, and claimed resurrection. Here, I will pick up just one intriguing evidential thread.

In his ground-breaking work *Jesus and the Eyewitnesses*, British scholar Richard Bauckham argues that Mark's Gospel was written "well within the lifetime of many of the eyewitnesses," while the other New Testament Gospels were written when living eyewitnesses were becoming scarce—just when their testimony would die out were it not put into writing.[14] Bauckham demonstrates that the frequency of names in the Gospels mirrors their frequency in other sources from first-century Palestine. (If you have ever wondered why there are so many Marys and Simons in the Gospels, those were very common names in the region at the time!) Bauckham then uses his knowledge of contemporary norms for citing eyewitnesses to illuminate name-dropping in the Gospels, arguing that many of those named were eyewitnesses who told their stories "as authoritative guarantors of their traditions."[15] This accounts for strange cameo appearances. For example, in Mark's crucifixion account, the soldiers press-gang a passerby to carry the cross when Jesus collapses. This man is identified by his place of origin as "Simon of Cyrene," but also described as "the father of Alexander and Rufus" (Mark 15:21). Bauckham argues that Simon's sons are mentioned because they were known within the early Christian community and could corroborate the account.[16]

The Resurrection

The discrepancies between the lists of named witnesses of the resurrection in different Gospels are often cited as evidence against their authenticity. But Bauckham argues that the differences actually demonstrate the "scrupulous *care* with which the Gospels present the women as witnesses."[17] He suggests that the writers named the eyewitnesses who were known to them personally. This is particularly significant in Matthew. Under Jewish law, three witnesses for any event were preferred,

---

14. Richard Bauckham, *Jesus and the Eyewitnesses: The Gospels as Eyewitness Testimony* (Grand Rapids, MI: Eerdmans, 2008), 7.
15. Bauckham, *Jesus and the Eyewitnesses*, 39.
16. Bauckham, *Jesus and the Eyewitnesses*, 51–52.
17. Bauckham, *Jesus and the Eyewitnesses*, 49.

but rather than bolstering his list, Matthew is "content with the only two women well known to him as witnesses."[18]

With our modern sensibilities, it is easy to miss the significance of women being the first witnesses to the resurrection at all. In contemporary Jewish culture, the testimony of women was not deemed credible. There is no way the Gospel writers would have chosen women as key witnesses in a fabricated story.[19] That would be like resting a vital legal claim today on the testimony of a few kids. We see this cultural bias against women in the reaction of the male disciples: "Now it was Mary Magdalene and Joanna and Mary the mother of James and the other women with them who told these things to the apostles, but these words seemed to them an idle tale, and they did not believe them" (Luke 24:10).

The authenticity of the Gospels is further attested by just how embarrassing they are to the first church leaders. All of Jesus's male disciples deserted him. Peter, one of his closest friends and a key leader in the early church, three times denied even knowing Jesus. On this and many other counts, the Gospels are extremely bad PR for the apostles. These details would surely have been airbrushed out if the Gospel writers were not keen to record what actually happened. Such particulars would certainly not have been made up! Who wants to be known for perpetuity as "doubting Thomas," or as the disciple who swore he would follow Jesus to death and a few hours later was swearing he did not know him?

N. T. Wright, another leading New Testament scholar and ancient historian, has shed significant light on the claim that Jesus rose from the dead. Carefully examining historical and cultural contexts—including the embarrassment of female witnesses—Wright upends many of the arguments typically used to discredit the resurrection. Some suggest, for example, that Jesus fainted on the cross but did not actually die. But Roman soldiers knew how to kill.[20] Crucifixion (the standard punishment for leaders of messiah movements) was one of their favored tools. Moreover, Wright observes that when contemporaneous

18. Bauckham, *Jesus and the Eyewitnesses*, 50.
19. N. T. Wright, *The Resurrection of the Son of God* (Minneapolis: Fortress, 2003), 607–8.
20. Wright, *Resurrection of the Son*, 709.

messiah movements ended in crucifixion, the followers either gave up and went home or found themselves a new messiah. The mantle was typically passed to a close relative or associate of the former leader. James, the brother of Jesus, would have been the obvious choice. But, while James was a leader in the early church, there was no attempt to claim his messiahship.[21] Rather, the disciples proclaimed that Jesus had been raised from the dead. Many died for this belief, which they would hardly have done for an elaborate lie.

In light of the Jewish context, Wright also dismisses the idea that Jesus was not physically raised, but that he simply lived on in the hearts of his disciples. Resurrection in Jewish terms always meant newly embodied life after a period of being dead. Many first-century Jews believed in the resurrection of all God's people on the last day. But the idea that one person should have been raised to a transformed, resurrection body in the middle of time was quite new and unexpected.

Today, we find bodily resurrection implausible. But as Wright explains, our first-century forebears also knew that people who died stayed dead. Even though Jesus warned his disciples he was going to die and be raised, none of them believed it until they saw it with their own eyes. In another embarrassing episode, Jesus's disciple Thomas refused to believe, even on the eyewitness testimony of all the other disciples, until he saw Jesus himself (John 20:24–29).

The resurrection seems as incredible to us as it did to Thomas. But if there is a God who created the universe, we cannot exclude the possibility of miracles. The One who made the laws of nature in the first place can surely intervene when he chooses. The One who brought life in the first place can surely bring life to the dead. In 2018, MIT professor Ian Hutchinson published a book called *Can a Scientist Believe in Miracles?*[22] He was not raised Christian but came to Christ when he was an undergraduate at Cambridge University. Now, years later, after decades of scientific work at the highest level, his answer to the question *Can a scientist believe in the resurrection?* is emphatically yes.

---

21. Wright, *Resurrection of the Son*, 700.
22. Ian Hutchinson, *Can a Scientist Believe in Miracles? An MIT Professor Answers Questions on God and Science* (Downers Grove, IL: InterVarsity Press, 2018).

7

Hasn't Science Disproved
Christianity?

In the opening pages of *The Atheist's Guide to Reality*, philosopher
Alex Rosenberg declares: "There's so much more to atheism than its
knockdown arguments that there is no God. There is the whole rest of
the worldview that comes along with atheism. It's a demanding, rigorous, breathtaking grip on reality, one that has been vindicated beyond
reasonable doubt. It's called science."[1] Other atheists pile on. Steven
Pinker states the negative case: "The findings of science imply that the
belief systems of all the world's traditional religions and cultures . . . are
factually mistaken."[2] Richard Dawkins sees a universe that "has precisely the properties we should expect if there is, at bottom, no design,
no purpose, no evil, no good, nothing but blind, pitiless indifference."[3]

Listening to New Atheists waxing lyrical, one might think that the
case for theism is closed. But there are other voices. MIT professor Daniel Hastings began following Jesus as a teenager in the United Kingdom:
"I start by saying that there is a God who created the universe," Hastings states, "and he is not an impersonal God."[4] MIT professor Jing

---

1. Alex Rosenberg, *The Atheist's Guide to Reality: Enjoying Life without the Illusions* (New York: Norton, 2011), viii.
2. Steven Pinker, *Enlightenment Now: The Case for Reason, Science, Humanism, and Progress* (New York: Penguin, 2018), 394.
3. Richard Dawkins, *River out of Eden: A Darwinian View of Life* (New York: Basic Books, 1996), 133.
4. Daniel Hastings, "Exploring True Life," The Veritas Forum (video), June 28, 2011, https://www.youtube.com/watch?v=OGmNPWsR7_I.

Kong, who grew up in China and became a Christian when she was a grad student at the University of California, Berkeley, declares: "[My] research is only a platform for me to do God's work. His creation, the way he made this world, is very interesting. It's amazing, really."[5] Andrew Gosler, Oxford professor of applied ethnobiology, became a Christian from a secular Jewish background when he was already a professor. He explains: "My coming to faith in Christ did not rest on a single issue, such as the value of life. It was a holistic redefining of perspectives that came together through every aspect of my life."[6] The list goes on. Cambridge professor of experimental physics Russell Cowburn expresses what the dozens of leading scientists I have had the privilege of working with feel: "Understanding more of science doesn't make God smaller. It allows us to see His creative activity in more detail."[7]

In this chapter, we will question the common assumption that science points to atheism. We will explore the Christian origins of science and how Christians have often been at the forefront of scientific discoveries. We will then take a snapshot of some emerging scientific fields that have been heralded as blows to faith and suggest that, far from validating secular humanism, they expose key weaknesses in a belief system that seeks, on the one hand, to reduce truth to that which is scientifically measurable and, on the other, to uphold the intrinsic value of life.

Bible-believing Christians have always held a range of views on the relationship between science and Scripture. The goal of this chapter is not to adjudicate between them. If you decide to follow Jesus, I trust you will undertake your own exploration and come to your own conclusions. My hope in these pages is simply to offer a taste of the fruitful relationship between science and Christianity—a relationship that gets submerged in the popular discourse—and to suggest that belief in a rational Creator God provides the first and best foundation for the scientific enterprise.

---

5. David L. Chandler, "In Search of New Ways of Producing Nanomaterials: Kong's Research Focuses on How to Make and Control Novel Forms of Thin-Film Carbon," *MIT News*, May 9, 2012, http://news.mit.edu/2012/profile-kong-0509.

6. Andrew G. Gosler, "Surprise and the Value of Life," in *Real Scientists, Real Faith*, ed. R. J. Berry (Oxford: Monarch, 2009), 182.

7. Russell Cowburn, "Nanotechnology, Creation and God," TEDxStHelier (video), August 27, 2015, https://www.youtube.com/watch?time_continue=3&v=UepCFseK_os.

Christianity and the Birth of Science

To hear New Atheists today, one would scarcely think that modern science was first developed by Christians. Two Franciscan friars, Roger Bacon (ca. 1214–ca. 1294) and William of Ockham (ca. 1285–ca. 1350), laid the empirical and methodological foundations for the scientific method. Francis Bacon (1561–1626) established and popularized it. In his essay "Of Atheism," he wrote, "It is true, that a little philosophy inclineth man's mind to atheism; but depth in philosophy bringeth men's minds about to religion."[8] Robert Boyle (1627–1691), whose name is memorialized in Boyle's law, was another key player in the development of science. Boyle was a devout Christian, heavily invested in evangelism and Bible translation. He considered becoming a minister but decided he could serve Jesus better as a scientist.

But was it just coincidental that the modern scientific method was first devised by Christians?

Historic Christianity prized the life of the mind. Medieval monasteries were centers of academic study. The first universities emerged from a need to train priests.[9] Oxford and Cambridge—and later, universities like Harvard and Yale—were founded as explicitly Christian institutions.[10] But early modern Europe was not the only locus of intellectual pursuit. China and parts of the Islamic world were in some ways more technically advanced and certainly valued academic study. So why was modern science invented in Christian Europe?

Princeton professor and world-class philosopher of science Hans Halvorson argues for an intrinsic connection between the theistic worldview and the scientific one. Scientists seek natural causes for natural phenomena, not divine intervention in a test tube. But Halvorson notes that this method did not arise from atheism. On the contrary, the first scientists believed our universe was designed and created by God "according to a blueprint that can be discerned by rational creatures like ourselves." Since God was free to create however he chose, "the

---

8. Francis Bacon, "Of Atheism," in *The Essays* (Harmondsworth: Penguin, 1986), 107.

9. While places of higher education outside medieval Europe are sometimes referred to as "universities," historian Jacques Verger argues that they were not properly so. See Verger, "Patterns," in *A History of the University in Europe*, vol. 1, *Universities in the Middle Ages*, ed. Hilde de Ridder-Symoens (Cambridge: Cambridge University Press, 2003), 35.

10. Harvard's motto, for example, is *Veritas Christo et Ecclasiae*, "Truth—for Christ and the Church."

only way to discover the blueprint of creation is by means of empirical investigation."[11] Indeed, Halvorson argues that theism still provides a better philosophical foundation for science than does atheism. Atheism *per se* does not offer a foundation for science at all.[12] This does not mean that atheists cannot be outstanding scientists. Many are. But just as atheism cannot ground our ethical beliefs, so it cannot justify our science.

Galileo and the Copernican Revolution

The idea that Christianity is science's enemy and atheism its ally biases our perception of many scientific breakthroughs. The discovery that the earth revolves around the sun is a case in point. Galileo's condemnation by the Catholic church in 1633 is presented as a win for atheism, when a conception of the cosmos based on a literal reading of Scripture was challenged by brave scientists willing to stand up to the church. Indeed, this episode is seen as paradigmatic of how Christianity and science have always interacted: science attacks, Christianity retreats. Sociologist Elaine Howard Ecklund interviewed scientists at elite universities and found that many cited "Galileo's torture at the hands of the Inquisition as a central piece of evidence that religion and science are in an entrenched conflict."[13] As Ecklund points out, the idea that Galileo was tortured is a widely believed myth unsupported by historical evidence. But there are three other problems with the notion that the Galileo affair proves the triumph of science over Christianity.

First, Galileo was a Christian. He argued vociferously that heliocentrism did not undermine the Bible. In fact, his attempt to make theological arguments was part of what got him in trouble with the pope, who had previously been Galileo's friend and supported his scientific work. In the wake of the Protestant Reformation, the Catholic church was highly sensitive to laymen making theological pronouncements.

11. Hans Halvorson, "Why Methodological Naturalism," in *The Blackwell Companion to Naturalism*, ed. Kelly James Clark (Chichester, West Sussex, UK: Wiley-Blackwell, 2016), 142.

12. As MIT philosopher and atheist Alex Byrne observes, "You can consistently hold atheism together with the idea that science tells you virtually nothing about the nature of reality, or any view you like about morality, or human nature, or anything else." Alex Byrne, "Is Atheism a Worldview?," The Veritas Forum (video), September 19, 2016, https://www.youtube.com/watch?v=oeynhmPHqB4.

13. Elaine Howard Ecklund, *Science vs. Religion: What Scientists Really Think* (Oxford: Oxford University Press, 2010), 149.

Galileo's argument that the biblical authors accommodated their language to the capacity of ordinary people was a standard principle of medieval theology. But while the theological battles of the Reformation were still raging, these questions were politically charged.[14]

Second, the prevailing cosmology before this controversy was not biblical but Aristotelian. Aristotle's model, in which the earth was at the center of the universe with the sun rotating around it, had been the standard paradigm taught in universities for centuries before Copernicus and Galileo rocked the cosmological boat. To be sure, Aristotle's model was more easily superimposed on some biblical texts than the heliocentric model. But his view that the earth was spherical does not map onto the ancient Near Eastern cosmology of the Old Testament, which envisages the earth being founded on pillars. Thus, the cosmology endorsed by the church before the Copernican revolution was not compatible with strict biblical literalism.

The third problem with the notion that Galileo overturned biblical literalism was that Christians had been exploring nonliteral views of biblical texts in relation to science for centuries. For example, the fourth-century theologian Augustine of Hippo cautioned his contemporaries not to make statements about science that might bring the Christian faith into disrepute: "It is a disgraceful and dangerous thing," he wrote, for a non-Christian "to hear a Christian, presumably giving the meaning of Holy Scripture, talking nonsense on these topics."[15] Some Christians today argue that not reading the Bible literally on every scientific question undermines the credibility of the resurrection claim. Augustine argued the opposite:

> If [unbelievers] find a Christian mistaken in a field which they themselves know well and hear him maintaining his foolish opinions about our books, how are they going to believe those books in matters concerning the resurrection of the dead, the hope of eternal life, and the kingdom of heaven?[16]

---

14. Galileo's case was further hindered by the fact that in his *Dialogue concerning the Two Chief World Systems* (1632), he put the pope's concerns about the heliocentric model in the mouth of Simplicio, who was, in the rest of the *Dialogue*, almost always speaking for the losing side.

15. St. Augustine, *The Literal Meaning of Genesis* (1.19.39), trans. John Hammond Taylor (New York: Paulist Press, 1982), 43.

16. Augustine, *Literal Meaning of Genesis*, 43.

Far from being a blow by atheist scientists against what had always been a literalist view of Scripture, therefore, the Copernican revolution could equally be heralded as a blow by Christian scientists against centuries of a misunderstanding based on pagan philosophy. To be sure, the Catholic church resisted at the time. But, as with practically every scientific controversy since, there were Christians on both sides.

A (Very) Brief History of Christians in Science

The importance of believers in the history of science is revealed by none other than Albert Einstein. Einstein kept pictures of three scientific heroes on the wall of his study: Isaac Newton, Michael Faraday, and James Clerk Maxwell. Newton (ca. 1642–1727) is one of the most influential scientists of all time, famous for formulating the laws of gravity and motion. While not an orthodox Christian, owing to his denial of the full divinity of Christ, Newton was an earnest believer in God and wrote more about theology than physics. Faraday (1791–1867) is best known for his work on electromagnetism, and his scientific contributions were so significant that he is considered one of the greatest experimental scientists ever. The Faraday constant is named after him, as is the Faraday effect, the Faraday cage, and Faraday waves. Faraday was a passionate Christian, deeply interested in the relationship between science and faith.[17] Maxwell (1831–1879) has been credited with the second great unification of physics, bringing together electricity, magnetism, and light. He was an evangelical Presbyterian, who became an elder of the Church of Scotland. For these men, science and faith went hand in hand, and studying God's creation was an act of worship.[18] But is this just a tiny minority report in the history of otherwise atheistic science? Not at all.

---

17. "I cannot doubt," wrote Faraday, excitedly, "that a glorious discovery in natural knowledge, and the wisdom and power of God in the creation, is awaiting our age, and that we may not only hope to see it, but even be honoured to help in obtaining the victory over present ignorance and future knowledge." Bence Jones, *The Life and Letters of Faraday*, vol. 2 (London: Longmans, Green and Co., 1870), 385.

18. See, for example, this prayer by James Clark Maxwell: "Almighty God, Who hast created man in Thine own image, and made him a living soul that he might seek after Thee, and have dominion over Thy creatures, teach us to study the works of Thy hands, that we may subdue the earth to our use, and strengthen the reason for Thy service; And so to receive Thy blessed Word that we may believe on Him whom Thou hast sent to give us the knowledge of salvation and the remission of our sins. All which we ask in the name of the same Jesus Christ our Lord." Quoted

Lord Kelvin (1824–1907), whose name is memorialized in the Kelvin unit of temperature, is another example of scientific excellence and serious faith. Kelvin was one of the first scientists to calculate the age of the earth in millions rather than thousands of years. In a speech to the Christian Evidence Society, of which he was president, he declared:

> I have long felt that there was a general impression in the non-scientific world, that the scientific world believes Science has discovered ways of explaining all the facts of Nature without adopting any definite belief in a Creator. I have never doubted that that impression was utterly groundless.[19]

In the nineteenth century as today, questions of science and faith were hotly debated. But there were serious Christians at the center of the "scientific world," arguing for belief in a Creator God.

The assumption that science is the tool with which atheists have gradually demolished Christianity is further exploded by the big bang. A Belgian Roman Catholic priest named Georges Lemaître was the first to propose the crazy-sounding idea that the universe had begun as an incredibly hot, incredibly dense point: a "cosmic egg." Like any scientific paradigm shift, the theory met with resistance. In this instance, some of the pushback was motivated by atheism. As Stephen Hawking observed, "Many people do not like the idea that time has a beginning, probably because it smacks of divine intervention. . . . There were therefore a number of attempts to avoid the conclusion that there had been a big bang."[20]

One of the scientists who opposed the theory was atheist physicist Fred Hoyle, who coined the term *big bang* in a radio interview, where he compared the theory to a party girl jumping out of a cake.[21] Along with many scientists of his day, Hoyle preferred the "steady state" theory, according to which the universe had always existed. With this

in Lewis Campbell and William Garnett, *The Life of James Clark Maxwell: With Selections from His Correspondence and Occasional Writings* (London: MacMillan, 1884), 237.

19. Lord Kelvin, quoted in *Twelfth Report of the Committee of the Christian Evidence Society* (London: G. Norman and Son, 1883), 46.

20. Stephen Hawking, *A Brief History of Time* (New York: Bantam, 1998), 49.

21. Walter Sullivan, "Fred Hoyle Dies at 86; Opposed 'Big Bang' but Named It," *New York Times*, August 22, 2001, https://www.nytimes.com/2001/08/22/world /fred-hoyle-dies-at-86-opposed-big-bang-but-named-it.html.

model, it was easier to avoid the idea that anything outside the universe brought it into being. Far from being yet another pointer toward atheism, the big bang is intriguingly congruent with the core Christian belief that God created the universe out of nothing.[22]

Perhaps the most controversial question in the realm of science and faith also has a complex history when it comes to Christianity. Darwin fluctuated in his own beliefs during his life, apparently progressing from deism to agnosticism. But Darwin's closest collaborator and "best advocate," Harvard professor and botanist Asa Gray, was a passionate Christian. Gray contributed his own research to Darwin's via a correspondence of more than three hundred letters. In a letter to Gray in 1881, Darwin wrote, "There is hardly any one in the world whose approbation I value more highly than I do yours."[23] Unlike Darwin, Gray saw nature as filled with "unmistakable and irresistible indications of design," and tried to persuade Darwin to return to Christianity, arguing, "God himself is the very last, irreducible causal factor and, hence, the source of all evolutionary change."[24]

The New Atheist story is further undermined by the history of genetics. Gregor Mendel (1822–1884) was a Roman Catholic friar who studied the heredity of pea plants in the gardens of St Thomas's Abbey. Dawkins recognizes Mendel as the "founding genius of genetics itself," but is careful to downplay his faith: "Mendel, of course, was a religious man, an Augustinian monk; but that was in the nineteenth century when becoming a monk was the easiest way for the young Mendel to pursue his science. For him, it was the equivalent of a research grant."[25] Such biased reporting is vital if one is to maintain the story of science as antithetical to faith, and in most instances, it is simply impossible to justify.

---

22. NASA scientist Robert Jastrow captures how disquieting the discovery that the universe had a beginning was to atheist scientists at the time: "For the scientist who has lived by his faith in the power of reason, the story ends like a bad dream. He has scaled the mountain of ignorance; he is about to conquer the highest peak; as he pulls himself over the final rock, he is greeted by a band of theologians who have been sitting there for centuries." Robert Jastrow, *God and the Astronomers* (New York: Norton, 1978), 107.

23. Charles Darwin, to Asa Grey, January 29, 1881, in the Darwin Correspondence Project, University of Cambridge, accessed October 17, 2018, https://www.darwinproject.ac.uk/letter/DCP-LETT-13031.xml.

24. Asa Gray, quoted in George Webb, *The Evolution Controversy in America* (Lexington: University Press of Kentucky, 2002), 19.

25. Richard Dawkins, *The God Delusion* (repr., Boston: Mariner, 2008), 125.

If the history of science from the sixteenth to the twentieth century gives us multiple examples of leading Christian scientists, have scientists come to their atheistic senses in the cool light of the twenty-first century?

Christian Scientists Today

I live a short walk from MIT, the sacred temple of scientific endeavor in the United States. Stop a student in the "infinite corridor" that meanders through its buildings and ask if he or she thinks there are any Christian professors at the Institute, and the answer will likely be no. Yet the roll call of Christian professors at MIT is impressive. I have already mentioned nuclear science professor Ian Hutchinson, professor of aeronautics and astronautics Daniel Hastings, and electrical engineering professor Jing Kong, none of whom was raised as a Christian. But there are more. Artificial intelligence expert Rosalind Picard, who invented the field of affective computing, became a Christian when she was a teenager. Chemistry professor Troy Van Voorhis came to Christ when he was a grad student at Berkeley. Biological and mechanical engineering professor Linda Griffith became a Christian when she was already an established scientist. Other Christians include professor of mechanical and ocean engineering Dick Yue; chemical engineering professor Chris Love; professor of biological engineering, chemical engineering, and biology Doug Lauffenburger; history professor Anne McCants; and even neuroscientist and former MIT president (the first female president of the Institute) Susan Hockfield. The list goes on. And it extends far beyond MIT to leading Christian scientists across the world. If science has disproved Christianity, no one has thought to notify them!

This is not to say that science professors are not more likely than the general population to be unbelievers. They are: 34 percent of science professors at elite universities say they do not believe in God, versus 2 percent of the general population, and a further 30 percent say they do not know if there is a God and there is no way to find out.[26] But we must be cautious about deriving causation from correlation.

---

26. Ecklund, *Science vs. Religion*, 17.

When interviewed, relatively few science professors at leading research universities tell stories of faith *lost* through science,[27] and the demographics of science professors bias strongly toward white male Americans, Asian Americans, and Jewish Americans—the demographics least likely to espouse belief in God—and away from the most religious demographics: African Americans and Latino Americans.[28] Perhaps because of increasing diversity, younger cohorts of scientists are getting progressively more religious—the opposite of the national trend.[29] Indeed, it is possible that the narrative that presents science as antithetical to Christianity is part of what is keeping underrepresented groups (African Americans, Latino Americans, and women) out of the sciences. Again, the New Atheist story in which science disproves Christianity turns out to be less compelling than it at first seemed.

The weakness of the claim that science has disproved Christianity is brought home by the testimony of one of the most influential scientists in America today, who came to faith when he was already a professional scientist. Francis Collins led the Human Genome Project and now directs the National Institutes of Health. He grew up in a secular home. Religion wasn't so much attacked as it was irrelevant. As a graduate student at Yale, he shifted from agnosticism to atheism, assuming that belief in God was rationally untenable. But his atheism was challenged during his time as a junior doctor, when the faith of his patients seemed to give them enviable help in the face of suffering. Collins was particularly shaken by one conversation with an older woman suffering from severe and untreatable pain, who shared her faith in Jesus and asked, "Doctor, what do you believe?" "I felt my

27. See Ecklund, *Science vs. Religion*, 17: "For the majority of scientists I interviewed, it is not engagement with science itself that leads them away from God."
28. In 2016, 82 percent of full professors at "very high-activity research universities" were white, versus 73 percent of the US population. Ben Myers, "Where Are the Minority Professors?," *The Chronicle of Higher Education*, February 14, 2016, https://www.chronicle.com/interactives /where-are-the-minority-professors. Whereas 13 percent of the US population is African-American and a national study of the top one hundred departments of science and engineering revealed that underrepresented minorities made up less than 5 percent of tenured or tenure-track faculty. Donna J. Nelson, "A National Analysis of Minorities in Science and Engineering Faculties at Research Universities" (n.p., 2007), 1, http://cheminfo.chem.ou.edu/faculty/djn/diversity/Facu lty_Tables_FY07/07Report.pdf. Moreover, 16 percent of science professors at elite universities are Jewish, compared with 2 percent of the general population, and among scientists who are Jewish, nearly 75 percent identify as atheists. See Ecklund, *Science vs. Religion*, 36.
29. The younger the cohort of scientists interviewed, the more likely they were to believe in God and to attend religious services. Ecklund, *Science vs. Religion*, 32.

face flush," he recalls, "as I stammered out the words, 'I'm not really sure.'"[30] In his discomfort, Collins realized that he had never really considered the evidence for God. This patient's simple question set him on a journey of exploration and research that ended in him accepting Jesus as his Savior. He now believes that "the God of the Bible is also the God of the genome."[31]

Does It Mean Anything?

In a very different doctor-patient conversation, Gregory House (the eponymous hero of the hit TV show *House, M.D.*) berates a performance artist who has finagled her way into his care. House realizes his patient intended to create a life-art piece, and challenges her: "I think you just figured out you're mortal, just a bag of cells and waste with an expiration date. You wanted to act out. You wanted people to notice. Maybe you even prayed for a different answer this time. I have a title for your piece—'It Doesn't Mean Anything.'"[32]

The idea that having a full scientific description of a human being ransacks our lives of meaning inspires House's nihilistic summary: we're all just bags of cells and waste with an unknown expiration date; it doesn't mean anything. Full-blown nihilism is one response to the reduction of humanity to component parts that some believe science has accomplished. But House's patient represents a different and perhaps more common view: sure, science has killed any cosmic sense of meaning, but that just frees us to create our own; each life is a performance piece. In both views, the premise is the same: if we have a complete scientific description of something, other descriptions are squeezed out. But what if this premise is wrong?

Eight years ago, I gave birth to my first child. Her conception was not miraculous. Her gestation was unremarkable. Had a scientist cared to document it, there would be no gaps in the script. And yet there was no doubt in my mind that this baby had been made by God, and that she was far more than a bag of cells and waste with an expiration date—not because she is not those things, but because

---

30. Francis Collins, *The Language of God: A Scientist Presents Evidence for Belief* (New York: Free Press, 2006), 20.
31. Collins, *Language of God*, 211.
32. "Moving On," *House, M.D.*, season 7, episode 23.

she is not *just* those things. Indeed, the Bible describes us in even less flattering terms than does Dr. House. "You are dust," declares God to the first man, "and to dust you shall return" (Gen. 3:19). From a Christian perspective, my daughter *is* a bag of cells. But she is not *just* cells. She is dust. But she is not *just* dust. Indeed, the Bible insists that our dust-formed selves have immense and inalienable value, not because we are *not* atoms and molecules, bags of cells, or dust, but because we are dust that has been fashioned by God and called to unique relationship with him. For Christians, therefore, the most important question is not *What does science say we are?* but *Who does God say we are?*

It's not that scientific knowledge doesn't matter. The scientific method has enabled us to fly planes, clean water, and cure disease. Our daily lives—at least in economically privileged parts of the world—depend on it. But much as I value science, I do not believe that scientific knowledge is the most important kind. The facts about ourselves and our world that are measurable by science may be the easiest to verify. What formula governs the speed at which an object falls to the ground? How high is the window ledge on which I'm standing? But were I to jump, no news report would confine itself to the exact distance from the ledge to the ground, or the precise effects of the impact on my body. The primary question people would ask would not be *how* but *why*. While discovering *how* can be important, knowing how someone died does not exhaust the story. Like the notes for the right and left hand in a piano sonata, the measurable script and the meaning script do not jostle for position. Both are needed to give us the full picture.

The primacy of meaning-seeking over fact-finding illuminates the biblical creation accounts. As I noted earlier, Christians hold a range of views regarding the genre of the creation accounts in Genesis and how they relate to science. But one thing is clear: Genesis is not *primarily* concerned with science. If it were, we would expect the accounts to be teeming with formulas and phenotypes. The God who made the universe must have scientific knowledge as far surpassing ours as a street lamp is surpassed by the sun! But the lack of scientific detail is not an oversight. Rather, it is a deliberate prioritization of a more important message. As a Christian, I believe that every detail of the creation accounts in Genesis is inspired by God and that these opening chapters are the first course in the Bible's feast of foundational answers to our deepest questions: *Who are we? What does life mean? And how do we relate to God and to each other?*

God could have begun the Bible with a detailed scientific description of the universe, just as I could tuck my kids in bed at night and tell them that they are mammals whose genetic identity arises from a combination of my DNA and that of their other progenitor. These statements are true. They communicate useful information that I would like my children to learn in the coming years. Perhaps one of them will go on to be a scientist and add to the pool of scientific information in which we twenty-first century Westerners swim. But right now, it's more important for my children to know that I am their mother and I love them. In fact, if I gave them the scientific information without the relational information, I would be robbing them of the truth and utterly failing to meet their needs.

Science and Human Value

In the West today, science in general, and evolution in particular, is often invoked to discredit Christian faith in favor of the form of secular humanism preferred by privileged elites. But stripping the meat of relational truth off the skeleton of scientific truth does not just undermine theism. It has consequences for any belief system that wants to preserve a concept of innate human value. This is evident even to Richard Dawkins, who describes himself as a passionate Darwinian when it comes to science and "a passionate anti-Darwinian when it comes to politics and how we should conduct human affairs."[33] Dawkins declares that "evolution gave us a brain whose size increased to the point where it became capable of understanding its own provenance, of deploring the moral implications and of fighting against them." But within a materialist worldview that rejects any supernatural storyline, there is no *reason* to think that the moral implications of evolution are to be deplored, or even that there are such things as

---

33. Richard Dawkins, *A Devil's Chaplain: Reflections on Hope, Lies, Science, and Love* (Boston: Mariner, 2004), 10–11.

moral implications. Using evolution to blast theism leaves the secular humanist stunned by the kickback.

The fact that evolution *per se* does not validate the specific form of liberal secular humanism preferred by New Atheist leaders is illustrated by the history of ideas. Evolutionary theory has been used at various times to justify a whole range of different beliefs. As we saw in chapter 5, Hitler invoked evolution to support his fascist agenda. But evolution was also claimed by Marx and Stalin as a scientific vindication of Communism, while capitalist leaders saw it as a vindication of capitalism. Likewise, in Darwin's day, while many atheists saw evolution as a proof of atheism, many Christian leaders disagreed.[34] Even some Calvinist leaders hailed evolution as "the Calvinistic interpretation of nature."[35] Such extreme ideological differences in its champions suggest that in this case, as in many others, the bare science can be viewed through different ideological lenses. But it cannot be the whole story.

If we are no more than the features that can be described by science, and our only story is the evolutionary story, we have no grounds for insisting on human equality, protection of the weak, equal treatment of women, or any of the other ethical beliefs we hold dear. To cite one example among thousands, female primates are routinely sexually assaulted by males. To say that this behavior is wrong for humans—that it should be vigorously resisted and rigorously punished, despite its evolutionary advantages—is to say that humans are distinct from other creatures at a fundamental level. Both Christians and secular humanists need an account of humanity that makes this distinction.

Christians ground human uniqueness on the biblical claim that we are made in the image of God. Just as God calls creation into being, so he calls humans to serve as his representatives on earth, in special relationship with their Creator and with each other, and

---

34. Historian James Moore observes that "with but few exceptions, the leading Christian thinkers in Great Britain and America came to terms quite readily with Darwinism and evolution." James Moore, *The Post-Darwinian Controversies: A Study of the Protestant Struggle to Come to Terms with Darwin in Great Britain and America, 1870–1900* (Cambridge: Cambridge University Press, 1981), 92.

35. George White, "Some Analogies between Calvinism and Darwinism," *Bibliotheca Sacra* 37 (January 1880): 76.

charged with moral responsibility. To maintain their beliefs about goodness, fairness, justice, and so forth, a secular humanist too must hold that humans are moral beings, distinct from other primates. The question is, on what grounds? And, ultimately, the answer cannot be scientific. Science can tell us how things are. It can explain why, for instance, a man might have the drive to commit a sexual assault as an effective means of propagating his genes. But it cannot tell us why he would be wrong to succumb to that drive. To be sure, we can conduct sociological calculations to see what behaviors turn out better for the group and decide that sexual assault yields a net negative in the overall happiness of the tribe. But to call rape *wrong*, we need a narrative about human identity that goes beyond what science or sociology can tell us.

One advantage of the biblical narrative is that it does not link human uniqueness to particular mental or physical characteristics. As we saw in chapter 4, basing our value on our characteristics or capacities jeopardizes human equality. And evolution has been co-opted to that end many times. For instance, if we rewind to the first half of the twentieth century, we see evolution being used to justify both racism and eugenics. Indeed, as anthropologist Matt Cartmill has observed, "From Darwin's time down to the beginning of World War Two, most scientists who studied human evolution . . . firmly believed that some living human races are closer to apes than others."[36] To be sure, that belief turned out to be scientifically groundless, and the ways in which evolutionary theory has been used for evil does not discredit science any more than the infamous Tuskegee syphilis study discredits medicine. Racial prejudice motivated both. But when atheists reject Christianity because of the evils done in the name of religion, we must recognize that evil has also been done in the name of science. And that it is ultimately only a religious worldview that enables us to diagnose evil *as* evil.

Reflecting on the difference between an atheistic approach to science and a Christian one, Stanford neuroscientist Bill Newsome poses this question:

---

36. Matt Cartmill, *A View to a Death in the Morning: Hunting and Nature through History* (repr., Cambridge, MA: Harvard University Press, 1996), 199.

Do we live in a universe where our highest values and intuitions about ethical behavior are in touch with the central reality of the universe and the reason the universe was built from the beginning? Or are our highest values and ethical intuitions kind of a joke—an accident—that really have nothing to do with what the universe is about?[37]

Science has its place—a vital one—in modern society. We can all benefit from the knowledge we have gained through the scientific method first devised by Christian scholars. But if we elevate scientific truth above all other kinds and believe that the scientific script rules out other stories, we have no grounds for morality and no basis for—in Dawkins's formulation—rebelling against our genes. We are bags of cells and waste with an expiration date, and it doesn't mean anything.

Are Humans Accidental or Designed?

In addition to evolution's perceived challenge to human uniqueness, another claim by which atheists seek to discredit Christianity is the idea that if you replayed the evolutionary tape over again, the results would be totally different.[38] This idea, along with the fact that death, suffering, and accidental circumstance are baked into the evolutionary story, has been used by atheists to argue that humans are not in any meaningful sense "designed" or intended by God.

Richard Dawkins uses the example of the recurrent laryngeal nerve, which takes a circuitous route in humans traveling from the brain to the larynx via the heart. In a public dissection of a giraffe's neck, where the same nerve takes the same journey at more extraordinary length, Dawkins observes: "The imperfections are exactly the kind of imperfections you'd expect from the accidents of history if there were no designer."[39] In Dawkins's view, while humans may look designed from the outside, if you lift the hood on the machine and start rooting around, you find that our insides tell a different story. As we have already noted, Christians differ in what they believe about how God

---

37. See Bill Newsome's reply to the question "How does faith affect your life?," in *Test of Faith*, (YouTube video interview), April 29, 2010, https://www.youtube.com/watch?v=PMIBfH0qS6Y.
38. This claim was popularized by Harvard professor and paleontologist Stephen J. Gould.
39. "Richard Dawkins Demonstrates Laryngeal Nerve of the Giraffe," YouTube (video), June 13, 2010, https://www.youtube.com/watch?v=cO1a1Ek-HD0.

went about creating humanity. But all Christians must believe that humans are ultimately designed, intended, and purposed by God. So, the argument goes, imperfections like this discredit the Christian story. But there are two main problems with this argument.

First, you could make the same argument about history. Many past events seem to depend on mishap, coincidence, and chance. But the Bible tells a story in which history—with all its seeming randomness, harshness, and mess—is divinely orchestrated, and in which suffering is baked into God's plan for salvation, which hinges on the suffering and death of a man on a cross.[40] Indeed, from a Christian perspective, there is no such thing as chance or historical accident: God rules over every circumstance of our lives.

Second, the replay-the-tape-for-difference claim may not even represent the best science. Simon Conway Morris, who holds the Chair of Evolutionary Paleobiology at Cambridge University, is best known for his groundbreaking study of the fossils of the Burgess Shale. These fossils are evidence for what is known as the Cambrian explosion: the 20–25-million-year period of accelerated diversification that started about 540 million years ago and produced most of the major animal phyla. Conway Morris is a Christian and highly critical of the claim that evolution validates atheism. Moreover, countering the claim that replaying the tape of life would produce different results, he cites multiple examples of convergence: the same characteristics evolving independently in different animals. Conway Morris argues that human beings were not a random accident but that something like a human is a predictable outcome of the evolutionary process: more like solving a puzzle than writing a novel.[41]

Again, Christians vary in their interpretation of the creation accounts in Genesis and my aim is not to gloss over theological complexity. But this emerging scientific frontier of convergence is questioning one of the key ways in which New Atheists have pitted science against creation. It will be fascinating to see how it unfolds in the coming years. It's also worth noting that while scientists have an account of

---

40. As we will see in chap. 11, Christians believe in a God who is incredibly good—but not in a God who always takes the shortest, straightest route from A to B: quite the reverse.

41. See Simon Conway Morris, *Life's Solution: Inevitable Humans in a Lonely Universe* (Cambridge: Cambridge University Press, 2004).

how more-complex life forms developed from simpler ones, we are all scratching around in the dark when it comes to the question of how the tape of life got started in the first place![42] But even if it were true that replaying the tape of life would likely produce a different result, and if we knew scientifically how the tape first started to play, this would have little relevance from a Christian perspective. Restart the sperm race that led to my conception, and the result would almost certainly not be me. Yet here I am, and I believe that God intended it so.

But is that belief itself just an artifact of my biological past?

Born Believers?

In his book *Why Would Anyone Believe in God?*, psychologist Justin L. Barrett argues that religious belief is a natural consequence of the kind of minds we have.[43] Barrett is widely regarded as the founding father of the field of evolutionary psychology of religion. He argues that the near universal propensity of humans to hold religious beliefs arises from our bias toward imputing agency. To give a simple example, if our forebears saw a shape that might have been a tiger, they were more likely to survive if they assumed it was a tiger intent on harming them than if they assumed it was just a tiger-shaped rock. Expect a tiger and get a rock: no harm, no foul. Expect a rock and get a tiger: game over! Paint that thinking on a larger canvas, so the reasoning goes, and you'll start seeing gods behind storms and droughts.

Atheists hail this with relief. It helps explain the stubborn refusal of most humans to abandon religion. But Barrett takes a different view. Formerly a senior researcher at the Institute for Cognitive and Evolutionary Anthropology at Oxford, and now a professor of psychology at Fuller Theological Seminary, Barrett sees the human propensity to believe in God as quite consistent with his Christian faith. "If there is a God with whom we are meant to be in a personal relationship," Barrett asks, "then how probable [is it] that engagement in such a relationship

---

42. If scientists figure out how this happened, it will have interesting implications for the possibility of finding life on other planets. For more on this, see Jack Szostak, "How Did Life Begin? Untangling the Origins of Organisms Will Require Experiments at the Tiniest Scales and Observations at the Vastest," *Scientific American*, June 1, 2018, https://www.scientificamerican.com/article/how-did-life-begin1/.

43. Justin L. Barrett, *Why Would Anyone Believe in God?*, Cognitive Science of Religion Series (Lanham, MD: AltaMira, 2004).

would happen to be good for us?"[44] Indeed, to see humanity's natural interest in God as proof of God's nonexistence seems rather obtuse! If a biological motive for human behavior discredits any deeper reality that behavior reveals, then my love for my husband and my children should be similarly dismissed: it doesn't mean anything.

Fine Tuning and the Multiverse

If we raise our gaze from humanity to the universe at large, we find another set of interesting questions broached by contemporary science. Just as the evidence that the universe had a beginning was unsettling to atheists in the twentieth century, the evidence that our universe is minutely fine-tuned for life raises some challenging questions for atheists today. Cosmologists have isolated key numbers that are fundamental to the physical universe. Some are extremely large. For example, N (1,000,000,000,000,000,000,000,000,000,000,000,000) measures the strength of the electrical forces that hold atoms together, divided by the force of gravity between them. Others are extremely small, like Q (0.00001), which represents the ratio between two fundamental energies.[45] Cambridge professor and world-class astronomer Martin Rees explained in his book *Just Six Numbers: The Deep Forces That Shape the Universe* that if any of these numbers were even fractionally different, there would be no stars, no earth, and no life.

Rees presents three possible explanations of this apparent fine-tuning. The first is pure chance. This is so incredibly unlikely that Rees does not find it plausible. The second possibility is that there is a God who intended for the universe to generate life. Rees acknowledges that this is a reasonable view, held by some of his colleagues.[46] But he himself prefers to believe that our universe is one among a mind-boggling number of parallel universes, each governed by different laws and defined by different numbers. Ours happens to be one that sustains

---

44. Justin Barrett, "Do Our Mental Tools Cause Belief in God?," The Veritas Forum (video), December 17, 2011, https://www.youtube.com/watch?v=hR3B9hIP0sE].

45. Martin Rees, *Just Six Numbers: The Deep Forces That Shape the Universe* (London: Phoenix, 2000), 166.

46. Rees specifically mentions the eminent theoretical physicist John Polkinghorne. For Polkinghorne's discussion of the same data, see John Polkinghorne and Nicholas Beale, *Questions of Truth: Fifty-One Responses to Questions about God, Science, and Belief* (Louisville: Westminster Knox Press, 2009), 44–45.

life. It is impossible to test this theory experimentally, because we are confined to this universe. But given the choice between believing in a Creator God and believing in a practically infinite number of parallel universes, Rees prefers the latter.

There is no theological problem with a so-called multiverse *per se*. In Psalm 8, the psalmist looks at the sky and wonders why God cares about humans, who are so seemingly insignificant in the grand sweep of God's creation. The infinite God who made billions of stars could easily have made billions of universes. But the idea of a Creator God does not sound quite so crazy when you realize that the best current alternative explanation for the apparent fine-tuning of the universe for life is the existence of an infinite number of parallel universes.

Are the Laws of Nature Enough?

In his 2010 book *The Grand Design*, the late Stephen Hawking declared:

> Because there is a law like gravity, the universe can and will create itself from nothing. . . . Spontaneous creation is the reason there is something rather than nothing, why the universe exists, why we exist. It is not necessary to invoke God to light the blue touch paper and set the universe going.[47]

Polemicists like Dawkins welcomed this statement with applause. But the book received substantial criticism, including from other secular scientists who saw it as making exaggerated claims and presenting highly speculative theories as established science.[48] Moreover, agnostic physicist Paul Davies pointed out, first, that the view of God as a touch-paper lighter misrepresents Christian theology (since Augustine, at least) and, second, that the scenario Hawking describes cannot provide a complete account of existence, because this view of reality "comes with a lot of baggage," including "sweeping 'meta-laws' that pervade the multiverse and spawn specific bylaws on a

---

47. Stephen Hawking and Leonard Mlodinow, *The Grand* Design (New York: Bantam, 2010), 180.

48. For example, atheist physicist Roger Penrose pointed out that the M-theory (a development of string theory that Hawking presents in *The Grand Design*) "enjoys no observational support whatever." Roger Penrose, review of *The Grand Design*, by Stephen Hawking, *Financial Times*, September 3, 2010, https://www.ft.com/content/bdf3ae28-b6e9-11df-b3dd-00144feabdc0.

universe-by-universe basis." Davies observes, "The meta-laws themselves remain unexplained—eternal, immutable transcendent entities that just happen to exist and must simply be accepted as given. In that respect, the meta-laws have a similar status to an unexplained, transcendent God."[49]

On this issue as on others, Christians and atheists are vulnerable to the same mistake: the idea that science will either prove or disprove theism. A more fruitful approach is to look at the world around us and ask ourselves, does this seem coherent with the possibility of God? Where Francis Collins marvels at God's creation through science, Richard Dawkins sees science as the faith-killing equivalent of insecticide. Where Stephen Hawking believed science rendered God unnecessary, Paul Shellard—who directs the Centre for Theoretical Cosmology at Cambridge and was one of Hawking's closest collaborators—sees the same science as quite consistent with his Christian beliefs. Describing the congruence he sees between science and his Christian faith, Nobel Prize–winning physicist William Phillips writes:

> I see an orderly, beautiful universe in which nearly all physical phenomena can be understood from a few simple mathematical equations. I see a universe that, had it been constructed slightly differently, would never have given birth to stars and planets, let alone bacteria and people. And there is no good scientific reason for why the universe should not have been different. Many good scientists have concluded from these observations that an intelligent God must have chosen to create the universe with such beautiful, simple, and life-giving properties. Many other equally good scientists are nevertheless atheists. Both conclusions are positions of faith.[50]

"The Unreasonable Effectiveness of Mathematics"

We are so used to science that we forget to marvel at the very fact that laws of the universe are comprehensible to us. Why should the neurons firing in a mammal's brain relate to the laws that shape the universe?

49. Paul Davies, "Stephen Hawking's Big Bang Gaps," *The Guardian*, September 4, 2010, https://www.theguardian.com/commentisfree/belief/2010/sep/04/stephen-hawking-big-bang-gap.
50. William D. Phillips, "Does Science Make Belief in God Obsolete?," *Fair Observer*, November 10, 2013, https://www.fairobserver.com/culture/does-science-make-belief-god-obsolete/.

Why should mathematics, which can in its purest form be undertaken in an armchair, relate to the workings of the world in ways that are both discoverable and beautiful to us?

Nobel Prize–winning physicist Eugene Wigner famously raised these questions in an article entitled "The Unreasonable Effectiveness of Mathematics in the Natural Sciences." Wigner observed that "the enormous usefulness of mathematics in the natural sciences is something bordering on the mysterious and that there is no rational explanation for it." He ends with gratitude: "The miracle of the appropriateness of the language of mathematics for the formulation of the laws of physics is a wonderful gift which we neither understand nor deserve."[51] Wigner was writing in 1960, but this marvel remains. It recalls the first hypothesis of the first modern scientists: that if a rational God made the universe and endowed humans with an intelligence that echoed his own, perhaps his image-bearing creatures would be able to discern his laws.

51. Eugene Wigner, "The Unreasonable Effectiveness of Mathematics in the Natural Sciences," *Communications in Pure and Applied Mathematics* 13, no. 1 (February 1960), dartmouth.edu (reading materials), https://www.dartmouth.edu/~matc/MathDrama/reading/Wigner.html.

8

Doesn't Christianity Denigrate Women?

At a pivotal moment in *Harry Potter and the Half-Blood Prince*, Professor Dumbledore makes a poignant request: "Severus . . . Please." Up to this point, we do not know whether Severus Snape is a double agent for Dumbledore or for the murderous antagonist Voldemort. Now Snape's loyalty is tested. Dumbledore, surrounded by enemies, pleads for help; and Snape kills him. The scene is devastating. We never liked Snape, but we hoped beyond hope that he was Dumbledore's man. Now Snape's betrayal of his mentor is complete.

It is not until the last Harry Potter book that we realize how wrong we were. When Harry extracts memories from Snape's dying mind and pours them into the magical Pensieve—where one can dive into another's past—we discover that Snape's love for Harry's mother, Lily, was the guiding principle of his life. We see Snape's anguish as Lily is murdered by Voldemort, and how Snape thenceforth commits himself to Dumbledore. Dumbledore tells Snape that he is dying from the slow working of an irreversible curse, and we hear Snape reluctantly pledge to kill him when the moment comes. Suddenly, we see Dumbledore's plea and Snape's actions in a new light. When we know the beginning and the end of the story, the meaning of "Severus . . . Please" is reversed.

To understand the Christian account of male and female, we must gaze into the "Pensieve" of the whole Bible. If we read texts only in the light of our own presuppositions, they will make little sense. But if we dive into the panorama of salvation history, the biblical view of men and women assumes new meaning. As with Snape, the key to understanding the Bible's view of men and women is a story of relentless love.

Before the Beginning

When we think about sex and gender, we instinctively start with culture, biology, and the backdrop of human history. But from a Christian perspective, we need to go further back. God is not constrained by biology. Rather than creating sex, in either sense of the word, he could have made humans capable of asexual reproduction—like copperhead snakes, when the feeling takes them! But God created male and female humans as a living metaphor.

Perhaps an analogy will help. In biblical terms, parenthood is designed to illustrate God's relationship with his children. Fatherhood metaphors are best known, not least because Jesus teaches us to call God "our Father" (Matt. 6:9). But the Old Testament also repeatedly figures God in maternal terms. The Lord says:

> Can a mother forget the baby at her breast
>   and have no compassion on the child she has borne?
> Though she may forget,
>   I will not forget you! (Isa. 49:15 NIV)[1]

I am four months pregnant as I write. When I drag my exhausted body out of bed to feed my infant in the night, I will catch a faint echo in my heart of the long-suffering love God has for me, and glimpse in my baby my utter dependence on God. If we examine the Bible, we will see that male and female form the raw material for another living, breathing metaphor.

Sex in Creation

As the Bible begins, God creates humanity "in his image" and "in his likeness." This language evokes three relationships that shed light on

---

1. The Old Testament features five other depictions of God as mother. For example:

    You were unmindful of the Rock that bore you,
        and you forgot the God who gave you birth. (Deut. 32:18)

    As a mother comforts her child,
        so will I comfort you. (Isa. 66:13 NIV)

our status before God: a child resembling a parent, a deputy representing a king, and a temple statue representing a god. This "image" language applies to male and female together, and God charges his humans to fill the earth and to rule over it (Gen. 1:26–29). Fulfilling these roles depends on man and woman relating to each other sexually. So we could say that God gives his people a three-orbed role: to rule, to relate, and to create.

Why did God design us so that both male and female were needed for procreation? Perhaps a relational God, who *is* love (1 John 4:8), could not truly be imaged by a solitary human. Like holograms impressed with 3-D images from the interference pattern of multiple beams of coherent light, God's image emerges not just from our rationality but also from our relationships.

This point is underscored when the story is retold in Genesis 2. God forms a man out of the dust, breathes life into him, and puts him to work in a garden. Then God declares, "It is not good that the man should be alone; I will make him a helper fit for him" (Gen. 2:18). God's constant refrain in Genesis 1 was that his creation was "good," and his creation of humans was "very good." So this assertion that a solitary human was "not good" is jarring. The man cannot image God alone; he needs a helper. This is our first Severus Snape moment. "Helper" sounds like a subordinate role. But in the Hebrew Scriptures, the word *helper* is overwhelmingly applied to God himself, so it cannot imply inferior status.[2]

We learn more about the connection between man and woman through a strange description of God making woman out of man's side. Woman is bone of man's bone and flesh of his flesh: they are different but fundamentally linked (Gen. 2:21–23). The next verse hammers the point home: "Therefore a man shall leave his father and his mother and hold fast to his wife, and they shall become one flesh" (Gen. 2:24). Sex joins man and woman in intimate relationship as they become fruitful and multiply. The God who exists in utter intimacy, with love across difference at the core of his being, creates image bearers who are of the same essence but different, and calls them into one-flesh unity.

---

2. E.g., Ex. 18:4; Deut. 33:26, 29; Pss. 20:2; 33:20; 54:4; 118:7; Hos. 13:9.

Broken Love

In Genesis 3, things go horribly wrong. Rather than applying God's rule to creation, the man and the woman break the only law God has given them: not to eat fruit from the tree of the knowledge of good and evil. The construction of this story is significant. The man is commanded not to eat from that tree before the woman is created, and God warns him that on the day he eats of it, he will die. When the mysterious, talking snake approaches the woman to question God's words, we wonder, *Where is the man?* The answer comes at the end of verse 6: he's right there with her. But rather than countering the snake's lies, the man eats the fruit too. This disobedience breaks both humanity's relationship with God and the fellowship between humans. Innocence and intimacy are replaced by shame and blame. Life yields to death.

The man and the woman are cursed by God in response to their rebellion in ways that affect the roles they were jointly given in Genesis 1. Ruling over creation is made hard by the curse on the man. Multiplying is made hard by the curse on the woman. Here, again, we hit upon a Severus Snape moment: the woman is not only cursed with pain in childbirth but also told that from now on, "your desire shall be contrary to your husband, / but he shall rule over you" (Gen. 3:16).[3] The word translated "desire" is rarely found in the Old Testament, but it occurs in the next chapter of Genesis, when God says to Adam and Eve's eldest son, Cain: "Sin is crouching at the door. Its desire is against you, but you must rule over it" (Gen. 4:7). Desire, here, communicates will to possess and master. Gone is the unashamed, united love story between men and women. Now there is conflict and power struggle. This is a result of rebellion, not God's original design. But how does this not lead to the denigration of women?

In one sense, it does. Throughout the Old Testament, we see sin resulting in appalling treatment of women by men—and vice versa. We see murder and rape and exploitation. But this is a diagnosis, not a prescription. The Bible does not endorse what it reports, as New Atheist mash-ups of Scripture would have us believe. But it does present a realistic picture of how human beings treat each other and, in

---

3. The exact meaning of the Hebrew here is contested, and the ESV margin has "toward." The ESV previously had "for" in the text and "against" in the margin.

particular, how we wield power. So how does the rest of the story make sense of what Genesis says about men and women in marriage? This time we must read on to understand.

The Love Song of God for His People

The relationship between man and woman finds fresh meaning when God's covenant with his people is pictured as a marriage. "For your Maker is your husband," declares Isaiah, "the LORD of hosts is his name" (Isa. 54:5).[4] Parenting metaphors sometimes liken God to a father and sometimes to a mother. But in the marriage metaphor the roles are never reversed: God is always the husband and never the wife. It may seem flimsy to hang the meaning of sex on a metaphor. But from a Christian perspective, metaphor is vital to theology: without it, we cannot hope to describe the invisible, transcendent, ungraspable God.

As we read on, we discover that this is not a happy marriage. God's people are unfaithful to him by worshiping idols.[5] The implication is not that women are naturally less faithful than men. The Old Testament paints a brutally real picture of male licentiousness.[6] But within the biblical metaphor, God is unrelentingly faithful. He desires the love and devotion of his people and hates when they give themselves to other gods. His love is jealous—the appropriate reaction of a loving husband to a cheating wife. But it is also forgiving. Though God has every right to reject his people, he wants them back, and the renewal of the covenant is pictured as a reconciling of husband and wife.[7] And yet this marriage never really seems to work. In this respect as in many others, the Hebrew Scriptures pose a question without ever quite yielding the answer. How can the holy, faithful, love-filled God live with his loveless, faithless, sin-filled people?

The Bridegroom Comes

Jesus is the living fulfillment of every Old Testament hope. When asked why his disciples do not fast, Jesus replies, "Can you make

---

4. See also, e.g., Isa. 54:5; Jer. 31:32; Ezek. 16:8; Hos. 2:7; Joel 1:8.
5. See, e.g., Isaiah 50; Jeremiah 3; Hosea 2.
6. For instance, King David's adultery and subsequent murder of Bathsheba's husband, King Solomon's straying from God by taking many wives, Samson's downfall through his desire for Delilah, etc.
7. See Isa. 54:6–8; 62:4–5; Jer. 31:31–33; Ezek. 16:62; Hos. 2:14, 16–19; 3:1.

wedding guests fast while the bridegroom is with them?" (Luke 5:34). John the Baptist picks up the metaphor: "The one who has the bride is the bridegroom. The friend of the bridegroom, who stands and hears him, rejoices greatly at the bridegroom's voice. Therefore this joy of mine is now complete" (John 3:29).

Where God was husband to his wandering people in the Old Testament, Jesus—the ultimate image of the invisible God—steps into history as a groom. Like a power line, grounded in Jesus, this metaphor returns in the New Testament letters written after his death and resurrection. But before we get to that, we must marvel at Jesus's relationships with women in the Gospels.

Women in the Gospels

The portrayal of women in the Gospels—particularly in Luke's Gospel—is stunningly countercultural. Luke constantly pairs men with women, and when he compares the two, it is almost always in the woman's favor. Before Jesus's birth, two people are visited by the angel Gabriel and told they are going to become parents. One is Zachariah, who becomes John the Baptist's father. The other is Jesus's mother, Mary. Both ask Gabriel how this can be. But while Zachariah is punished with months of dumbness for his unbelief, Mary is only commended. The prominent role of women in Luke continues as Mary and her cousin Elizabeth prophesy over Jesus in the womb, and as a prophet (Simeon) and a prophetess (Anna) prophesy over the infant Jesus.

The adult Jesus consistently weaves women into his preaching. In his first sermon, he enrages his audience with two Old Testament examples of God's love reaching beyond the Jews: one is a woman, the other is a man (Luke 4:25–27). In Luke 15, the female-oriented parable of the lost coin is nestled between the male-oriented parables of the lost sheep and the lost (or prodigal) son. In Luke 18, the female-oriented prayer parable of the persistent widow is paired with the male-oriented prayer parable of the Pharisee and the tax collector. Even as he approaches crucifixion, Jesus stops to address female mourners (Luke 23:27–31). In a male-dominated culture, his attention to women throughout his preaching is remarkable.

This male-and-female thread works its way through Luke's healing accounts. First, Jesus heals a man with an unclean spirit (Luke 4:33–35). Then he heals Simon's mother-in-law (Luke 4:38–9). In chapter 7, Jesus heals a centurion's servant and then raises a widow's son, out of compassion for the grieving mother. In chapter 8, Jesus heals a man with a demon, then a bleeding woman, and then a synagogue ruler's daughter. Jesus's last healing in Luke is of a woman with a disabling spirit. She praises God. When the male synagogue ruler objects, Jesus calls him a hypocrite and reminds him of the woman's status as a "daughter of Abraham" (Luke 13:16–17).

Jesus's elevation of women as moral examples is yet more striking. In Luke 7, he is dining at Simon the Pharisee's house, when a "sinful woman" (likely a prostitute) disrupts the party. She weeps on Jesus's feet, wipes them with her hair, and anoints him with ointment. Simon is appalled: surely if Jesus were a prophet, he would know this woman is utterly unworthy of touching him! But Jesus turns the contrast on its head and holds this woman up as an example to shame Simon. In cultural terms, Simon has every advantage. He is a man; she is a woman. He is religiously admired; she is despised. He's hosting a dinner party; she is a weeping, prostrate embarrassment. But according to Jesus, she surpasses Simon on every count (Luke 7:36–50). Jesus elevates another low-status woman as a moral example in Luke 21, when he commends the poor widow for her gift of two small copper coins. In Jesus's eyes, this offering exceeds the much larger gifts the rich are putting in the offering box (Luke 21:1–4).

Jesus's valuing of women might seem to be compromised by his choice of twelve male apostles, mirroring the twelve tribes of Israel. But Luke emphasizes the women who followed Jesus too: "The twelve were with him, and also some women who had been healed of evil spirits and infirmities: Mary, called Magdalene, from whom seven demons had gone out, and Joanna, the wife of Chuza, Herod's household manager, and Susanna, and many others, who provided for him out of their means" (Luke 8:1–3 mg.). Like Jesus's male disciples, these women were in for the long haul (see Luke 23:49, 56). They were there at the beginning of Jesus's ministry and at the end. But can these women legitimately be called disciples?

Jesus answers that question for us in Luke 10 when we first meet two of Jesus's female friends: Mary and Martha. Martha is playing a traditionally female role, serving her guests, while her sister Mary is assuming a traditionally male role, sitting at Jesus's feet with the other disciples. Martha asks Jesus to correct this, to tell Mary to get up and help with the serving. But Jesus affirms Mary: "Mary has chosen the good portion, which will not be taken away from her" (Luke 10:42).

Luke's final comparison surrounds Jesus's resurrection. In Luke 24, some of his female disciples visit the tomb to anoint his body. There, they encounter angels who announce the resurrection. The women report this to the apostles, who don't believe them. Peter runs to the tomb to check the facts. But even then, they are not convinced. When two male disciples meet Jesus on the road to Emmaus, they recount the women's tale but do not seem to have absorbed it. Jesus rebukes them, "O foolish ones, and slow of heart to believe all that the prophets have spoken!" (Luke 24:25).

Luke is not the only Gospel to elevate women. In a moving account in John, Jesus shocks his disciples by crossing ethnic, religious, gender, and moral boundaries to talk with a sexually compromised Samaritan woman, who becomes an evangelist to her people (John 4:1–30). Later, Jesus saves a woman caught in adultery from being stoned, forcing her male accusers to acknowledge that they are not morally superior to her (John 8:7). Then, in John 11, we see Jesus's tender interaction with Martha and Mary after the death of their brother, Lazarus. Jesus speaks some of his most famous recorded words to comfort Martha, and then cries with her and her sister before miraculously raising Lazarus from the dead.[8] In Matthew 9, Jesus commends the faith of a woman suffering from unrelenting menstrual bleeding who touched him to be healed. In Matthew 19 he protects women from unwarranted divorce, which would in many cases leave them destitute.

Jesus's valuing of women is unmistakable. In a culture in which women were devalued and often exploited, it underscores their equal status before God and his desire for personal relationship with them.

---

8. We will explore this story in detail in chap. 11, "How Could a Loving God Allow So Much Suffering?"

But is Jesus's life and ministry an oasis of equality in a desert of biblical misogyny?

The Offense of the Marriage Metaphor

When the marriage metaphor first re-fuses with human marriage in Paul's letter to the church in Ephesus, it strikes us like Snape muttering magic under his breath during Harry's first Quidditch match. We think it's a curse, when in fact it's a protective charm. "Submit yourselves to one another," writes Paul, "out of reverence for Christ."

> Wives, submit yourselves to your own husbands as you do to the Lord. For the husband is the head of the wife as Christ is the head of the church, his body, of which he is the Savior. Now as the church submits to Christ, so also wives should submit to their husbands in everything. (Eph. 5:22–24 NIV)

I was an undergraduate at Cambridge when I first wrestled with these words. I came from an academically driven, equality-oriented, all-female high school. I was now studying in a majority-male college. And I was repulsed. "Wives, submit to your husbands, as to the Lord"? You have got to be kidding me. I had three problems with these verses. The first was that wives should submit. I knew women were just as competent as men. If there was wisdom in asymmetrical decision-making in marriage, surely it should depend on who was more competent in the relevant area. My second problem was with the idea that wives should submit to their husbands *as to the Lord.* It is one thing to submit to Jesus Christ, the self-sacrificing King of the universe. It is quite another to offer that kind of submission to a fallible, sinful man. My third problem was the idea that the husband was the "head" of the wife. This seemed to imply a hierarchy at odds with men and women's equal status as image bearers of God.

This all seemed to pull against the countercultural message of the gospel. The Bible had offered me a radical narrative of power inversion in which the Creator God laid down his life, the poor outclassed the rich, and outcasts became family. The gospel was a consuming fire of love across differences to burn up racial injustice and socioeconomic exploitation. And yet here were these horrifying verses promoting the subjugation of women. Jesus had elevated women to an equal status with men. Paul, it seemed, had pushed them down.

At first, I tried to explain the shock away. I tried, for instance, to argue that in the Greek, the word translated "submit" appears only in the previous verse, "Submit to one another out of reverence for Christ" (Eph. 5:21 NIV), so the rest of the passage must imply mutual submission. But the command for wives to submit occurs three times in the New Testament (see also Col. 3:18; 1 Pet. 3:1), while husbands are called four times to love (Eph. 5:25, 28, 33; Col. 3:19) and once to honor their wives (1 Pet. 3:7).

Indeed, when I trained my lens on the command to husbands, the Ephesians passage started to come into focus. "Husbands, love your wives, as Christ loved the church and gave himself up for her" (Eph. 5:25). How did Christ love the church? By dying on the cross; by giving himself, naked and bleeding, to suffer for her; by putting her needs above his own; by sacrificing everything for her. I asked myself how I would feel if *this* were the command to wives: *Wives, love your husbands to the point of death, putting his needs above yours, and sacrificing yourself for him?* Ephesians 5:22 is sometimes critiqued as a mandate for spousal abuse. Tragically, it has been misused that way. But the command to husbands makes that reading impossible. How much more easily could an abuser twist a verse calling his wife to suffer for him, to give herself up for him, to die for him?

When I realized the lens for this teaching was the lens of the gospel itself, it started to make sense. If the message of Jesus is true, no one comes to the table with rights. The only way to enter is flat on your face. Male or female, if we grasp at our right to self-determination, we must reject Jesus, because he calls us to submit to him completely. And while Christians are certainly called to sacrifice in response to Christ, we are primarily called to accept his sacrifice for us.

With this lens in place, I saw that God created sex and marriage as a telescope to give us a glimpse of his star-sized desire for intimacy with us. Our roles in *this* great marriage are not interchangeable: Jesus gives himself for us, Christians (male or female) follow his lead. Ultimately, my marriage is not about me and my husband any more than *Romeo and Juliet* is about the actors playing the title roles.

Recognizing that marriage (at its best) points to a much greater reality relieves the pressure on all concerned. First, it depressurizes single people. We live in a world where sexual and romantic fulfillment are paraded as ultimate goods. Miss out on sex, we are told, and you miss out on life. But within a Christian framework, missing marriage and gaining Christ is like missing out on playing with dolls as a child, but growing up to have a real baby. When we are fully enjoying the ultimate relationship, no one will lament for the loss of the scale model. It also takes the pressure off married people. Of course, we have the challenge of playing our roles in the drama. But we need not worry about whether we married the right person, or why our marriages are not flinging us to a constant state of Nirvana. In one sense, human marriage is designed to disappoint. It leaves us longing for more, and that longing points us to the ultimate reality of which the best marriage is a scale model. Ephesians 5 used to repulse me. Now it convicts me and calls me toward Jesus: the true husband who satisfies my needs, the one man who truly deserves my submission.

Mishearing Paul on Marriage

Desiring to justify God's commands, Christians sometimes try to ground this picture of marriage in gendered psychology. Some suggest that women are natural followers, while men are natural leaders. But the primary command to men is to love, not to lead, and I have never heard anyone argue that men are naturally better at loving. Some claim that men need respect while women need love, or that we are given commands corresponding to natural deficiencies: women are better at love; men are better at respect. But to look at human history and say that men naturally respect women is to stick your head in the sand with a blindfold on!

At best, these claims about male and female psychology are generalizations. At worst, they cause needless offense and give way to exceptions: if these commands are given because wives are naturally more submissive, and I find that I am a more natural leader than my husband, does that mean we can switch roles? Ephesians 5 grounds our roles in marriage not on gendered psychology but on Christ-centered theology.

I have been married for a decade, and I am not naturally submissive. I am naturally leadership-oriented. I hold a PhD and a seminary degree, and I am the trained debater of the family. Thank God, I married a man who is man enough to celebrate this! And yet it is a daily challenge for me to remember my role in this drama and to notice opportunities to submit to my husband *as to the Lord*, not because I am naturally more or less submissive or because he is more or less naturally loving, but because Jesus went to the cross for me.

No Mandate for "Traditional" Gender Roles

Ephesians 5 sticks like a burr in our twenty-first-century ears because centuries of "traditional" gender roles have often meant wives contorting around the needs of their husbands, while husbands assert their dominance. We think of the stereotypes gently mocked by the relationship between Mr. and Mrs. Banks in *Mary Poppins*.

But Paul does not say that the husband's needs come first, or that women are less gifted in leadership than men, or that women should not work outside the home. At least one of Paul's key ministry partners was a woman who did just that,[9] as did the idealized wife described in the Old Testament book of Proverbs. Paul does not specify that wives should earn less than their husbands, or that families should privilege the husband's career over the wife's. A man may work for a nonprofit, pastor a church, or study for a PhD and earn a fraction of his wife's corporate salary. Paul is clear elsewhere that men cannot abdicate their responsibility to ensure that their families are provided for. But this does not mean the husband must be the primary breadwinner. In biblical terms, the value of work is measured not in dollars but in service. Indeed, Jesus himself, the archetypal leader, did not earn money, and he was financially dependent on some of his female followers (Luke 8:2–3).

Viewed closely, Ephesians 5 is a withering critique of common conceptions of "traditional" gender roles that have often amounted to privileging men and patronizing women. In the drama of marriage, the wife's needs come first, and the husband's drive to prioritize himself

---

9. See Lydia, "a seller of purple goods," in Acts 16:14.

is cut down with the brutal axe of the gospel. This is no return to Victorian values. Rather, it is a call to pay attention to the character of Christ. If we hear the call to husbands as a mandate to oppress and dominate, we are forgetting that Jesus came not to be served but to serve, not to lead an army but to give his life as a ransom. When husbands are called to love their wives "as Christ loved the church and gave himself up for her," the word translated "gave up" is the same one the Gospels use when Jesus is handed over to be crucified.[10]

Behold, the Man!

We will never understand the Bible's call on men and women unless we see Jesus as the ultimate man. He had strength to command storms, summon angel armies, and defeat death. But his arms held little children, his words elevated women, and his hands reached out to heal the sick. Jesus drove traders out of the temple with a whip. But he tenderly welcomed the outcast and weak.

After he had been mocked, beaten, and abused by his guards, Jesus was displayed to the crowds wearing a crown of thorns and a purple robe to ridicule his kingly claim. The Roman governor Pilate announced, "Behold the man!" (John 19:5). These words drip with irony. Jesus, beaten and humiliated out of love for his people, was and is the perfect man. No one who uses the Bible's teaching on marriage to justify chauvinism, abuse, or denigration of women has looked at Jesus.

The End of Marriage

The marriage metaphor finds its fulfillment in the Bible's final book. The apostle John hears what seems like the voice of a great multitude crying out,

> The marriage of the Lamb has come,
>   and his Bride has made herself ready. (Rev. 19:7)

Here, two massive metaphors collide. Jesus as husband is the sacrificial Lamb, reinforcing the link between husbanding and loving

---

10. See Matt. 27:26; Mark 15:15; John 19:16.

sacrifice. An angel declares, "Blessed are those who are invited to the marriage supper of the Lamb" (Rev. 19:9). Later in Revelation, Jerusalem is pictured as Christ's bride: "Then I saw a new heaven and a new earth," writes John, "for the first heaven and the first earth had passed away, and the sea was no more. I saw the holy city, new Jerusalem, coming down out of heaven from God, prepared as a bride adorned for her husband" (Rev. 21:1–2; see also 21:9–10). After long ages of failure and unfaithfulness, God's people are finally married to Jesus, their sacrificing Husband-King.

The marriage metaphor finds its last outlet in the final chapter of the Bible, bonded with another visceral metaphor: "The Spirit and the Bride say, 'Come.' And let the one who hears say, 'Come.' And let the one who is thirsty come; and let the one who desires take the water of life without price" (Rev. 22:17).

Jesus offered living water first to a woman: a woman who, because of her race, religion, sex, and sexual history, would have been beneath the contempt of a respectable rabbi. He asked her for a drink. Then he claimed that whoever drank the water he could give would never be thirsty again, but that that water would become in them a spring of water, welling up to eternal life (John 4:13–14).

Women in the Church

Springing from this well, this strange new first-century faith flowing out of Judaism proved highly attractive to women. Sociologist Rodney Stark has shown from a wide array of textual and archaeological sources that the early church was majority female.[11] This is particularly striking, given that the Greco-Roman world in the first and second centuries was disproportionately male, due to selective infanticide of baby girls and the high proportion of maternal deaths in child birth.[12] Indeed, early Christianity was mocked by outsiders for its appeal to women. The second-century Greek philosopher Celsus snarked that Christians "want and are able to convince only the foolish, dishonor-

---

11. Rodney Stark, *The Rise of Christianity: How the Obscure, Marginal Jesus Movement Became the Dominant Religious Force in the Western World in a Few Centuries* (Princeton, NJ: Princeton University Press, 1996).

12. Michael J. Kruger, *Christianity at the Crossroads: How the Second Century Shaped the Future of the Church* (Downers Grove, IL: IVP Academic, 2018), 36.

able and stupid, only slaves, women, and little children," while the third-century Christian apologist Minucius Felix records critics saying that Christianity attracted, "the dregs of the populace and credulous women with the inability natural to their sex."[13]

The status of women was raised in the church. Paul's inclusion of nine women among the ministry partners he lists at the end of his letter to the Romans is one evidence among many that women played a major role in the first-century spread of the Christian message.[14] Roman families often gave their prepubescent daughters away in marriage, but Christian women could marry later. They also "benefited from Christian condemnation of traditional male prerogatives in regard to divorce, incest, infidelity, polygamy, and female infanticide."[15] If Paul's instructions on marriage are shocking to our modern ears, they would have shocked his first hearers for precisely opposite reasons: their radical elevation of women. Indeed, for many Gentiles, the Christian expectation that men be faithful to their wives and sacrificial in their approach to them would have seemed quite unreasonable.

Just as we cannot cling to a white-centric perception of Christianity in the face of the global church, so we cannot maintain a male-oriented view. To this day, more women than men are Christians. Globally, women are generally more religious across a range of indices, but the difference is more pronounced for Christians, both in affiliation and in practice. For example, Christian women are 7 percent more likely than Christian men to attend church on a weekly basis.[16] And as Yale professor Stephen Carter points out, "around the globe, the people most likely to be Christians are women of color."[17]

---

13. Kruger, *Christianity at the Crossroads*, 34–35.

14. Phoebe, Prisca, Mary, Junia, Tryphaena and Tryphosa, Rufus's mother, Julia, and Nereus's sister (Rom. 16:1–15).

15. Stark quotes from a letter dating from 1 BC written by a seemingly devoted husband, Hilarian, to his wife, Alis, to illustrate the pagan world's casual disregard of female infants: "I ask and beg you to take good care of our baby son, and as soon as I receive payment I shall send it up to you. If you are delivered of a child, if it is a boy keep it, if a girl discard it. You have sent me word, 'Don't forget me.' How can I forget you. I beg you not to worry." Stark, *Rise of Christianity*, 97–98.

16. "The Gender Gap in Religion around the World," Pew Research Center, March 22, 2016, http://www.pewforum.org/2016/03/22/the-gender-gap-in-religion-around-the-world/.

17. Stephen L. Carter, "The Ugly Coded Critique of Chick-fil-A's Christianity," *Bloomberg*, April 21, 2018, https://www.bloomberg.com/view/articles/2018-04-21/criticism-of-christians-and -chick-fil-a-has-troubling-roots.

Christianity and Women's Rights

But let's not paint too rosy a picture. As in every other ethical area, the church has under-delivered on its promise to women. Denigrating and patronizing attitudes have all too often infected church culture, and selective readings of Scripture have enabled men to propagate misogynistic views. Yet Christians have also played a leading role in championing women's rights, from the early church to the present day. As Wendy Alsup reminds us, first-wave feminism in the early 1920s, which gained American women the right to vote and inherit land, was due in large part to Christian activism.[18] We saw seeds of this activism in the abolitionist movement, as Christian leaders like Sojourner Truth advocated for women's rights.[19] We also see it in the global spread of Christianity. For example, women have played a key role in the development of the church in China, stepping out beyond the confines prescribed by Confucian tradition and becoming evangelists and disciplers beyond the home.[20]

True Christianity flips the script on the marginalization of women that characterizes many traditional cultures and gives them equal status before God, with a whole new role to play of witnessing to the gospel of Jesus and loving others in his name. But it is nonetheless true that biblical frameworks diverge from some core doctrines of modern feminism around the kinds of freedom women (or men, for that matter) should enjoy.

I say "should enjoy," because in a modern Western context, we must contend with some challenging data on women's self-reported happiness. Steven Pinker finds it "not entirely surprising that as women gained in autonomy relative to men, they also slipped in happiness."[21] But *is it* not surprising? Our modern mantras teach us that freedom and happiness go hand in hand: just give us more choice and we will

---

18. See Wendy Alsup, *Is the Bible Good for Women? Seeking Clarity and Confidence through a Jesus-Centered Understanding of Scripture* (Colorado Springs: Multnomah, 2017).

19. See, for example, Sojourner Truth's stunning impromptu speech, "Ain't I a Woman?," delivered at the Women's Convention in Akron, Ohio, on May 29, 1851, where she cites Jesus's relationship with Mary and Martha as evidence of the value of women.

20. See Alexander Chow, "The Remarkable Story of China's 'Bible Women,'" *Christianity Today*, March 16, 2018, https://www.christianitytoday.com/history/2018/march/christian-china-bible-women.html.

21. Steven Pinker, *Enlightenment Now: The Case for Reason, Science, Humanism, and Progress*, (New York: Penguin, 2018), 285.

optimize! But extensive psychological data tells a different story. Some degree of freedom certainly enhances happiness, but too many options seem to deflate the balloon.

I first encountered this data through Harvard professor Dan Gilbert, whose work we explored in chapter 1.[22] Gilbert describes one study in which subjects were allowed to choose a print from a selection of beautiful paintings. Those who were told they could change their minds ended up less satisfied with their prints than those who made clear choices. This and many similar studies have shown that commitment, not unlimited choice, breeds happiness. Loosening commitment (e.g., telling the subjects they could come back any time in the next week and trade in their prints) decreases satisfaction, as does increasing choice beyond a certain point.

At the trivial end of the spectrum, if someone is offered a large array of chocolates to choose from (say thirty, rather than six), he or she is less likely to choose or to be satisfied with the choice made.[23] But this psychological instinct also illuminates the benefits of marriage over either extensive switching between sexual partners or semi-committed cohabitation. Most people today see cohabitation as a wise precaution against future divorce. But the data tells another story. People who live together before they marry are more likely to divorce than those who do not,[24] and there is a gender differential in how men and women tend to view cohabitation, with men expressing significantly less commitment to the relationship on average.[25] Moreover, while marriage correlates with a range of mental and physical health

---

22. See Dan Gilbert, "The Surprising Science of Happiness," TED2004 (video), February 2004, https://www.ted.com/talks/dan_gilbert_asks_why_are_we_happy; and Daniel Gilbert, *Stumbling on Happiness* (New York, Vintage, 2007), 202.

23. Jonathan Haidt, *The Happiness Hypothesis: Finding Modern Truth in Ancient Wisdom* (New York: Basic Books, 2006), 101.

24. "Premarital cohabitation has consistently been found to be associated with increased risk for divorce and marital distress in the United States." Scott M. Stanley, Galena Kline Rhoades, Howard J. Markman, "Sliding versus Deciding: Inertia and the Cohabitation Effect," *Family Relations* 55 (October 2006): 499. For an analysis of potential causes, see https://onlinelibrary.wiley.com/doi/epdf/10.1111/j.1741-3729.2006.00418.x?referrer_access_token=wu1Z1URtk23jrD7fqRNn5ota6bR2k8jH0KrdpFOxC66SF1aJDraJRypyD_sck7_fW2s-LYZlHy-79jDt6UFiXOG2q1LxkIIPm3DLwQ6GVisgj5zvpPAQwJeduNrr4dcDM7BDn4uAW_txQF34J11V-A%3D%3D.

25. Meg Jay, "The Downside of Cohabiting before Marriage, *New York Times*, April 14, 2012, https://www.nytimes.com/2012/04/15/opinion/sunday/the-downside-of-cohabiting-before-marriage.html?pagewanted=all&_r=0. See also, Michael Pollard and Kathleen Mullon Harris, "Cohabitation and Marriage Intensity: Consolidation, Intimacy, and Commitment," Rand Labor & Population, June 2013, https://www.rand.org/content/dam/rand/pubs/working_papers/WR1000/WR1001/RAND_WR1001.pdf.

benefits for both men and women, for women at least, increasing our number of sexual partners can have negative psychological effects.[26]

Pinker attributes the decline in female happiness to the multiple competing demands on Western women today. There may well be truth in this. But is it possible that what women have gained in freedom and professional opportunity many have lost in the sexual revolution that cloaked what many men wanted—commitment-free sex—under the mantle of liberating women? Two years ago, an agnostic friend who teaches at a world-class university told me that she routinely has female students ask her why they are having all the (sometimes barely consensual) sex expected of a modern woman but not experiencing the promised happiness.

I have no desire to make sweeping statements about the mental health or happiness of women who chose to have multiple sexual partners. Some of my smartest non-Christian friends have chosen that path, and some of my dearest Christian friends were saved out of that lifestyle. But from a purely biological perspective, it would not take a rocket scientist to hypothesize that women are biased toward commitment from a man who will protect them and their children, rather than moving on and spawning more children with other women.[27] Another agnostic friend, who had lived a *Sex and the City* lifestyle in New York for a decade, told me she had reached the same conclusions about commitment-free sex as I have, but for experiential rather than religious reasons. She described having to suit up in impregnable emotional armor to sustain the lifestyle and grieved that no one had told her sooner. "Why are girls not given this data in high school?" she asked.

---

26. See, for example, Tyree Oredein and Cristine Delnevo, "The Relationship between Multiple Sexual Partners and Mental Health in Adolescent Females," Community Medicine & Health Education, December 23, 2013, https://www.omicsonline.org/the-relationship-between-multiple-sexual-partners-and-mental-health-in-adolescent-females-2161-0711.1000256.pdf, which found that "the prevalence of sadness, suicide ideation, suicide plans and suicide attempts increased with the number of sexual partners across all racial/ethnic groups"; and Sandhya Ramrakha et al., "The Relationship between Multiple Sex Partners and Anxiety, Depression, and Substance Dependence Disorders: A Cohort Study," NCBI, February 12, 2013, https://www.ncbi.nlm.nih.gov/pmc/articles/PMC3752789/, which found "a strong association between number of sex partners and later substance disorder, especially for women."

27. As an academic study of sex and happiness rather clinically puts it, "The happiness-maximizing number of sexual partners in the previous year is calculated to be 1." David G. Blanchflower and Andrew J. Oswald, *Money, Sex and Happiness: An Empirical Study* (Cambridge, MA: National Bureau of Economic Research, 2004), 2, https://www.nber.org/papers/w10499.pdf.

To be clear, I am not suggesting that women are not really interested in sex. Quite the reverse. But on average, married people have more and better sex than their unmarried peers.[28] Particularly for women, whose sexual process is often more complicated than men's, lasting commitment can be the key to true arousal. In the New Testament, husbands and wives are instructed to have sex regularly—prioritizing the woman's sexual desire as much as the man's (1 Cor. 7:3–5)—and one whole book of the Bible explores marital love though a wide range of erotic expression, giving voice to female sexual desire as well as male.[29] Sex is to be valued, treasured, and enjoyed. But sex is not an ultimate good: it is a mark of a particular covenant, a means of multiplying image bearers of God, and a glimpse of a greater reality.

"Pro-Life? That's a Lie!"

The redefinition of sexual ideals connects with another ethical area where many Christian women feel alienated from contemporary feminism, and where many of my secular friends feel alienated from Christianity. Abortion is far too large an issue to explore in any depth here, and it is one of the hardest questions to discuss meaningfully across differing views. But I will touch on it nonetheless, as no exploration of women's rights would be complete without it.

In my early twenties, I took part in a silent pro-life protest in London. Protesters on the other side were not silent. They repeated a chant: "Pro-life? That's a lie! You don't care if women die!" That accusation was so far from my own position that I found silence almost unbearable. But I did not want to fight back with equivalent slurs. I knew these pro-choice chanters cared deeply about women's agency and about the millions of vulnerable women affected by unwanted pregnancies. I care too.

I do not romanticize the past. Women have disposed of unwanted babies in various ways since time immemorial. Indeed, as pediatric physician Paul Offit discovered to his surprise, it was only the advent

---

28. Summarizing several studies are Linda Bloom and Charlie Bloom, "Want More and Better Sex? Get Married and Stay Married," *Huffpost*, July 13, 2017, https://www.huffingtonpost.com /entry/want-more-and-better-sex-get-married-and-stay-married_us_5967b618e4b022bb9372aff2 See also Blanchflower and Oswald, *Money, Sex and Happiness* on levels of sex enjoyed by married people versus unmarried people.
29. See the Old Testament Song of Songs.

of Christianity that made infanticide seem morally problematic.[30] Unmarried mothers have been ostracized. Illicit abortions have caused many maternal deaths. I am keenly aware of the hypocrisy of people who advocate for unborn life but neglect the vulnerable after birth, and I think the "blame" for abortion lies primarily not at the feet of women who make that choice in desperate circumstances but rather at the feet of all of us who are part of a society that separates sex from commitment, creates an ecosystem of unplanned pregnancy, and fails to support women who find themselves in that situation.

But while the slogan that a woman has the right to do what she wants with her own body is powerful, we must all agree that a person's right to decide what to do with his or her own body has limits when those actions implicate another person's body. Therefore, however uncomfortable the answer may be, the question we must all ask is whether unborn infants count as humans, and if so, when their humanity starts.

Atheist philosopher Peter Singer, whose work I touched on in chapter 4, questions the idea that birth is a meaningful break point in the person/nonperson divide. Rather than looking for a starting point for personhood before birth, however, he comes to the distressing conclusion that human infants are not persons, and that infanticide should trouble us no more than abortion. This view is not unique to Singer. In 2012, medical ethicists Alberto Giubilini and Francesca Minerva published a paper in the *Journal of Medical Ethics* arguing that "after birth abortion (killing a newborn) should be permissible in all cases where abortion is, including cases where the newborn is not disabled."[31] Few reading this book would agree. Our moral frameworks have been so inscribed with Christian valuing of the young and the weak that killing a baby feels horrific. But the logic is sound: if humans are not in a special category of personhood by virtue of their creation in the image of God, perhaps we should judge their value according to their capacities.

As I write this, I am pregnant with my third child. I am blessed with a stable marriage and a fulfilling career. But each pregnancy has

30. Paul Offit, *Bad Faith: When Religious Belief Undermines Modern Medicine* (New York: Basic Books, 2015), 127. See also my discussion of Offit in chap. 4 (p. 67), under "Bad Faith."

31. Alberto Giubilini and Francesca Minerva, "After-Birth Abortion: Why Should the Baby Live?," *Journal of Medical Ethics* (2012): 1, https://jme.bmj.com/content/medethics/early/2012/03/01/medethics-2011-100411.full.pdf.

reminded me of the precarious nature of how our society counts humans. After a few months of pregnancy, my baby had all his features and organs in place. He was moving independently in ways that I and my family could feel. His body is within mine and dependent on mine, but he is not part of my body. And yet he has no rights under Massachusetts law. Laws developed under the seemingly common-sense principle of the age of viability are constantly being called into question by scientific advances that enable younger babies to survive outside the womb. But to reduce the legal limit would mean to look over our shoulder and wonder if babies aborted in the past beyond the new limit should have been counted as human. And is scientific advancement the right measuring stick for human value?

As with many of the questions explored in this book, I believe that intelligent, well-meaning people can come to different conclusions on this topic because they are coming from fundamentally different starting points. I have many non-Christian friends who disagree with me on abortion. They see the pro-life movement as oppressive to women—though most of those same friends would want to limit a woman's right to choose when it comes to the selective abortion of females, which has resulted in a gender gap of twenty-five million in India and thirty-five million in China, likely mirroring the gender discrepancies due to female infanticide in the first century, before Christianity disrupted the scene.[32] Many would also balk at the selective abortion of babies with Down syndrome. We all ultimately recognize that what we say about human life at any stage has wider implications and that much of ethical history has been determined not by whether humans should be valued but by who counts as human in the first place.

Despite the complex and, at times, heartrending challenges raised by unwanted pregnancy, I do believe that Christian faith entails a pro-life position, and while there are certainly some who oppose abortion for misogynistic reasons, the claim that being pro-life implies being anti-women is unsustainable.

---

32. Elaine Storkey, "Violence against Women Begins in the Womb," *Christianity Today*, May 2, 2018, https://www.christianitytoday.com/women/2018/may/violence-against-women-begins-in -womb-abortion.html.

Like every other element of the Christian worldview, however, the recognition that unborn babies are fully human and therefore infinitely valuable belongs within a much larger story, a story in which the most vulnerable are the most important, a story in which no human being is unwanted, a story in which all of us are sexual sinners and only Jesus has the right to judge, a story in which sacrifice for others is the only path to joy, and a story that ends—for those willing to accept the offer—with a marriage of such beauty and intimacy that it makes the best human marriage seem like a heart emoji compared with a Shakespeare sonnet. Like Dumbledore's "Severus . . . please," the Bible's words on women are the words of a man who lays down his life. The ultimate man laid down his life for the billions of women who have trusted him with theirs. Does Christianity denigrate women? On the contrary. It lifts us into fellowship with God himself.

9

Isn't Christianity Homophobic?

Rachel and I are that fizzy mix of alike and opposite that makes for a great relationship. I'm an extrovert; she's an introvert. I'm an optimist; she's a pessimist. I'm impulsive; she's risk-averse. I'm from London; she's from California. I grew up in a fiercely academic, church-going family. She is a self-made scholar, raised religion-free. We both studied arts subjects at swanky universities. We both love books and poetry and debating fresh ideas. We are both passionate Christians with seminary degrees, trying to grapple with the Bible in the original languages and apply it to our complicated lives. We make each other laugh, we push each other to do better, and we are both primarily attracted to women.

Our stories of same-sex attraction are as different as our stories of faith. Mine is the story of a girl who found herself from childhood falling in love with older, inaccessible girls, but hoped and prayed she would grow out of it—a dream that finally died in grad school. It's a story of silence and quiet loss, as my heart got stuck to people who could not want me back. It's a story of never touching another woman in a sexual way, but always longing for more intimacy—sometimes more than I knew I could have. And, like many Christians of my generation who felt more drawn to those of their own sex, it's a story of carrying the burdens of legitimate needs and complex desires, and a cavernous fear that disclosing my feelings would ruin my friendships.

Rachel's story is the opposite. It's a story of growing up without a Christian framework and realizing at fifteen that she was drawn to a beautiful senior girl. It's a story of pursuing and seducing that girl and establishing an intimate, ongoing, open relationship. It's a story of sleeping with many other supposedly straight women—even developing a conquest mentality—and of despising Christians for being stupid and easily lured into bed. But then it's a story of reading her way into Yale, being left by her high school girlfriend, plunging into existential angst, stealing a book called *Mere Christianity* from a lapsed-Catholic friend, and being overpowered by the gospel of Jesus. It's a story of trying to reconcile her lifestyle with the Bible and failing; of committing to Jesus above sex with women and failing; and then gradually growing in obedience and ability to resist temptation. It's a story of dependence on Jesus's love and trusting that his no to sexual relationships with women meant a better yes to a deeper relationship with him.[1]

Rachel and I are both now married to men—men we love and respect and depend on. Our marriages are good and true, and tempered by all the usual ups and downs that arise when two sinful people bind themselves to each other for life. We both consider our husbands to be among the greatest blessings God has given us. We would not change them for the world, and their Christlike love has shaped and changed us in a thousand ways. But we both chose to marry men because of our commitment to Christ over our emotional and sexual preferences, and when we feel drawn to people outside our marriages (as most married people do from time to time), that draw is always toward women. For Rachel, the challenge is one of not wandering back to well-trodden roads. For me, it's not leaning against hitherto unopened gates. A decade into marriage, neither of us expects these lures to evaporate. We believe that God could change our instincts, but we have no promise that he will, because blue-blood heterosexuality is not the goal of the Christian life: Jesus is.

This chapter may be the most controversial yet. It will argue for a view that is profoundly unpopular in twenty-first-century Western

1. You can read Rachel's beautiful account of her own story in Rachel Gilson, "I Never Became Straight. Perhaps That Was Never God's Goal," *Christianity Today*, September 20, 2017. https://www.christianitytoday.com/ct/2017/october/i-never-became-straight-perhaps-that-was-never-gods-goal.html.

society, and increasingly unpopular in some church settings. But I do not write this because I am a homophobic bigot who just doesn't get how two women or two men could want each other in an all-consuming way, or because I don't believe that same-sex couples can be faithful partners, responsible citizens, and loving parents: I have friends who are all those things.

You can say that I have been enculturated from an early age to resist homosexual intimacy and that my beliefs are biased by my faith. They are. But hearing Rachel's story confirmed my suspicion that these facts do not discredit my beliefs. I write this chapter not because I want to believe that following Jesus precludes same-sex marriage. That is, for me, an inconvenient truth. I write because I believe in a greater truth than my small mind can fathom, a deeper desire than my weak heart can muster, and a closer relationship than the best human marriage can attain.

Two Ways to Be One Body

If you have read the first paragraph of chapter 1 and jumped straight to here, please scroll back up! This chapter will make little sense without the foundation of the last, which argued that just as God created parenthood to show us how he loves his children, so he created sex and marriage to give us a glimpse of what it means to be united to Christ.[2] As we saw, the Bible presents marriage as a one-body experience: a man and a woman knit together in a spiritual one-flesh reality, illustrated in the fleshiness of sex, and manifested by the combining of two parents' DNA in each child. But there is another biblical dimension to being one body, and if we don't take time to ponder this, we will never grasp the logic of the Christian boundaries around sex.

People sometimes say that the Bible condemns same-sex relationships. It does not. The Bible *commands* same-sex relationships at a level of intimacy that Christians seldom reach. Jesus preached a gospel of radical intimacy: with him first and foremost, but through him also with each other. Building on Jesus's words at his Last Supper with his disciples, Paul argues that Christians are inextricably bound to together: "The bread that we break, is it not a participation in the body

---

2. If you could stretch to reading chap. 6 on biblical metaphor, that would be even better!

of Christ? Because there is one bread, we who are many are one body, for we all partake of the one bread" (1 Cor. 10:16–17).

Within the Christian framework, one-body unity is not just for husbands and wives: it's for everyone.[3] Christians are not designed to work alone any more than lungs can work without a heart. "Just as the body is one and has many members, and all the members of the body, though many, are one body," Paul explains, "so it is with Christ" (1 Cor. 12:12). He concludes, "If one member suffers, all suffer together; if one member is honored, all rejoice together" (1 Cor. 12:26).

In a biblical framework, therefore, friendship is not the consolation prize for those who fail to gain romantic love. Like marriage and like parenthood, it is another way in which God manifests an aspect of his love for us. Christians are "one body" (Rom. 12:5), brothers and sisters (Matt. 12:50), "knit together in love" (Col. 2:2), comrades in arms (Phil. 2:25). Paul calls his friend Onesimus his "very heart" (Philem. 12) and likens his affection for believers in Thessalonica to that of "a nursing mother taking care of her children" (1 Thess. 2:7). Nursing a baby is vitally different from a sexual act, but it too is a true comingling of two people in mutual vulnerability and dependence. New Testament Christians are seen sharing their resources, living communally, bearing one another's burdens, loving each other deeply, and expressing love physically. The command "Greet one another with a holy kiss" appears in the New Testament five times.[4]

As we will see later in this chapter, the Bible is clear that sexual intimacy belongs exclusively to heterosexual marriage. But the one-body reality of gospel partnership—best experienced in same-sex friendships—is not a lesser thing. We have this on the authority of Jesus himself, who never married, invested deeply in friendship, and declared, "Greater love has no one than this, that someone lay down his life for his friends" (John 15:13).

While not being less in biblical terms than marriage, friendship plays a different role. The one-flesh intimacy of marriage expresses Christ's jealous love for his people. It is, in an important sense,

---

3. Paul uses the same language in Rom. 12:4–5 and Eph. 4:15–16.
4. Rom. 16:16; 1 Cor. 16:20; 2 Cor. 13:12; 1 Thess. 5:26; 1 Pet. 5:14.

exclusive. Christian friendship, by contrast, is designed to include. Paul's breastfeeding metaphor points to this.

When I was pregnant with my second daughter, I worried that I would not love her as much as I loved my first. But when she came, God expanded my heart. I trust that God will stretch my heart to love our third child just as much. My love for my children is powerful and intimate, but not exclusive. Likewise, the deep, vulnerable, and joyous love that God pours out in same-sex friendships does not have the exclusive, one-and-done boundaries of marriage. In my own experience, the more I grow in intimacy with one friend, the more I need to press into other relationships to be the person God calls me to be, and not fall prey to inwardness and insecurity. Understanding the different kinds of boundaries that operate in marriage and in friendship will help us understand the purpose of each.

The Benefits of Boundaries

We humans thrive on boundaries. We need freedom, to be sure. But we need boundaries to create the right kind of spaces for the different parts of our lives. These boundaries can be spatial: this venue is for baseball; that one, for football. Both games can be played simultaneously, but not on the same field. They can be temporal: these hours are for sleeping; these are for working; these are for play. Sleeping in the middle of the work day or playing in the middle of the night is seldom for our good. They can also be relational: it's not okay for strangers to touch my body, but this stranger can touch my body in this way because she is my doctor. If we listen closely to the Bible's sexual ethics, we find that its clear boundaries create both a safe space for sex and a whole arena for different kinds of intimate connection.

Within a Christian framework, opposite-sex marriage is set apart as the only place for sexual intimacy. This boundary cuts off the possibility of sex with anyone else. It is highly restrictive and, in some respects, against our inclinations: few married people never have the desire for sexual intimacy with someone other than their spouse. Thus, every Christian is called at times to sacrifice his or her desires. But marriage also creates immense freedom and security for loving, sexual intimacy without fear of critique or abandonment. The boundaries of friendship fall in a different place: they prohibit sex, but they create space for intimacy with multiple people who will touch our hearts, minds, and bodies in different ways.

We see different kinds of love and boundaries operating most clearly in family structures. Close family relationships are marked by deep love and physical intimacy. My daughters, who are eight and six, come to me often for physical touch. Holding my girls brings me delight and satisfies my mother-love desires. But as my friends who experienced abuse as children can painfully attest, introducing sexual intimacy into a parent-child bond destroys that love. The boundaries that operate within a family create space for different forms of intimacy. In the best case, children get to experience physical and emotional closeness with their parents and their siblings. But before long, they realize they also need friends—not to replace their family relationships, but to complement them.

By the same token, physical intimacy can play a key role in friendship. Often, it's the ritual of greeting. Hugs to say hello and goodbye to my friends punctuate my daily life and bring me joy. But sometimes the role of touch in friendship is more specific. In the past month, I've held two close friends at length: in one instance, to offer comfort for a broken heart; in another, to wordlessly express forgiveness and restored relationship. To make either of these moments sexual would have destroyed their worth. It would also have missed the point: within the boundaries of those relationships, extended hugs are the highest expression of physical love, and can leave a lasting impression.

Two years ago, I spoke publicly about my own history of same-sex attraction for the first time. I was chairing a panel at our church's women's retreat, and I felt in the moment that the group would be served by my alluding to this part of myself. It was a big step. Not long before, I hadn't talked about this with even my dearest friends. After the session, I sat down with a woman who was new to the church and had questions, and while I was responding to her concerns, a close friend who knew my history came to join the conversation and put her arm around me. I had been so focused on what I was doing that I hadn't been attending to my own emotional needs. But this simple act of physical affection hit me like a wave and met a need I didn't even realize I had.

In our sexualized world, we might think that a deeply meaningful hug with a friend or a loving arm around our shoulders is inevitably dwarfed by the greater physical intensity of sex. But while sexual contact may involve a more powerful physiological response, it is not necessarily more truly intimate. In fact, it is all too common for people to gain physical pleasure from sex without deep emotional connection. And while a good sexual relationship should also involve deep friendship and nonsexual touch, there will always be ways in which particular friends "get" us differently than our spouse—ranges of interest and emotion that they can uniquely access. Rather than seeing sexual and romantic love as the high point on a scale where friendship laps at the low-water mark, the Bible invites us to pursue human love in different forms, governed by different boundaries. The same Scriptures that say no to same-sex sexual intimacy say a massive *yes* to intimacy of other kinds. Indeed, deep, Jesus-centered intimacy around shared mission should leave any cheap, hook-up versions of sexual intimacy in the dust.

How do these boundaries relate to same- versus opposite-sex relationships? If we operate in a framework that sets half the human race aside from the possibility of a sexual relationship, we have great freedom to pursue nonsexual intimacy. Of course, this is more complicated for same-sex-oriented people. The feelings I sometimes experience in friendship mean that I need to examine my heart and be quick to repent and redirect if I find myself in dangerous territory. But given that most women do not share my attractions, and those close to me who do also share my beliefs, I can largely feel free to pursue intimacy in friendship without risking compromising my marriage. Like any other Christian, I need safe friends with whom I can be utterly honest, and who will call me out and help me make corrections when the pendulum of my heart has swung too far in one direction. And I need a level of intimacy with my husband that allows me to bring my struggles *to* him and refocus my desires *on* him. But while it is tempting for same-sex-attracted Christians to retreat from friendship for fear of messing up, I believe this is quite the wrong approach.

Whatever our sexuality, we are all more prone to eat junk food when we are hungry, and we are all more prone to seek illicit relationships when our core relational needs are not being met. For Christians capable of experiencing attraction to same-sex friends, the solution is not friendship starvation but healthy nourishment.

As I have gone on in life and pondered the wisdom of what is for many the hardest command of the Christian faith, I have come to believe that closing off half the people we encounter from the possibility of a sexual relationship opens up other possibilities. Just as human beings are omnivorous and thrive on a range of foods, so we thrive on a range of relationships. And while sexual and romantic relationships may have the intensity of meat, a vegetarian will thrive and flourish where a human carnivore sickens. In modern society, we are led to believe we cannot live without sex. In fact, I believe we are more likely to wither without friend and family love.

A Call to Longing but Not Loneliness

Last summer, I took a long walk with a friend who was considering dating women. She'd had bad experiences with men. She'd been inspired by a lesbian couple who seemed to model all sorts of Christian goods, and she was finding herself attracted to certain women. I brought up Jesus's call on all Christians to deny themselves, take up their cross, and follow him—irrespective of the cost. She said it seemed unfair that same-sex-attracted Christians should be sentenced to loneliness. I was reading the book of Acts at the time. I observed that, while the first Christians faced every kind of suffering, even being stoned to death, there was one struggle they did not face: loneliness. If we reduce Christian community to sexual relationships and the nuclear family, we are utterly failing to deliver on biblical ethics.

This point is underlined by the Bible's view of singleness. Jesus himself never married. While Paul commends marriage, he values singleness *more* (1 Cor. 7:38). Single people are vital to the church family—which is the primary family unit in Christian terms—and should experience deep love and fellowship with other believers. Where church culture inhibits this by overemphasizing marriage and parenting, Christians need to fight for culture change and embody the biblical reality that the local church is truly their family. Enabling same-sex-attracted Christians who choose to remain single to thrive in church means becoming more biblical, not less.[5]

I do not mean to minimize the pain. Some of my same-sex-attracted friends experience a drum-like beat of sexual temptation. But this is also true for many heterosexual Christians, whether they are married and struggling to be faithful to their spouses, or single and longing for marriage. Ultimately, every Christian is called to sexual self-restraint. Except in the case of a spouse's death or an extreme scenario warranting biblical divorce, Christians are called to, at most, one sexual partner. Saying yes to Jesus means saying no to sexual freedom. But it does not mean missing out. At its best, marriage is meant to leave us wanting more: it is a gateway drug to a far more fulfilling relationship.

This does not diminish the longing that many single people feel. Rather, it gives it meaning. Within the Christian worldview, there is intentionality to unfulfilled longing. As a predominantly same-sex-attracted woman happily married to a man, I myself am increasingly convinced that the longing I at times have felt is ultimately a longing not for another woman but for the One who created that person. Like a print of the *Mona Lisa*, a human being created in God's image can never be as stunning as the original. Jesus is, by definition, infinitely more beautiful, compelling, and capable of love.

In a moment of characteristic brilliance, Shakespeare puts these words into the mouth of Enobarbus, reflecting on whether Anthony will leave his lover Cleopatra:

> Never; he will not:
> Age cannot wither her, nor custom stale
> Her infinite variety: other women cloy
> The appetites they feed: but she makes hungry
> Where most she satisfies.[6]

---

5. Rosaria Butterfield's excellent book *The Gospel Comes with a House Key: Practicing Radically Ordinary Hospitality in our Post-Christian World* (Wheaton, IL: Crossway, 2018) illustrates this. I have written much less extensively on how this biblical mentality should inform our practices in church gatherings; see Rebecca McLaughlin, "Why I Don't Sit with My Husband at Church," *Christianity Today*, April 19, 2018, https://www.christianitytoday.com/women/2018/april/why-i-dont-sit-with-my-husband-at-church.html.

6. William Shakespeare, *Anthony and Cleopatra*, act 2, scene 2.

But, lyrical as this is, it's ultimately untrue. If we want infinite delight, a finite being will not satisfy.

As with all other aspects of faith, this is a gamble. I once confessed to Rachel a sense of grief—envy even—that she had experienced all the intimacy with women I had grown up wanting, and more. I will always remember her response: "Trust me, all of that was nothing compared to knowing Christ."

What Does the Bible Really Say about Homosexuality?

When Rachel was first considering Christianity, she consulted a lesbian friend who was training to be a Lutheran minister. This friend assured Rachel that a monogamous same-sex marriage was not incompatible with Christian faith and gave her a book that made that case. Rachel read it ravenously and found it compelling. But when she looked up the Bible passages the book referenced, its arguments crumbled in her hands.

The Bible is unequivocal on the question of homosexual sex. First, men sleeping with men is prohibited in the Jewish law (e.g., Lev. 18:22; 20:13). This does not prove the case for Christians. Many Old Testament laws are specifically declared not binding in the New Testament (for example, food restrictions). But the logic of opposite-sex marriage and the prohibition on homosexual sex are reaffirmed multiple times.[7]

Let's start with Jesus's framework. Jesus is sometimes caricatured as a prophet of free love, unconcerned about sexual ethics. But his teaching on sexual morality was consistently stricter than the Old Testament law.[8] For instance, when the Pharisees asked Jesus whether a man may divorce his wife "for any cause," he replied:

> Have you not read that he who created them from the beginning made them male and female, and said, "Therefore a man shall leave his father and his mother and hold fast to his wife, and the

---

7. See Robert A. J. Gagnon, *The Bible and Homosexual Practice: Texts and Hermeneutics* (Nashville: Abingdon, 2001) for a detailed treatment of the prohibitions on homosexual sex in the Hebrew Scriptures and how they relate to New Testament texts.

8. For example, "You have heard that it was said, 'You shall not commit adultery.' But I say to you that everyone who looks at a woman with lustful intent has already committed adultery with her in his heart" (Matt. 5:27–28).

two shall become one flesh"? So they are no longer two but one flesh. What therefore God has joined together, let not man separate. (Matt. 19:4–6)

Jesus reaffirms God's creation of humans male and female, his one-flesh design for marriage, and its high demands: a man may not divorce his wife except for unfaithfulness (Matt. 19:9). Jesus's hearers are shocked by the strictness of this teaching (Matt. 19:10). To be sure, Jesus routinely scandalized those around him by associating with those known for their sexual immorality. But far from expanding the options on sexual relationships, Jesus tightened the Old Testament law.

We are tempted to think that today's sexual possibilities did not exist in the first century. But the repeated references to all sorts of sexual immorality in the New Testament remind us that the Judeo-Christian restrictions on sex were always countercultural. Ancient Greek culture allowed sex between males—typically between grown men and teenage boys—and celebrated homoerotic desire. Plato, while not approving of homosexual sex, wrote of one student,

> Star-gazing Aster, would I were the skies,
> To gaze upon thee with a thousand eyes.[9]

His epitaph for another mentee hails "Dion, whose love once maddened the heart within this breast."[10] Moreover, in Plato's *Symposium*, Aristophanes articulates a founding myth for sexual orientation, in which humans began as composite creatures: some male-male, some female-female, and some male-female. Zeus split them up and left them with a desire to find their other half—be it in heterosexual or homosexual union.[11]

There was typically an asymmetry to gay sex in the ancient world, with an age or status differential between the penetrator and the penetrated. But this was also true of heterosexual marriage, which often paired a man in his thirties with a woman in her early teens. And while much gay sex was exploitative and promiscuous, there were cultural

---

9. Quoted in Louis Crompton, *Homosexuality and Civilization* (Cambridge, MA: Harvard University Press, 2003), 55.
10. Quoted in Crompton, *Homosexuality and Civilization*, 56.
11. See Plato's *Symposium*, 189c–93e.

models for committed homosexual relationships. In the fourth century BC, a Greek army known as the Sacred Band of Thebes was formed, consisting of a 150 pairs of male lovers. The theory was that the added sexual bond would motivate soldiers to fight for each other.[12]

Roman culture was more restrictive, in that sex between male citizens was frowned upon. But men were free to sleep with male slaves and prostitutes. However, as Louis Crompton (himself a gay man and pioneer of queer studies) argued in *Homosexuality and Civilization*, the exploitative nature of much gay sex in the ancient world does not open the door to reinterpreting the New Testament: "Nowhere does Paul or any other Jewish writer of this period imply the least acceptance of same-sex relations under any circumstances. The idea that homosexuals might be redeemed by mutual devotion would have been wholly foreign to Paul or any other Jew or early Christian."[13]

When we examine the New Testament, we find explicit prohibitions of homosexual sex. But we also find a surprising weakness in the claim that Paul, who wrote most of the relevant texts, was a judgmental homophobe. In a letter to his mentee Timothy, Paul reaffirms the scriptural prohibitions on sexual sin—heterosexual and homosexual. But he refuses to stand on any moral high ground. Reflecting on how false teachers were twisting the law, Paul writes:

> The law is not laid down for the just but for the lawless and disobedient, for the ungodly and sinners, for the unholy and profane, for those who strike their fathers and mothers, for murderers, the sexually immoral, men who practice homosexuality, enslavers, liars, perjurers, and whatever else is contrary to sound doctrine. (1 Tim. 1:9–10)

Sexual immorality, including homosexual immorality, is listed here between the sins of murder and slave catching. The phrase "men who practice homosexuality" also appears in 1 Corinthians 6:9, where it translates two Greek words that seem to specify the active and passive partners.[14] While there was shame for a man in being penetrated

---

12. For more details on the Sacred Band of Thebes, see Crompton, *Homosexuality and Civilization*, 69–73.

13. Crompton, *Homosexuality and Civilization*, 114.

14. *Malakoi* (effeminate) and *arsenokoitai* (men bedders).

in Roman culture, Paul condemns both roles. But he also repeatedly declares that *no one* is holy according to the law. A few verses later in 1 Timothy he writes, "Christ Jesus came into the world to save sinners, of whom I am the foremost" (1 Tim. 1:15). Far from thinking he is *better* than those whose sin he lists, Paul presents himself as *worse*: "a blasphemer, persecutor, and insolent opponent" of Jesus (1 Tim. 1:12), saved only to prove that the *least* deserving person can be redeemed. Indeed, in this chapter, Paul refers to himself as the "foremost" of sinners twice (1 Tim. 1:15, 16)!

When Paul references homosexual sex in his letter to the church at Rome, it flows out of a description of idolatry. This makes sense in the broader biblical logic of marriage as a picture of God's relationship with his people, and in the broader cultural context of the role of sex in some pagan worship rituals. Paul describes people abandoning worship of God and throwing themselves into sexual relationships:

> For this reason God gave them up to dishonorable passions. For their women exchanged natural relations for those that are contrary to nature; and the men likewise gave up natural relations with women and were consumed with passion for one another, men committing shameless acts with men and receiving in themselves the due penalty for their error. (Rom. 1:26–27)

These verses condemn homosexual sex for women and for men. They are unquestionably offensive. But the reality is that the Bible is offensive from beginning to end.

When Rice professor Jim Tour was a student, a Christian friend started telling him about Jesus. Jim wasn't convinced. He thought he was a pretty good guy, so all the talk of sin cutting him off from God confused him. But then his friend pointed him to Matthew 5:27–28, where Jesus asserts that anyone who looks at a woman lustfully has committed adultery in his heart. Jim realized that his pornography addiction placed him squarely in that category, and he ultimately came to recognize Jesus as the Messiah his Jewish upbringing had taught him to await. With or without pornography, if you are a straight man, it's unlikely that you can plead "not guilty" to Jesus's charge. Worse still, Jesus says that if your right eye causes you to lust, you are better to gouge it out and enter the kingdom of God than to stay in your sin (Matt. 5:29). No one can listen to Jesus and not be shocked, offended, and broken by his stance on sexual sin. But Jesus's most offensive words strike at the most scrupulously chaste people of his day.

In a massive tirade against the hyper-religious Pharisees, Jesus calls them hypocrites, blind guides, whitewashed tombs, sons of murderers, and serpents: "You brood of vipers," he yells, "how are you to escape being sentenced to hell?" (Matt. 23:33). We cannot read the Bible and not be offended—condemned even—unless we come as broken sinners. If we come like that, we are tenderly embraced. Indeed, while Jesus's condemnation of sexual sin is terrifying, his consistent welcome of repentant sexual sinners is equally shocking. We see this in the Gospels, and in the early Christian movement.

In Paul's letter to the Corinthians, we get a glimpse of a church composed of repentant sinners of all kinds—sexual and otherwise. Corinth was the Vegas of the Roman Empire, with party-city ethics. "Do you not know," writes Paul, "that the unrighteous will not inherit the kingdom of God?" He then lists illustrative examples:

> Neither the sexually immoral, nor idolaters, nor adulterers, nor men who practice homosexuality, nor thieves, nor the greedy, nor drunkards, nor revilers, nor swindlers will inherit the kingdom of God. And such were some of you. But you were washed, you were sanctified, you were justified in the name of the Lord Jesus Christ and by the Spirit of our God. (1 Cor. 6:9–11)

According to this passage, some of the very first Christians entered the church with homosexual histories and desires. This is as true today as it was then.

No Room for "Them and Us" in the Church

Despite Paul's refusal to cast himself as morally superior, Christians have often confused the Bible's clear boundaries around sex with a license for unloving, superior, and judgmental attitudes toward gay and lesbian people. But while the New Testament is clear on its no to homosexual relationships, it leaves no room for a "them and us" approach. By Jesus's definition, every adult Christian is guilty of sexual sin, and Christians with homosexual desires and histories helped to launch the early church. While I do not believe that upholding biblical sexual ethics is innately homophobic (defined by the *Oxford English Dictionary* as "Having or showing a dislike of or prejudice against homosexual people"), many Christians today do need to repent of their unbiblical attitudes.

When my husband and I moved to America and joined our current church, we knew one man in the congregation who was open about his same-sex attraction. Lou was raised in the church and first realized he was attracted to other guys when he was a teenager. He bravely told his youth leader. That leader dropped everything to tell the senior pastor, who insisted Lou wake his parents immediately to tell them. These leaders may not have meant ill. They evidently had no experience or framework from which to support their younger brother in Christ. But I doubt they would have had the same reaction if he had confessed a heterosexual pornography addiction—a far more destructive sin problem than a young man finding himself attracted to other boys and seeking help. Thankfully, Lou bore with the failures of his leaders and held on to his faith in Christ, and today he is a tremendous gift to our church as a single, servant-hearted man who is sacrificing sexual and romantic fulfillment for the greater prize of faithfulness to Christ.

Countless Christians have faced treatment similar to Lou's—and worse—on confessing their same-sex attraction. Many, fearing rejection, have not spoken up at all. While I have never had a Christian react badly when I've shared my own struggles, I suffered in silence for much of my Christian life, and a culture that isolates believers in loneliness and shame is deeply unbiblical. As Nazi-era German theologian and resistance leader Dietrich Bonhoeffer put it, "The Christian needs another Christian who speaks God's Word to him. . . . The Christ in his own heart is weaker than the Christ in the word of his brother."[15] The further I go on in life, the more convinced I am that every Christian is a struggling Christian, dependent on help from brothers and

---

15. Dietrich Bonhoeffer, *Life Together*, trans. John W. Doberstein (New York: HarperCollins, 1954), 23.

sisters who know their needs and vulnerabilities. Lungs don't work without hearts, or legs without feet. We're simply not designed for solo flight.

When Paradigms Break

But there is another sense in which there is no room for "them and us" when it comes to homosexuality. Psychology professor Lisa Diamond, herself a lesbian activist, has extensively researched the nature of sexual orientation and drawn surprising conclusions. First, she has found that bisexuality is far more widespread than anyone has realized. Drawing on the 2002 National Survey of Family Growth, Diamond notes that around 14 percent of women and 7 percent of men reported experiencing same-sex attraction, but that less than 2 percent of men and less than 1 percent of women were exclusively same-sex attracted.[16] It turns out I belong to by far the largest sexual minority: women who experience same-sex attraction, but not exclusively. If you watched a documentary of my heart well into adulthood, you would conclude that I was same-sex-oriented. And yet here I am, happily married to a man.

Diamond notes that preconceptions of sexual identity have stopped researchers from asking people about desires and experiences that do not conform to their label. She has found that when asked just about the last year of their lives, 42 percent of self-identified lesbians report having fantasized about sex with a man, 26 percent report having desired sex with a man, and 9 percent have engaged in heterosexual sex. Likewise, 31 percent of gay men report having fantasized about a woman in the last year, 20 percent confess to wanting sex with a woman, and 12 percent have slept with a woman in the past year. Furthermore, 15 percent of self-identified lesbians reported having had romantic feelings for a man in the previous year, and 31 percent of self-identified gay men reported having had romantic feelings for a women. Meanwhile, 50 percent of self-identified heterosexual women and 25 percent of heterosexual men reported having experienced a

---

16. Professor Diamond summarizes her data in a fascinating lecture at Cornell University entitled "Just How Different Are Female and Male Sexual Orientation?," YouTube (video), October 17, 2013, https://www.youtube.com/watch?v=m2rTHDOuUBw. This survey was repeated in 2008 with very similar results.

same-sex attraction in the past year, while 35 percent of women and 24 percent of men reported a same-sex sexual fantasy.[17]

To complicate the picture further, Diamond observes that it is quite common for our attractions to change over time—both from heterosexual to homosexual and vice versa. My younger self's hope that I would simply grow out of my same-sex attractions was not completely unfounded. As Diamond puts it, "Perhaps the only way to be certain whether an adolescent's same-sex attractions will persist into adulthood is to observe whether they actually *do*."[18] Conversely, people who enter homosexual relationships later in life are not necessarily acknowledging desires they have always had. When *Sex and the City* star Cynthia Nixon left her long-term partner and father of her children and started dating a woman whom she subsequently married, she reflected:

> In terms of sexual orientation I don't really feel I've changed. I don't feel there was a hidden part of my sexuality that I wasn't aware of. I'd been with men all my life, and I'd never fallen in love with a woman. But when I did, it didn't seem so strange. I'm just a woman in love with another woman.[19]

After years of study, Diamond has concluded that, when we categorize people as gay or straight, "We are not in fact cutting nature at its joints, we are kind of imposing some joints on a very messy phenomenon."[20]

Diamond recognizes how challenging this data is for contemporary conceptions of sexual identity. With remarkable honestly, she concludes: "We've advocated for the civil rights of LGBT people on the basis of them being LGBT. We have used categories as a part of our

---

17. Diamond, "Just How Different?"

18. See Lisa Diamond and Ritch C. Savin-Williams, "The Intimate Relationships of Sexual-Minority Youths," in *The Blackwell Handbook of Adolescence*, ed. Gerald R. Adams and Michael D. Berzonsky (Oxford: Blackwell, 2008), 396.

19. Quoted in John Hiscock, "Sex and the City's Cynthia Nixon: 'I'm Just a Woman in Love with a Woman,'" *The Telegraph*, May 13, 2008, https://www.telegraph.co.uk/culture/film/starsand stories/3673343/Sex-and-the-Citys-Cynthia-Nixon-Im-just-a-woman-in-love-with-a-woman.html.

20. Diamond, "Just How Different?" See also L. M. Diamond and C. J. Rosky, "Scrutinizing Immutability: Research on Sexual Orientation and U.S. Legal Advocacy for Sexual Minorities," *Journal of Sex Research* 53 (2016): 363–91, where the authors suggest that "arguments based on the immutability of sexual orientation are unscientific, given what we now know from longitudinal, population-based studies of naturally occurring changes in the same-sex attractions of some individuals over time."

strategy for social policy and for acceptance, and that is really, really tricky, now that we know it's not true."[21]

To be clear, this does not deny that many people experience consistently homosexual attractions throughout their lives; nor does it deny the possibility of a genetic component to sexual orientation (a debate that has always been a red herring when it comes to moral questions);[22] nor does Diamond's data imply that we choose our attractions. I have friends who wish they could summon enough opposite-sex attraction to make heterosexual marriage work, and others who long to be free of seemingly uncontrollable heterosexual lust. But it does highlight our agency in our sexual choices. As Rachel puts it, "The object of attraction is to some extent beside the point. I could find myself attracted to a potted plant! The question is, what do I *do* with that attraction?"

Disentangling Sexuality and Race

Our ability to make choices about what we do with our attractions is part of what makes the rhetorical entanglement of racial diversity and diversity of sexual lifestyle so problematic. The gay rights movement is often heralded as the new civil rights movement, and those who question gay marriage are equated with sixties segregationists: prejudiced bigots on the wrong side of history. But while there are certainly commonalities between the ways in which racial and sexual minorities have experienced ill-treatment, equating these two groups is problematic in at least five ways.

First, unlike racial heritage, sexual activity involves choice. My Myers-Briggs personality profile is called "the Campaigner." I enjoy public speaking, and my high school class in the UK voted me "most likely to become prime minister." But I now live in America, and because I was not born here, I could never run for president. My birthplace, like my racial heritage, was given to me. I had no choice in the matter, and it is not susceptible to change. My natural attraction toward public speaking is more like sexual orientation. It's a mix of

---

21. Diamond, "Just How Different?"
22. Many behaviors that are morally negative (e.g., alcoholism) can be linked to genetic predispositions.

innate predispositions and life experiences, a blend of chosen and unchosen, and I now make decisions about what I do with it. Ultimately, while we do not choose our sexual *attractions*, we do choose our sexual *actions*. They therefore carry moral weight in a way that racial heritage does not.

Second, though twentieth-century scientists tried long and hard to find significant biological differences between races, they failed. But, except in rare cases (which I will touch on shortly), there are real biological differences between men and women—differences that are highly relevant in the context of sex. Comparing same-sex marriage to mixed-race marriage is, therefore, quite illegitimate. Whereas mixed-race marriages are positively advantageous when it comes to having kids (greater genetic diversity being correlated with lower risk of genetic disease), same-sex marriage is a biological dead end. This difference does not prove any ethical case. Childbearing is not the sole purpose of marriage, but it is a relevant consideration and another reason we cannot equate same-sex and interracial marriage.

Third, if you sample the global population today, white Westerners are far more likely to affirm gay marriage than people of color.[23] Accusing everyone who does not affirm gay marriage of being backward and bigoted is not a strike in favor of tolerance and diversity. Undoubtedly, some people oppose gay marriage out of bigotry. But I am not one, and nor are most people I know who hold to heterosexual marriage on religious grounds.

Fourth, while the Bible cuts strongly and emphatically in favor of racial equality and integration, it cuts equally firmly against same-sex marriage. From a Christian perspective, therefore, it is entirely consistent to support racial equality, integration, and mixed-race marriages while opposing same-sex marriage. The stance against mixed-race marriages taken by many white Christians in American history represented an utter failure to listen to the Scriptures. It should be a cautionary tale to Christians today not to try to cloak their sinful prejudices in biblical garments. But the past failure of Christians to listen to the

---

23. David Masci and Drew DeSilver, "A Global Snapshot of Same-Sex Marriage," Pew Research Center, December 8, 2017, http://www.pewresearch.org/fact-tank/2017/12/08/global-snapshot-sex-marriage/.

Bible when it reaches conclusions they do not like does not license Christians today to do the same.

Finally, opposition to homosexual sex is common to the two largest global worldviews—Christianity and Islam—as well as to most other religious traditions. Given the global population trends, the claim that those who oppose gay marriage will be "on the wrong side of history" is likely to be inaccurate. Rather than assuming that the arc of history bends a certain way, we must all pay careful attention to what forms our moral stances and give each ethical question consideration on its own terms.

None of this proves that the biblical view is correct or that it should necessarily dictate secular laws. Just as church participation, prayer, and generosity to the poor are required of Christians but should not be forced on non-Christians, so the Bible's prohibitions on sex outside the boundaries of heterosexual marriage do not necessarily imply that this ethic should be imposed on those outside the church. But we must stop equating racial heritage with sexual behavior, and we must stop assuming that all traditional Christians are hateful bigots simply because they restrict marriage to male and female.

What about Those Born Intersex?

A few years ago, a friend of mine gave birth to an intersex child, whom I'll call Jamie. This child is chromosomally male, but presents predominantly female outwardly and was assigned female at birth. Exactly how Jamie will develop in puberty is hard to predict. It is equally unclear whether Jamie will *feel* more male or female through the maturation process, or will be attracted to men, women, or both. Space here does not allow proper theological consideration to situations like this, nor am I qualified to provide such. My instinct says that biologically intersex children should be given plenty of time, freedom, and support to figure things out. But I will address one question that naturally arises. Does the existence of beautiful intersex kids, like my friend's, undermine the biblical boundaries that preclude same-sex marriage? I believe not.

My first daughter is a natural lawyer: she finds exceptions to every rule. When she was five, I told her she should never jump out of the window of our apartment. She shot back, "Unless the house is on fire, in which case you should." I agreed. Does this exception invalidate the rule? Not at all. I was still right to tell her not to jump out of the window. Likewise, when my younger daughter once ran across a road without looking first, I yelled at her in the harshest terms and made her promise never to do that again. This rule is for her good. Disobedience could be deadly. But if she were being chased by a murderous child snatcher, crossing a road without looking first may be the right choice. Almost every good rule has exceptions.

Why can we not say, therefore, that people who are exclusively same-sex attracted are exceptions to the biblical rule? Because the Bible is clear in its no to homosexual sex. For the intersex child, the rules may need to be applied differently, because the child's starting point is different. Of course, this becomes more complicated when we consider people who identify on the transgender spectrum. Feeling that one's sex has been misassigned can have a clear biological source, for example, having chromosomes that do not match your genitalia. We must not oversimplify. But just as sexual attraction is often fluid over time, many people experience changes in their sense of themselves as male and female, and we must be careful (whatever our beliefs) about letting children whom we consider too young to vote, drink, or marry make permanent, life-changing decisions about their bodies.

What does this mean for Christians? On the one hand, Christians must beware of allowing feelings to dictate actions. According to the Bible's unflattering diagnosis, we are all naturally sinful and confused, and God calls us all to roles that require self-forgetfulness. This at first sounds frustrating. Modern Western society teaches me to prioritize discovering my authentic self, peeling back the onion layers of my identity and living out of what I find there at all costs. But from a Christian perspective, who I am in relation to God *is* my authentic self. I find myself not in the depths of my psychology but in the depths of his heart. And when he calls you or me "child," "beloved," "friend," that's who we are, and any other identity—male, female, father, mother, child, friend—flows out of that.

At the same time, Christians must resist defining manhood and womanhood according to unbiblical gender stereotypes. As we explored in the previous chapter, the Bible calls men and women to distinct roles in some contexts. But our gender stereotypes are not prescribed by Scripture. Like paleontologists sifting through the dirt, we must excavate what the Bible actually says, while dusting off the cultural dross.

Last Words, from Jesus

The Bible is not silent on the question of people who, for biological or experiential reasons, are not straightforwardly male or female. In Matthew 19, after Jesus's declaration that marriage represents an unbreakable bond between a man and a woman, his disciples respond, "If such is the case of a man with his wife, it is better not to marry" (Matt. 19:10). Jesus replies:

> Not everyone can receive this saying, but only those to whom it is given. For there are eunuchs who have been so from birth, and there are eunuchs who have been made eunuchs by men, and there are eunuchs who have made themselves eunuchs for the sake of the kingdom of heaven. Let the one who is able to receive this receive it. (Matt. 19:11–12)

First-century eunuchs were typically males who had been castrated in childhood. They performed specific roles, ranging from singing, to guarding high-status women.[24] But, as Jesus notes, some people are simply born without the potential to reproduce, and others choose lifelong celibacy for the sake of the kingdom of heaven. In Jesus's estimation, whether you are born intersex, lose sexual function, or embrace celibacy for other reasons, your life and service are of immense value.

Later in Matthew, Jesus explains that when he returns to bring heaven and earth back together, there will be no marriage (Matt. 22:30). Why? Because marriage is a temporary state, designed to point us to a greater reality. At the resurrection, no one who has chosen Jesus over sexual fulfillment will have missed out. Compared with that relationship, human marriage will seem like a toy car next to a Tesla, or a kiss on an envelope versus a lover's embrace.

---

24. The Ethiopian eunuch of Acts 8, whose conversion story we explored in chap. 2, was one example of this.

10

Doesn't the Bible Condone Slavery?

In 1881, escaped-slave-turned-abolitionist-intellectual Frederick Douglass published his final autobiography. In it he describes growing up a lonely and destitute child. But aged thirteen, he heard a white minister preach that all people, slave or free, rich or poor, were sinners in need of Christ. "I cannot say that I had a very distinct notion of what was required of me," recalls Douglass, "but one thing I did know well: I was wretched and had no means of making myself otherwise."[1] Douglass sought counsel from an older black Christian, who told him to cast all his cares upon God. Douglass responded:

> This I sought to do; and though for weeks I was a poor, broken-hearted mourner, traveling through doubts and fears, I finally found my burden lightened, and my heart relieved. I loved all mankind, slaveholders not excepted, though I abhorred slavery more than ever. I saw the world in a new light, and my great concern was to have everybody converted.[2]

Douglass's story exposes a deep tension in the history of slavery, particularly in America. First, how did so many white people who identified as Christians embrace slavery? Second, how did so many

---

1. Frederick Douglass, *The Life and Times of Frederick Douglass* (Radford, VA: Wilder, 2008), 49.
2. Douglass, *Life and Times*, 49.

black people, oppressed and abused in a supposedly Christian country, come to embrace Jesus?

In this chapter we will explore why slaves throughout the centuries have been drawn to Christianity. We will examine the horror of the transatlantic slave trade, the sinful blot of slavery on American history, and the ways in which the Bible has been used at times to condone slavery. But we will also see how biblical ethics radically undermines human slavery and creates a whole new paradigm, within which every Christian is both a slave and deeply free.

The God Who Sees

When we hear the basic story of the first slave described in the Old Testament, it confirms our worst suspicions: the patriarch Abraham slept with his wife's slave girl. This rings in our ears as clear proof that the Bible endorses slavery—even sex slavery. As with many Old Testament narratives, however, we must read the whole story to grasp its meaning. From Genesis 3 onward, the Bible describes human sin, and in many instances it is clear that description is not prescription, as even the Bible's heroes make terrible moral mistakes.

Abraham and Sarah were old and infertile. But God promised Abraham descendants that would outnumber the stars. Rather than trusting God for a miracle, Sarah urged Abraham to sleep with her Egyptian slave girl, Hagar. In ancient Near Eastern culture, sleeping with a slave would not have raised so much as a moral eyebrow. Indeed, becoming an additional wife of Abraham was a status raise for Hagar. But within the narrative, Abraham's decision to sleep with Hagar clearly goes against God's will and reveals a lack of faith in God's promises.

When Hagar conceived, she embraced her new status and started looking down on her barren mistress. Sarah "dealt harshly" with Hagar in response, and Hagar fled. Then comes the most extraordinary part of the story: the angel of the Lord appeared to Hagar and made promises to this escaped slave girl that mirrored God's promises to Abraham himself. Indeed, Hagar is the first person in the Scriptures to name God: "You are a God of seeing," she declares, "Truly here I have seen him who looks after me" (Gen. 16:13). In Genesis 21, when Sarah's son Isaac is born, Sarah again drives Hagar away. Again, God appears to her. He takes care of her and her son, Ishmael, and reiterates his promises.

We do not know Hagar's full story or how she came to be Sarah's handmaid in the first place. Being part of Abraham's household may have been preferable to being an unprotected woman in the ancient Near East. But we do know that Abraham's sleeping with her went against God's promise, and that Hagar was seen and heard and validated by God himself in an astonishing way.

Slavery in the Old Testament

Hagar's story is the first in a line of slave narratives in the Old Testament. Notably, Abraham's great-grandson Joseph was sold into slavery by his brothers. But God redeemed this sinful act by leading Joseph to become a ruler in Egypt.[3] This illustrates three differences between ancient slavery and its more modern incarnations. First, ancient slavery was not yoked to racial hierarchy. Hagar was an Egyptian slave to Hebrews; Joseph was a Hebrew slave to Egyptians. Second, it was common for people to sell themselves into slavery, as it represented a form of employment and was preferable to destitution. Third, while many slaves in the ancient world undoubtedly suffered the kind of brutality and exploitation experienced by many enslaved Africans in America, advancement was also possible within the slave status and beyond—even to the point of becoming a senior civil servant.

However, the Bible devotes significant attention to the oppressive nature of enforced slavery. After Joseph's death, his descendants multiplied in Egypt and finally became enslaved as a people within a foreign land. They were worked to the bone by a subsequent pharaoh, who ordered the mass slaughter of their infant sons (Exodus 1). God did not let this go unpunished. When God called Moses to redeem his people, and Pharaoh refused to let them go free, the angel of death killed the firstborn sons of the Egyptians, while Hebrew homes were protected by the blood of a Passover lamb. Thenceforth, the story of God's people was a story of emancipated slaves.

When God gave his people the law, it included repeated reminders that they were once slaves, and this was to inform how they would

---

3. Joseph later explained to his brothers, "You meant evil against me, but God meant it for good, to bring it about that many people should be kept alive, as they are today" (Gen. 50:20).

treat slaves, immigrants, widows, and orphans.[4] Slave catching was a capital offense: "Whoever steals a man and sells him, and anyone found in possession of him, shall be put to death" (Ex. 21:16). Slaves were given a range of protections and privileges: for example, slaves were included in the day of rest (Ex. 20:10); if their masters did them permanent bodily harm, they had to be released (Ex. 21:26); and any Hebrew man or woman sold into slavery had to be released after six years and given gifts—unless he or she chose to remain (Ex. 21:2; Deut. 15:12–16). Israelites were also commanded to offer refuge to escaped slaves: "You shall not give up to his master a slave who has escaped from his master to you. He shall dwell with you, in your midst, in the place that he shall choose within one of your towns, wherever it suits him. You shall not wrong him" (Deut 23:15).

Protections extended to those captured in warfare. It was standard practice for ancient armies to rape the women of conquered peoples, or to keep them as sex slaves. But the Old Testament specifies that if an Israelite soldier desired a captive woman, he must give her a month to mourn for her family and then marry her. It also forbade him from subsequently deciding that he was done with her and selling her to someone else (Deut. 21:10–14). In our cultural framework, where arranged marriage of any kind seems oppressive, these verses sound abhorrent. But at a time when women did not expect to choose their husbands, and where a woman's livelihood depended on the provision of a male relative, this framework offered captive women protection and respect.

In summary, the Old Testament bans slave catching, provides protections for slaves, and invites us to see the world through enslaved eyes: from Hagar, to Joseph, to the whole people of Israel at their exodus from Egypt. But it does not ban slavery itself. So, what does the New Testament have to offer?

Paul's Letter to Philemon

It may shock you to hear that the New Testament includes a letter written to return a runaway slave to his master. Or perhaps that aligns with your expectation that the Bible justifies slavery. Paul writes from prison in Rome, where he has encountered an escaped slave, Onesimus, and he is

---

4. E.g., Deut. 5:15; 16:12; 24:18.

sending Onesimus back to his master, Philemon. These facts seem to make an ironclad case for the Bible's support of slavery. Until you read the letter.

Paul asserts his right to command Philemon, but he chooses persuasion instead: "I appeal to you," Paul writes, "for my child, Onesimus, whose father I became in my imprisonment" (Philem. 10). This is the first blow. Slaves were not sons; they were property. But Paul calls this runaway slave his child. Then he goes further: "I am sending him back to you, sending my very heart" (Philem. 12). Paul's words of affection for Onesimus surpass any other expression of love for an individual Christian in his writings. He wishes Onesimus could stay with him, but sends him back to Philemon, "no longer as a bondservant but more than a bondservant, as a beloved brother" (Philem. 16). Paul instructs Philemon to receive Onesimus is if he were Paul himself: this runaway slave is worth as much as an apostle, and Philemon had better treat him as such. Paul offers to pay anything Onesimus owes Philemon (Philem. 19) and concludes, "Confident of your obedience, I write to you, knowing that you will do even more than I say" (Philem. 20).

According to Roman law, Philemon could have branded Onesimus, deliberately broken his joints, or administered some other form of brutal punishment. But Paul writes in such a way that if Philemon does not welcome Onesimus back with honor and love—as a beloved brother, not a bondservant—he will be flat out rebelling against his most respected mentor. And Paul addresses this letter not just to Philemon but also "to Apphia our sister and Archippus our fellow soldier, and the church in your house" (Philem. 2). Philemon could not harm Onesimus without incurring public shame.

Jesus, the Slave

Paul's intense identification with Onesimus grows from roots put down by Jesus himself. When his disciples were jostling for position in his future kingdom, Jesus declared, "Whoever would be great among you must be your servant, and whoever would be first among you must be your slave, even as the Son of Man came not to be served but to serve, and to give his life as a ransom for many" (Matt. 20:26–28). Jesus had come to be a slave: a slave whose own life was to be traded in exchange for others. Status in his kingdom lies at the bottom of the pile.

Jesus embraced a slave status again during his Last Supper with his disciples. Foot washing was a role usually performed by slaves, and Jesus dressed for the part. He took off his outer clothing, wrapped a towel around his waist, poured water in a basin, and washed his disciples' feet. They were horrified. But Jesus explained: "You call me Teacher and Lord, and you are right, for so I am. If I then, your Lord and Teacher, have washed your feet, you also ought to wash one another's feet" (John 13:13–14).

Preparing for his crucifixion—his ultimate act of service—Jesus claimed the role of a slave and commanded his followers to do likewise. This point is not lost on Paul, who describes Jesus's incarnation itself as his "taking the form" of a slave, and his crucifixion as "becoming obedient to the point of death, even death on a cross" (Phil. 2:5–8). Crucifixion was a fitting death for a slave who stood up to the empire. When a rebellion known as the Third Servile War was quelled by Rome in 71 BC, approximately six thousand slaves were crucified along the Appian way.

Christians as Slaves

Two years ago, I met a woman with a tattoo on her wrist written in Greek characters. It read *doulos*, the Greek word for slave. Knowing that she was a Christian, I understood the message. In New Testament terms, every Christian is a slave of Christ—starting with the apostles.

In the first century, a slave would be known by his belonging to someone: for example, Onesimus, slave of Philemon. Paul routinely applies the term *doulos* to himself:[5] for example, "Paul, a slave of Christ Jesus" (Rom. 1:1); "Paul and Timothy, slaves of Christ Jesus" (Phil. 1:1); "Paul, a slave of God and an apostle of Jesus Christ" (Titus 1:1). Peter, James, and Jude also introduce themselves as slaves in their letters, and the epithet is stretched further. In his list of ministry partners in Colossians, Paul calls Tychicus his "fellow bondslave of the Lord" (Col. 4:7) and Epaphras "a slave of Christ Jesus" (Col. 4:12). But, in a tenderly tactful move, Paul does not use that language of Onesimus. Rather, he calls the one person in the list we know to have been an actual slave "our faithful and beloved brother, who is one of you" (Col. 4:9).[6]

---

5. The English Standard Version provides the contextual rendering "servant" in these verses.
6. It is also interesting that Paul calls Phoebe "our sister Phoebe, a servant [*diakonos*] of the church at Cenchreae" (Rom. 16:1), rather than a slave (*doulos*).

Why was this slave language so favored among the early church leaders? First, to communicate their utter belonging to Christ: "You are not your own," writes Paul; "you were bought at a price!" (1 Cor. 6:19–20). Just as slaves lived to do their master's work, Christians lived to serve Christ. Second, the slave title communicated the cost of following Jesus. The first Christian leaders suffered persecution, beatings, hunger, shipwreck, and death. Their lot was hard. But a third motivation for the apostles' using this slave language must surely have been the reality that many early Christians were slaves. Hearing leaders refer to themselves in this way must have been sweet to the ears of first-century Christians in bondage. Far from being subhuman possessions, they had status equal with the foremost leaders of the church.

Slaves as Christians

The New Testament insists on the equality of slave and free within the church. Paul writes to the Corinthians: "For in one Spirit we were all baptized into one body—Jews or Greeks, slaves or free—and all were made to drink of one Spirit" (1 Cor. 12:13). Likewise, he writes to the Colossians, "Here there is not Greek and Jew, circumcised and uncircumcised, barbarian, Scythian, slave, free; but Christ is all, and in all" (Col. 3:11). And to the Galatians: "There is neither Jew nor Greek, there is neither slave nor free, there is no male and female, for you are all one in Christ Jesus" (Gal. 3:28). In line with statements like this, one of the earliest non-Christian sources we have concerning the persecution of Christians suggests it may not have been uncommon for slaves to hold leadership roles in the early church. In an early second-century letter to the Emperor Trajan, Pliny the Younger recounts trying to find out more about Christianity by torturing "two female slaves who were called deaconesses."[7]

Given Paul's theological convictions and the way he embraced and empowered the runaway slave Onesimus, we might expect him to urge slaves to rebel against their masters and assert their equal status. But he does not. Paul writes to the Colossians:

---

7. See Michael J. Kruger, *Christianity at the Crossroads: How the Second Century Shaped the Future of the Church* (Downers Grove, IL: IVP Academic, 2018), 32. While the word translated "deaconess" can simply mean servant, Paul's designation of Phoebe as both a "deaconess" and a patron suggests that early Christians used this language theologically.

Bondservants, obey in everything those who are your earthly masters, not by way of eye-service, as people-pleasers, but with sincer-
ity of heart, fearing the Lord. Whatever you do, work heartily, as
for the Lord and not for men, knowing that from the Lord you will
receive the inheritance as your reward. You are serving the Lord
Christ. (Col. 3:22–24)

Far from urging slaves to rebel, Paul encourages them to serve. But this
is not for the sake of their earthly masters (*kyriois*): it is for the Lord
(*ton kyrion*). Jesus, their true Master, sees their service and will reward
them with an inheritance. They serve not because they are subhuman.
They serve as sons and daughters of God.

Some slaves were able to purchase their freedom, and Paul encourages
them to do so if they can (1 Cor. 7:21). But many would not have had
agency over their status, and encouraging them to run away could have
caused them great harm. But Paul gives their work eternal significance
and tells them they are seen and valued by the Lord. In the next breath,
Paul commands Christian masters to treat their slaves justly and fairly,
because their treatment of their slaves is being watched by their Master.
Slaves were not necessarily poorly treated. Many were. But we see examples in the Gospels of even Roman masters caring for their slaves (e.g.,
Luke 7:1–10), and the roles performed by slaves encompassed a range
well beyond our expectations: for example, slaves could be doctors or
teachers, as well as menial laborers. Many first-century slaves lived es-
sentially normal lives and were paid for their work—sometimes enabling
them to buy their freedom.[8] But Paul is clear that, regardless of their kind
of work, every ethical command Christian masters have received from
the apostles applies to their slaves, who are now their siblings in Christ.

Paul does not write to slaves glibly, dictating to the oppressed from
a position of comfort. While the apostle was highly educated and a
Roman citizen, his slavery to Christ had come with the price tag:
imprisonment, beatings, hunger, rejection, and the looming prospect
of execution. In his letter to Timothy, moreover, we see a specific
condemnation of the foundational practice that created slavery in
America. Building on Exodus 21:16, where slave catching is a crime

---

8. For more on this, see the discussion of ancient slavery in Andrew T. Lincoln, *Ephesians*,
Word Biblical Commentary (Waco, TX: Word), 415–20.

leading to capital punishment, Paul lists "enslaving" alongside other lawbreaking sins (1 Tim. 1:10). These verses blow a hole in the side of any attempt to justify the transatlantic slave trade on biblical grounds.

But why did Paul not explicitly condemn slavery itself?

A Pound of Flesh

In a climactic scene in Shakespeare's *The Merchant of Venice*, the merchant Antonio stands in court in fear for his life.[9] Not thinking all his ships could be wrecked, bringing him financial ruin, Antonio has signed a contract entitling the money lender Shylock to a pound of his flesh if Antonio defaults on a loan. Now Shylock wants to take his bond. Portia, a brilliant woman who has cross-dressed as a lawyer, first pleads with Shylock for mercy. When her persuasion fails, she acknowledges that the pound of flesh is owed. Shylock is delighted. But as he prepares his knife, Portia stops him: the bond, she points out, says nothing about blood. He can take his pound of flesh. But if Shylock sheds one drop of Antonio's blood, his own goods will be forfeited to the state.

Setting aside the complex anti-Semitism of the play (complex because Shylock is both caricatured as a mean-hearted money lender and given the most devastating speech against racism in Shakespeare's corpus), this scene offers us a powerful paradigm.[10] Portia affirms the law she cannot change: Shylock can take his pound of flesh. But she construes the law in a way that makes it impossible for him to harm Antonio. She is unquestionably on Antonio's side, and her argument saves his life.

The New Testament argues against slavery the way Portia argues against Antonio's death: by cutting the legs out from under it. Jesus inhabited the slave role. Paul calls himself a slave of Christ, loves a runaway slave as his very heart, and insists that slave and free are equal in Christ. With no room for superiority, exploitation, or coercion, but rather brotherhood and shared identity, the New Testament created a tectonic tension that would ultimately erupt in the abolition of slavery.

Has the Church Endorsed Slavery?

The volcano did not lay dormant between the first century and the nineteenth-century abolitionist movement. In the fourth century, when

---

9. Act 4, scene 1.
10. See act 3, scene 1.

Christians were wielding political power for the first time, theologian Gregory of Nyssa launched an attack on the notion of slavery that was unprecedented in the ancient world, where slavery was taken for granted as a fact of life:[11]

> If a man makes that which truly belongs to God into his own private property, by allotting himself sovereignty over his own race, and thinks himself the master of men and women, what could follow but an arrogance exceeding all nature from the one who sees himself as something other than the ones who are ruled?[12]

Gregory further attacked slavery by lambasting the sale of slaves: "How much does rationality cost?" he asked, "How many obols for the image of God? How many staters did you get for selling the God-formed man?"[13] Likewise, Gregory's contemporary theologians Augustine and John Chrysostom saw slavery as not ordained by God but a result of sin.[14] Nonetheless, many Christian leaders accommodated slavery, caught up in the current of the ancient world that saw slavery as entirely normative. Even the leading Stoic philosopher Epictetus, himself once a slave, made no attempt to argue against the institution.[15]

Gregory's critique seems to have had no direct impact on broader thinking, but a stand taken by his brother Basil of Caesarea paved the way for legislative protection of slaves from one of their most common abuses. The sexual exploitation of both male and female slaves was rampant in Roman culture. Indeed, sex with slaves and prostitutes was deemed a necessary outlet for the male libido. Basil upheld the innocence both of slaves used for sex and of women forced into prostitution. In 428, the Eastern emperor issued a decree condemning "pimps, fathers, and slave-owners who impose the necessity of sinning on their daughters or slave women," and offering protection to "slaves and daughters and others who have hired themselves out on account

---

11. Kyle Harper, "Christianity and the Roots of Human Dignity in Late Antiquity," in *Christianity and Freedom*, vol. 1, *Historical Perspectives*, ed. Timothy Samuel Shah and Allen D. Hertzke, Cambridge Studies in Law and Christianity (Cambridge: Cambridge University Press, 2016), 132.

12. Gregory of Nyssa, *Homilies on Ecclesiastes* 4.1, quoted in Harper, "Roots of Human Dignity," 133.

13. Gregory of Nyssa, *Ecclesiastes* 4.1, quoted in Harper, "Roots of Human Dignity," 133.

14. See John Chrysostom, *Homily on Ephesians*, hom. 22, and Augustine, *City of God*, bk. 19.

15. Kyle Harper makes this point in "Roots of Human Dignity," 129.

of their poverty" to appeal for help to bishops and judges.[16] Historian Kyle Harper observes of this decree, "The translation of Christian ideology into statutory law could hardly be clearer."[17] During the course of the fifth century, Christian emperors expanded the ban, and all sexual procurement became illegal.

Large-scale Christian abolitionism started to take hold in the seventh century, and over time the Christianization of Europe effectively eliminated slavery. Saint Bathild, wife of King Clovis II of Burgundy (who had once been a slave herself), campaigned for abolition of the contemporary slave trade and the freeing of all slaves. In the ninth century, Saint Anskar campaigned against the Viking slave trade. The influential thirteenth-century theologian Thomas Aquinas argued that slavery was a sin, and a succession of popes upheld this view, including Pope Paul III, who explicitly prohibited slavery in 1537. Nonetheless, the practice crept back. Between 1562 and 1807, European colonial expansion included a horrific explosion of slavery. During that period, British traders alone transported over three million slaves.

As we look at Britain's role in the slave trade, however, we must be careful not to assume that the horrors of slavery were the fruits of Christianity. At the time of William Wilberforce, whose evangelical convictions propelled him to lead the abolitionist campaign, Christianity in England was at a low ebb. Church attendance was sparse, and preaching poor. After surveying the best preachers in London, a contemporary of Wilberforce noted, "Not one of the sermons contained more Christianity than the writings of Cicero."[18] Indeed, Wilberforce's passionate faith was seen as religious fanaticism. "If to be feelingly alive to the sufferings of my fellow-creatures is to be a fanatic," he replied, "I am one of the most incurable fanatics ever permitted to be at large."[19] Wilberforce believed he had been called by God to shipwreck the slave trade. He led a squadron of Christian abolitionists, whose refusal to give up campaigning for the lives of their fellow humans finally carried the day.

---

16. Quoted in Shah and Hertzke, *Christianity and Freedom*, 1:138.
17. Shah and Hertzke, *Christianity and Freedom*, 1:138.
18. Quoted in William Hague, *William Wilberforce: The Life of the Great Anti-Slave Trade Campaigner* (New York: HarperCollins, 2007), 10, which offers a broader discussion of the state of the established church in England at the time.
19. Quoted in Robert Isaac Wilberforce, Samuel Wilberforce, and Caspar Morris, *The Life of William Wilberforce*, vol. 4 (Philadelphia: Henry Perkins, 1841), 290.

Turning our gaze to America, it is a tragic irony that a country founded on the "self-evident" truth that "all men are created equal" and "endowed by their Creator with certain unalienable Rights" including "Life, Liberty and the pursuit of Happiness," so radically failed to deliver on these ethics. It is similarly tragic that many Christian leaders abused Scripture to endorse race-based chattel slavery. In some cases, whites condoned practices so blatantly at odds with Christian ethics that there is no way their reading of Scripture could have been sincere. In others, Scripture was selectively invoked to allow for "benevolent" slave owning. For example, nineteenth-century Baptist pastor Richard Fuller, who prided himself on his care for his slaves, argued that both the Old and the New Testaments regulate slavery rather than repudiating it, and that while the abuse of slaves was clearly against the Bible, the possession of slaves *per se* was not. In contrast, Baptist pastor and Brown University president Francis Wayland argued that holding slaves was fundamentally sinful. Their debate was published in 1847.[20] A key plank of Fuller's case was that the Jewish patriarchs (including Abraham) owned slaves, so it cannot be innately sinful. But the patriarchs were sinful in many ways. Specifically, Wayland argued that the patriarchs also practiced polygamy, which was consistently portrayed in a negative light in the Old Testament and is effectively outlawed in the New.

As we noted in chapter 4, Jesus warned that not everyone who claimed to be a follower of his would indeed follow him, and that he specifically highlights care for the poor and oppressed as a litmus test for authentic Christianity. But we must reckon with the fact that some theological heroes in America owned slaves, including Reformed pastor Jonathan Edwards, who is widely acknowledged as one of America's greatest theologians and intellectuals. Any complicity by a Christian leader in the practice of slavery is great cause for lament and must not be glossed over. Yet, as leading black theologian Thabiti Anyabwile observes, while Edwards was wrong to argue that slave-

---

20. Richard Fuller and Francis Wayland, *Domestic Slavery Considered as a Scriptural Institution,* ed. Nathan A. Finn (Macon, GA: Mercer University Press, 2008). For a tight summary of this debate, see Aaron Menikoff, "How and Why Did Some Christians Defend Slavery?," The Gospel Coalition, February 24, 2017, https://www.thegospelcoalition.org/article/how-and-why-did-some-christians-defend-slavery/.

holding is not innately sinful, he rightly condemned the transatlantic slave trade, rejected the idea that Israel's history could be invoked to justify colonial abuse in Africa, argued that God would not "wink" at manstealing, and recognized Africans and Native Americans as spiritual equals. Edwards was the first pastor in Northampton to allow full church membership to black Christians, and he argued in the 1740s that there could be no advance of evangelism in Africa until the slave trade had ended.[21] We all have blind spots in our beliefs, often created by the cultures that surround us. Edwards was no exception.

This blindness was characteristic of many other Christian slaveholders. Solomon Northup, whose story was told in the 2013 feature film *12 Years a Slave*, described the Baptist preacher who was his second master like this: "In my opinion, there never was a more kind, noble, candid, Christian man than William Ford. The influences and associations that had always surrounded him, blinded him to the inherent wrong at the bottom of the system of Slavery."[22]

The boundaries of slaveholder benevolence are poignantly described by slave-turned-author Harriet Jacobs. Jacobs recalls a happy childhood. She loved her white mistress and was well treated by her. Indeed, Jacobs did not realize she was a slave until her mother died when she was six. But when her mistress died, it turned out she had broken her promise to set Jacobs free. In devastating lines that strike at the heart of Christian failure in the era of slavery, Jacobs wrote: "My mistress had taught me the precepts of God's Word: 'Thou shalt love thy neighbor as thyself.' 'Whatsoever ye would that men should do unto you, do ye even so unto them.' But I was her slave, and I suppose she did not recognize me as her neighbor."[23] Given that Jesus's parable of the good Samaritan answers the question "Who is my neighbor" with a story of love across racial difference, the failure of white Christians to recognize black people as their neighbors is without excuse.

---

21. Thabiti Anyabwile, "Jonathan Edwards, Slavery, and the Theology of African Americans" (lecture delivered at Trinity Evangelical Divinity School, February 1, 2012), https://s3.amazonaws.com/tgc-blogs/wp-content/uploads/sites/2/2012/02/12151529/Thabiti-Jonathan-Edwards-slavery-and-theological-appropriation.pdf.

22. Solomon Northup and David Wilson, *Twelve Years a Slave: Narrative of Solomon Northup* (New York: Miller, Orton and Mulligan, 1855), 90.

23. Harriet Jacobs, *Incidents in the Life of a Slave Girl*, ed. L. Maria Child (New York: Washington Square, 2003), 10.

Key Christian Abolitionists

The abhorrent nature of American slavery ultimately led to its denunciation by key Christian leaders in the United States and Europe. For example, while on a preaching tour in America, influential British preacher Charles Spurgeon denounced slavery as "the foulest blot that ever stained a national escutcheon," and declared that it would be far better "that north and south should be rent asunder, and the states of the union shivered into a thousand fragments, than that slavery should be permitted to continue." To American pastors who defended slavery as a "peculiar institution," Spurgeon responded, "It is, indeed, a peculiar institution, just as the devil is a peculiar angel, and hell is a peculiarly hot place."[24] Likewise, Methodist leader John Wesley denounced slavery as "that execrable villainy which is the scandal of religion . . . and of human nature."[25]

The impact of women in the movement is particularly striking. In Britain, for example, poet and activist Hannah More played an important role in shaping public thinking on this issue.[26] Likewise, in America, Harriet Beecher Stowe wrote the best-selling novel *Uncle Tom's Cabin* with the explicit goal of making her whole nation "feel what an accursed thing slavery is." Stowe—a passionate believer—declared, "I wrote what I did because as a woman, as a mother, I was oppressed & broken-hearted, with the sorrows & injustice I saw, because as a Christian I felt the dishonor to Christianity—because as a lover of my country I trembled at the coming day of wrath."[27] Her book was not perfect. Despite its clear-eyed view of the sin of slavery, *Uncle Tom's Cabin* reified some stereotypes about black people that illustrate how hard it was for white Americans to shed prejudice entirely. But its author's sincere faith enabled her to see that slavery in America was antithetical to Christianity.

Yet more remarkable was the role played by black Christians, who overcame white bigotry to embrace Christ and change culture. Black

---

24. Quoted in Lewis A. Drummond, *Spurgeon: Prince of Preachers*, 3rd ed. (Grand Rapids, MI: Kregel, 1992), 480.

25. John Wesley, to William Wilberforce, February 24, 1791, in *John Wesley*, ed. Albert Outler (New York: Oxford University Press, 1964), 86.

26. For a brilliant biography of this lesser-known abolitionist, see Karen Swallow Prior, *Fierce Convictions: The Extraordinary Life of Hannah More—Poet, Reformer, Abolitionist* (Nashville, Thomas Nelson, 2014).

27. Quoted in Joan D. Hendrick, *Harriet Beecher Stowe: A Life* (Oxford: Oxford University Press, 1995), 237.

abolitionist David Walker decried "pretended preachers of the gospel of my Master" who held and abused slaves; and Walker delivered one of the first sustained public attacks on slavery by a black American.[28] Likewise, Frederick Douglass (whose story I touched on at the beginning of this chapter) went from runaway slave to leading abolitionist public intellectual, denouncing the hypocrisy of supposedly Christian, abuse-perpetrating slaveholders in the harshest of terms. Henry Highland Garnet, a minister and abolitionist who was born into slavery but escaped as a child with his family, served as another key abolitionist orator. For these men and many others, faith and education united to propel them into public service. Emancipation was a gospel issue.

If there is a prize for overcoming adversity, however, it must go to the black abolitionist women. Harriet Tubman is the most famous today. Tubman had been told Bible stories by her mother as a child and modeled her efforts to free slaves on Moses's leading of the Israelites out of Egypt. Indeed, she was nicknamed "Moses" by her contemporaries for her many secret missions to help slaves escape their captivity. Douglass commended Tubman thus: "The midnight sky and the silent stars have been the witnesses of your devotion to freedom and of your heroism."[29] Likewise, Sojourner Truth escaped slavery to become one of the most effective orators in the movement—despite her lack of education. When she met Stowe, Truth was asked whether she preached from the Bible. Truth answered that she did not, because she could not read. "When I preaches," she said, "I has just one text to preach from, an' I always preaches from this one. My text is, 'When I found Jesus.'"[30]

For many ex-slaves, however, emancipation, education, and evangelism went hand in hand. Their faith propelled them to speak for Jesus and against slavery, and their hunger to read Scripture made them thirst for education. Recalling his conversion, Douglass wrote, "My desire to learn increased, and especially, did I want a thorough acquaintance with the contents of the Bible."[31] The stories of Christian

---

28. See Peter P. Hinks, ed., *David Walker's Appeal to the Coloured Citizens of the World* (University Park: Pennsylvania State University Press, 2002), 40.

29. Frederick Douglass, to Harriet Tubman, August 29, 1868, quoted in Sarah H. Bradford, *Harriet: The Moses of Her People* (New York: Lockwood, 1886), 135.

30. Quoted in "Sojourner Truth: Abolitionist and Women's Rights Advocate," *Christianity Today*, September 2018, www.christianitytoday.com.

31. Douglass, *Life and Times*.

slaves expose the lies that enabled many a white Christian to partici-
pate in the slave system, and their advocacy awakened the hearts and
minds of many white Americans to its evils. But the desire of Christian
slaves for people of all races to come to saving faith in Jesus often went
beyond even their desire for slavery to be overturned. In 1852, Henry
Highland Garnet and his wife moved to Jamaica to serve as missionaries and educators. Former slave Thomas Johnson was mentored by
Charles Spurgeon and became one of American's first missionaries to
Africa in 1878. Likewise, after gaining her freedom, Amanda Berry
Smith traveled to India and Africa to preach the gospel and to do
what she could to meet physical and educational needs. Back home
in America, she funded the Amanda Smith Orphanage and Industrial
Home for Abandoned and Destitute Colored Children.[32] For Smith
and many others, loving Jesus meant loving justice. But the gospel was
more than a convenient rhetorical means to a just end. Winning people
for Jesus was, for many, the first call.

The Miracle of the Black Church

If slavery is the founding sin of America, the existence of the black
church is perhaps its greatest miracle. Many Christian leaders failed
to denounce slavery. Many abusive slave owners called themselves
Christians. Yet Christian faith penetrated deeply into slave communities. Some whites invested in and encouraged the faith of their slaves.
Others banned their worship gatherings and punished those who par-
ticipated. Many slave churches met in secret. The Jesus of the Scriptures—who cared for the oppressed and marginalized, embraced a
slave role, spoke truth to power, and suffered torture, rejection, and
death—appealed to slaves. Seeing through the hypocrisy of their op-
pressors, many found hope in the knowledge that they were loved,
redeemed, and treasured by an everlasting God, who would one day
bring justice.

The man who inspired Harriet Beecher Stowe's character "Uncle
Tom" was a case in point. Josiah Henson was, in Stowe's penetrating

---

32. Smith's autobiography, *An Autobiography, The Story of the Lord's Dealing with Mrs.
Amanda Smith, the Colored Evangelist Containing an Account of Her Life Work of Faith, and
Her Travels in America, England, Ireland, Scotland, India, and Africa, as An Independent Mis-
sionary*, was published in 1893.

description of eighteenth-century Maryland, "Born a slave—a slave in effect in a heathen land and under a heathen master."[33] Henson was eighteen years old before he heard the gospel of Jesus. When he finally heard that the Son of God had died for all—"the bond, the poor, the negro in his chains"—his response was this: "I stood and heard it. It touched my heart and I cried out: 'I wonder if Jesus Christ died for me?'"[34] Henson was overwhelmed by the idea that he, "a poor, despised, and abused creature, deemed by others fit for nothing but unrequited toil—but mental and bodily degradation"—was known and loved by Jesus himself: "Oh, the blessedness and sweetness of feeling that I was loved! I would have died that moment with joy, and kept repeating to myself, 'The compassionate Savior about whom I have heard "loves me."'" Henson escaped slavery and went on to set up a refuge for escaped slaves in Canada and to become a Christian preacher himself, proclaiming the gospel of Jesus and lending his rhetorical skill to the abolitionist movement.

This thread of faith ran through the experience of slaves, through the abolitionist movement, and through the subsequent waves of oppression and resistance that have too often plagued black American experience. When Martin Luther King stepped forward to lead the civil rights movement, he spoke spiritual truth to a country still failing to deliver on the promise of Christianity, and he led with the weapons of Jesus: faith, hope, love, and nonviolence. While many white Christians once again failed to see the sinfulness of segregation and denied equal rights to their black brothers and sisters, King insisted that this equality sprang from the Scriptures and could not be withheld by anyone who owned the name of Christ.

What about today? The complicity of white Christians in the history of slavery, segregation, and racial injustice in America stands as a blot on the record of Christianity. The current racism of many white Christians is its residual stain and must be countered by biblical truth and the raising up of more leaders of color within majority-white churches. But we must not make the mistake of allowing the racism

33. Josiah Henson, *Autobiography of Josiah Henson: An Inspiration for Harriet Beecher Stowe's Uncle Tom* (New York: Dover, 1969), 3.
34. Henson, *Autobiography*, 24.

of many white Christians to define Christianity itself. Today, black Americans are almost 10 percent more likely to identify as Christians than whites and are more religious across a range of measures. For instance, 75 percent of black Americans say that religion is very important in their lives versus only 49 percent of whites. In addition, 47 percent of black Americans say they attend religious services weekly, compared with 34 percent of whites.[35] While surveys typically separate out "historically black churches" from "evangelical churches," most black churches are theologically evangelical, and many have a strong evangelistic heartbeat, unashamedly calling others to repentance and faith in Jesus.[36]

In the second chapter of this book, we exploded the myth that Christianity is a white Western religion. In this chapter we have seen how the Bible invites us to see the world through the eyes of slaves and to embrace slave status ourselves. We have noticed the role played by Christians in the gradual abolition of an institution that was unquestioned in the ancient world, the pioneering role played by early slave evangelists, and the extraordinary spread of Christianity among slaves in America. The church must face its moral failures: many Christians have sinned with respect to slavery, and many white Christians have sinned against black victims of that oppressive and dehumanizing institution. But we must also ask, how many generations of faithful black believers do there need to be in America before we stop associating Christianity with white slave-owners and start listening to the voices of black believers that echo down to us through the blood-stained centuries? And how long will it be before we listen to the longing of Frederick Douglass and thousands of other slave evangelists, whose conversions made them abhor slavery more than ever, but whose "great concern was to have everybody converted"?

---

35. David Masci, "5 Facts about the Religious Lives of African Americans, Pew Research Center, February 7, 2018, http://www.pewresearch.org/fact-tank/2018/02/07/5-facts-about-the-religious-lives-of-african-americans/.

36. For example, 93 percent of Christians in historically black churches believe in heaven, and 82 percent in hell; 82 percent believe the Bible is the Word of God; 61 percent read the Bible at least once a week. "Members of the Historically Black Protestant Tradition Who Identify as Black," Pew Research Center, 2018, http://www.pewforum.org/religious-landscape-study/racial-and-ethnic-composition/black/religious-tradition/historically-black-protestant/.

11

How Could a Loving God
Allow So Much Suffering?

Nadia Murad's systematic rape at the hands of an ISIS judge. Three million Africans forcibly transported by the British slave trade. Six million Jews murdered in the Holocaust. The Rwandan Genocide. The ethnic cleansing of Rohingya Muslims. The trafficking of more than two million children this year in the global sex trade, while 1.5 million children died of diarrhea. Famines in South Sudan, Somalia, Nigeria, and Yemen. The 2004 tsunami in Indonesia that left 230,000 dead. The quiet stealth of cancer. Children abused by their parents.

Richard Dawkins looks at all of this, combined with the impersonal forces that have forged our bodies through suffering, violence, and death, and declares that our universe "has precisely the properties we should expect if there is, at bottom, no design, no purpose, no evil, no good, nothing but pitiless indifference."[1] In this chapter, we will face the question that haunts us all at one time or another. How can we reckon with suffering?

For many, this question torpedoes the Christian faith. How can the hypothesis of a loving, powerful God stand under the crushing weight of human distress? Does Christianity work only for those whose lives

---

1. Richard Dawkins, *A River out of Eden: A Darwinian View of Life* (New York: Basic Books, 1996), 133.

are not shipwrecked? Must we gloss over others' distress to believe in an omnipotent, benevolent Creator?

This chapter will examine three broad frameworks for suffering: suffering without God, suffering from a Buddhist perspective, and suffering in the Christian worldview. It will suggest that suffering is not the wrecking ball that knocks Christianity down but rather the cornerstone on which, painfully, brick by brick, it has always been built.

Suffering minus God

For some, removing God from the equation promises relief. Suffering happens. There is no meaning, no reason, no hope; so we can stop trying to read the tea leaves. At first, this may seem like a mature approach. Make what meaning you can out of your life, and don't expect a higher power to help or care. Stephen Hawking, who lived with debilitating motor neuron disease for his whole adult life, believed the brain is a computer that stops working when its components fail: "There is no heaven or afterlife for broken down computers," he declared; "that is a fairy story for people afraid of the dark."[2]

Many atheists today anchor themselves on humanism, believing in the human spirit and a capacity for progress, creativity, and love without any need for a "God hypothesis." But Dawkins's relentless chain—"no design, no purpose, no evil, no good"—illuminates a problem. This bleak view of the universe erodes the foundations on which we balance life and humanness itself. If there is no good or evil, why do we lament? If our sympathy for others is just a byproduct of evolutionary kinship, why empathize with the suffering of those outside our tribe? And if our sense of self is just a delusion, the meaningfulness of life in the face of suffering evaporates along with our moral agency. The irony at the heart of today's secular humanism is that spokesmen like Sam Harris believe in human beings no more than they believe in God: ultimately, both are delusions. Removing meaning from the equation of suffering does not solve the riddle. Rather, it unravels our very self.

---

2. Stephen Hawking, "There Is No Heaven," interview by Ian Sample, *The Guardian*, May 15, 2011, https://www.theguardian.com/science/2011/may/15/stephen-hawking-interview-there-is-no-heaven.

This view is not the necessary outcome of science. With the same belief in science but different beliefs about God, Cambridge paleobiologist Simon Conway Morris poses this question: "Suppose that the moral structure, the ethical voice . . . the endless yearning for a world made good are not the fantasies of a deracinated ape but rather are signposts to deep realities in which our destiny may be involved."[3] Atheism amputates this hope. We are just children making sandcastles in the face of a relentless tide. Or rather, we are not children. We are computers with delusions of personhood. "So imperious is the materialist approach to reality," writes Pulitzer Prize winner Marilynne Robinson, "that it considers what it cannot capture by its limits as effectively non-existent: for example, the human self."[4]

Many who have lost confidence in the idea of God are still clinging to a delusion of universal meaning. A few years ago, I was walking through suffering with a dear nonreligious friend. She talked hopefully about the universe having some kind of plan. Because I loved my friend, I pleaded with her—gently—not to reach for that placebo. If there is no God, we still suffer, but there is no "universe" to care. There is no design, no purpose, no evil, no good—nothing but blind, pitiless indifference. We must stare into that abyss and not fool ourselves with platitudes. There is too much at stake.

A Buddhist Approach to Suffering

My suffering friend had grown up in a Jewish home but had moved away from theism to atheism and thence to Buddhist practices. This is a well-trodden path for disillusioned Westerners. Buddhism (at least in its Westernized forms) offers refuge from the bleakness of atheism without the strictures of "organized" religion. It begins with the challenge of suffering and offers us a way to cope. The combination is attractive. In his best-selling book *The Happiness Hypothesis*, atheist-Jewish psychologist Jonathan Haidt recalls:

---

3. Simon Conway Morris, "Except Where It Matters," in *Does Evolution Explain Human Nature?* (West Conshohocken, PA: John Templeton Foundation, n.d.), 10, https://www.issuelab.org/resources/9030/9030.pdf.

4. Marilynne Robinson, *What Are We Doing Here? Essays* (New York: Farrar, Straus and Giroux, 2018), 128.

When I began writing this book, I thought that Buddha would be a strong contender for the "Best Psychologist of the Last Three Thousand Years" award. To me, his diagnosis of the futility of striving felt so right, his promise of tranquility so alluring. But in doing research for the book, I began to think that Buddhism might be based on an overreaction, perhaps even an error.[5]

Haidt goes on to recount the Buddha's story.[6] The man who became the Buddha was a prince. But a prophecy declared that he would one day leave the palace and turn his back on the kingdom. To avert this, the king did everything in his power to keep his son happy. The young prince married a beautiful princess, was given a stunning harem, and was prevented from leaving the comforts of the palace. But he grew bored and eventually persuaded his father to let him go out in a chariot.

To ensure that his son continued to avoid unhappiness, the king ordered all his aged, sick, and disabled subjects to stay at home. But one old man remained on the street, and the prince discovered that everyone ages. The next day, the prince saw a sick man and discovered disease. On the third day, the prince saw a corpse and learned, to his horror, that everyone dies. As predicted, he left the palace and entered the forest to begin his journey of enlightenment. When he emerged, the Buddha proclaimed that life is suffering, and that the only means of escape is to break the ties of attachment that bind us to life.

Haidt poses an interesting question: What would have happened if the prince had left his chariot and talked with the aged, disabled, and sick? He cites research showing that even people in deeply undesirable circumstances tend to be more satisfied than dissatisfied with their lives. Robert Biswas-Diener, the scholar whose research Haidt invokes, interviewed people in hard situations, including sex workers living in the slums of Calcutta. He concludes, "While the poor of Calcutta do not lead enviable lives, they do live meaningful lives" as they "capitalize on the non-material resources available to

---

5. Jonathan Haidt, *The Happiness Hypothesis: Finding Modern Truth in Ancient Wisdom* (New York: Basic Books, 2006), 102–3.
6. The details of the story vary, depending on the source. Here, I am following Haidt's summary.

them."[7] Perhaps the key to facing suffering is not detachment and removal but meaning and love. Nonattachment may shield us from suffering. To love is to be vulnerable. To desire and strive is to risk disappointment. But as Haidt notes, nonattachment also deprives us of our greatest joys. Striving, desire, and deep attachment can lead us to the precipice. But they can also bring us to treasures nonattachment cannot find.

Is there another option for coping with suffering? Can we pursue desire, cling to attachment, and strive for good things while finding meaning in the suffering that comes?

A Christian Perspective on Suffering

There are many possible entry points to a discussion of Christianity and suffering. Philosophers through the ages have offered defenses for the idea of a loving, omnipotent God in the face of suffering.[8] Arguments address different kinds of suffering, from suffering caused by human sin (e.g., Nadia Murad's rape) to suffering by natural causes (e.g., motor neuron disease), and suggest that inability to see a reason for any given experience of suffering does not mean a reason cannot exist. To return to the Harry Potter illustration of chapter 8, Severus Snape had a morally defensible reason for killing his mentor, a reason that Harry could see only when he accessed the broader story. But rather than focusing on philosophical arguments, we will start with the Gospel story to which I have most often clung in the face of suffering. It's a story of Mary and Martha, whom we first met in chapter 8, when Martha was serving, while Mary sat at Jesus's feet. And it offers an entry point to a whole biblical theology of suffering.

When Jesus Doesn't Come

In John 11, Mary and Martha's brother Lazarus falls sick. But the sisters are lucky: they are close friends with a miracle-working healer, so they dial 911 for Jesus. The text claims, "Jesus loved Martha and

7. Robert Biswas-Diener and Ed Diener, "Making the Best of a Bad Situation: Satisfaction in the Slums of Calcutta," *Social Indicators Research* 55, no. 3 (September 2001): 329–52, quoting 337.

8. See, for example, Alvin Plantinga's early classic, *God, Freedom, and Evil* (Grand Rapids, MI: Eerdmans, 1989).

her sister and Lazarus" (John 11:5). But then comes a stunning *non sequitur*: "So, when he heard that Lazarus was ill, he stayed two days longer in the place where he was" (John 11:6). Jesus frequently healed strangers. He even healed long-distance. But this time, when his closest friends cry out, he waits. This is the first reality with which Christians must grapple. Sometimes, we call for Jesus through our tears, and he does not come.

Three years ago, I rubbed up against an internal seam that left me in deep pain. Parts of myself that I had hidden for years and then tried to bring out into the light had been beaten back by a broken relationship. I had thought God was healing me, inviting me to not believe my fears, but now all the fears about myself that had hung around the periphery of my vision were coming true, and I was devastated. This was not earth-shattering grief: no one had died. But it was shattering to me. My husband witnessed more of my tears in the space of a month than in the previous ten years. One night, he tried to comfort me by reading from Psalm 121:

> I lift up my eyes to the hills.
>> From where does my help come?
> My help comes from the LORD,
>> who made heaven and earth. (vv. 1–2)

But I just cried more. "I feel like I am crying out to the Lord," I explained, "and he is not helping me."

In biblical terms, we have models for our seemingly unanswered cries. On the night he was arrested, Jesus pleaded with God, "Father, if you are willing, remove this cup from me" (Luke 22:42). But he went to the cross nonetheless. Paul was tormented by a "thorn in his flesh." He prayed repeatedly for the Lord to take it away. But God answered, "My grace is sufficient for you, for my power is made perfect in weakness" (2 Cor. 12:9). As Oxford professor C. S. Lewis grieved for the wife God had unexpectedly given him—complete with the death sentence of her terminal cancer—he reflected, "Not that I am (I think) in much danger of ceasing to believe in God. The real danger is of coming to believe such dreadful things about Him. The conclusion I dread is not 'So there's no God after all,' but 'So this is what God's really like.'"⁹ At times, belief in an omnipotent God adds one more desperate tear on the face of suffering. Jesus could have come when Mary and Martha called. But he did not. Does Jesus not love these sisters after all?

When Jesus Comes

Lazarus has been in his tomb for four days by the time Jesus arrives. Ever proactive, Martha goes out to meet him. "Lord," she says, "if you had been here, my brother would not have died. But even now I know that whatever you ask from God, God will give you" (John 11:21–22). Perhaps we sense reproach in these words. And yet Martha's faith in Jesus is complete: Lazarus is dead, but she still believes her Lord can help.

Jesus responds, "Your brother will rise again" (John 11:23). Like many first-century Jews, Martha believes in an end-time resurrection of God's people. "I know that he will rise again," she replies, "in the resurrection on the last day" (John 11:24). But we can almost hear this grieving woman think, *But what about now, Jesus? What about now? Why won't you help me now?*

In this moment, Martha stands where many Christians stand when faced with suffering. We have ultimate promises: one day Jesus will return and put the world to rights. But we are much more like children than philosophers. Our pain is real and urgent. It refuses to be soothed by faraway hope. Neat, theological answers will not do. But neither are they all that Christianity offers.

When Jesus finally comes, he does not fix Martha's problem. Instead, he changes the terms of engagement. Jesus looks into this grieving woman's eyes and says: "I am the resurrection and the life. Whoever believes in me, though he die, yet shall he live, and everyone who lives and believes in me shall never die. Do you believe this?" (John 11:25–26). Is Jesus talking about Lazarus? Perhaps. Though he is physically dead, he trusted in Jesus, so he is truly, spiritually alive. But Jesus is not talking to Lazarus—not yet. He is talking to Martha, who is reeling from Lazarus's death—a death that has cost her emotionally, and likely also jeopardized her security at a time when most

---

9. C. S. Lewis, *A Grief Observed* (New York: HarperCollins, 2009), chap. 1, ebook.

women depended on male relatives for support. Martha longs to have Lazarus back. But Jesus looks her in the eye and says, "I am the resurrection and the life." As you stand here in your desperate grief, your greatest need is not to have your brother back again. It's to have me.

This statement is yet more shocking than Jesus's failure to come in the first place. Far from being the "good moral teacher who never claimed to be God" of modern mythology, Jesus here claims not that he is offering good guidelines for life but that he himself *is* life: life in the face of suffering, life in the face of death.

All parents know that, at times, they must let their children suffer. We hold our crying babies still while strangers stick needles into their healthy flesh. They look at us through tears of betrayal, and we cannot explain that we are making them suffer now to save them from future disease. Some parents are faced with a far harder task: allowing doctors to poison their children with drugs that ravage their bodies, making them vomit and lose their hair as they lie shut up in a hospital for days, or weeks, or months. The pain is bitter, but with this cruel course these parents hope to save their child's life. The question we must always ask of suffering is this: What could possibly be worth it? Jesus's flabbergasting claim is that he is. But this play has two more acts.

Jesus Wept

Martha responds with stunning faith: "Yes, Lord; I believe that you are the Christ, the Son of God, who is coming into the world" (John 11:27). But then she calls Mary, who falls at Jesus's feet, weeping, and repeats her sister's reproach, "Lord, if you had been here, my brother would not have died" (John 11:32). Jesus is deeply moved and troubled. He asks where Lazarus has been laid. And then we encounter one of the shortest and most confusing verses in the Bible: "Jesus wept" (John 11:35). These words are strange because we know how easily these tears could have been spared. If Jesus had only come when he was called, no one would be crying. The bystanders observe, "See how he loved him!" But some also wonder, "Could not he who opened the eyes of the blind man also have kept this man from dying?" (John 11:36–37).

We have all had the experience of being comforted by someone who does not truly understand what we are going through. It is often unsatisfying. But Jesus is no remote deity, watching suffering from a safe distance. He is the God who inhabits our suffering. The prophet Isaiah calls the Messiah, "a man of sorrows, and acquainted with grief" (Isa. 53:3), and we see in the Gospels how Jesus is moved with compassion for suffering people. This compassion goes beyond sympathy. Jesus does not just feel sorry for us in our weakness and pain. He takes that agony on himself.

> Surely he has borne our griefs,
>   and carried our sorrows.

Isaiah continues,

> He was pierced for our transgressions;
>   he was crushed for our iniquities;
> upon him was the chastisement that brought us peace,
>   and with his wounds we are healed. (Isa. 53:4–5)

In this prophecy, grief, suffering, and sickness are rolled up together with sin and guilt and loaded onto the Messiah's back. And when Jesus comes, he carries that load. He bears the moral weight of guilt and sin in our place. But he also bears the heartbreak of our suffering. Jesus holds us close as we lament. He weeps with us as we weep. He knows the end of the story, when he will wipe every tear from our eyes. But this does not stop him from cleaving to us in our pain. In fact, pain is a place of special intimacy with him.

We see this in our own lives. We can laugh with anyone. But we cry with those closest to us; and the bond is strongest when their suffering connects with ours. In Jesus, we find the one person who knows all our heartache and all our pain. Left by those closest to him, beaten by strangers, stripped and abused and hung up on a cross to die—there is no wound of ours he cannot touch. He has even experienced abandonment by his Father. On the cross he cried out with the words of Psalm 22:1, "My God, my God, why have you forsaken me?" (Matt. 27:46).

Jesus knows his resurrection is coming. And yet he cries out in his distress. Jesus knows the end of Mary and Martha and Lazarus's story. And yet he weeps.

"Lazarus, Come Out!"

When Jesus comes to Lazarus's tomb, he is deeply moved again, and he commands that the stone be taken away. Martha cautions him, "Lord, by this time there will be an odor, for he has been dead four days" (John 11:39). But Jesus insists. He prays. Then he shouts, "Lazarus, come out!" And the man who has died comes out (John 11:43–44).

I often tell my daughters this story. Unlike most children in most of human history, they have had little experience with death so far. But I want them to know that one day, when their bodies have rotted and their lives have been forgotten, Jesus will call them out of their graves—not to float as disembodied souls in the sky, but to walk in resurrected bodies on the earth. The one who called stars into being will also call them from death to life.

Jesus's power over death is absolute. I believe it is the only hope we have in the face of our inevitable end. But what fascinates me about this story is how little focus there is on Lazarus himself. Rather, the narrative draws our gaze to profound questions: Why, if Jesus planned to heal Lazarus, did he not just do so in the first place? Why did he let Lazarus die, and leave Mary and Martha mourning for days? Why not tell Martha what he was planning to do right away? In this strange stretching of the story, we get a glimpse of the whole biblical framework for suffering. The space between Lazarus's death and Jesus's calling of him out of the tomb is the space in which Martha sees Jesus for who he really is: her very life.

This story illuminates both suffering and prayer. We often see prayer as a means to an end: God is a cosmic vending machine; insert prayer and expect results to drop into your hand—or kick the machine in anger when they don't. But the story of Lazarus upends this idea. Jesus is not a means to an end, a mechanism through which Martha can change her circumstances. He is the end. Her circumstances drive her to him. It's not that her suffering or our suffering doesn't matter: it matters enough to bring tears to the eyes of the Son of God! But it matters like a first meeting matters to marriage, or like birth matters to motherhood. It is an entry point to relationship, a relationship formed through suffering as much as through joy. If, as Jesus claims, the goal of our existence is relationship with him, finding him in our suffering is the point.

Suffering and Sin

Recognizing the role of suffering in our relationship with Christ helps us see through a common misconception about suffering from a Christian perspective. We are tempted to believe that suffering is a punishment for sin. But the Bible is clear that—while sin and suffering are clearly connected in a universal sense, and living in rebellion against God can cause us heartache now—the amount of suffering a person endures is not proportional to his or her sin. The Old Testament book of Job dramatizes this point. Jesus reinforces it. Earlier in John's Gospel, Jesus encounters a man who was blind from birth, and his disciples ask, "Rabbi, who sinned, this man or his parents?" (John 9:2). Jesus replies, "It was not that this man sinned, or his parents, but that the works of God might be displayed in him" (John 9:3). Then Jesus heals the man.

This teaching sets Christianity apart from the versions of Buddhism that teach karma and reincarnation. Within that logic, our present circumstances are the result of past actions: sins in a past life can determine suffering here and now. Not so in Christianity. Indeed, if anything, Christianity reverses that paradigm: those who live in privilege now are warned of an afterlife of suffering if they do not take the radical medicine of Christ. Those who suffer now are closest to God's heart. This dynamic is explored in one of Jesus's most uncomfortable parables—a story guaranteed to send chills down the spine of every person reading this book—the parable of the rich man and another Lazarus (Luke 16:19–31). While we can absolutely look for meaning in our suffering, we should not use it as a measuring stick for guilt, or think that if we only prayed harder or had more faith or did better, our lives would be suffering-free.

Suffering and Love

From a biblical perspective, we must also reject the idea that if God loves us, he cannot intend for us to suffer. This premise crumbles on every scriptural page. Time and again, we see those who are chosen and beloved by God suffering. When Jesus comes, we see that script played out on a cosmic stage: God's beloved Son, the One in whom the Father is well pleased, comes expressly to suffer and to die out of love for his people. Indeed, our beliefs about God and suffering expose the fault lines between our natural assumptions and the biblical narrative.

The loving, omnipotent God of our imagination would move swiftly from creation to new creation, from the garden of Eden of Genesis to the heavenly Jerusalem of Revelation. But the God of the Bible charts a different course. He spreads his story out over thousands, even millions, of years and weaves in all the mess of human history—sin and sex and death and historical accident. And at the center of history, he stakes the cross of his beloved Son. Jesus's death is no accident. It is not even Plan B. It is the lynchpin around which all human history revolves, the central peg of reality itself. This brutal death of an innocent man—bearing a world's weight of sin and guilt and suffering—is the focal point of the story. Indeed, it is the lens through which we visualize the narrative itself. But it is not the last word.

Suffering and Story

The Lord of the Rings kindled my imagination as a child. My father read it to me. Now I'm reading it to my eight-year-old—much to our mutual delight. At a low point in the narrative, two central characters, Frodo and Sam, discuss where they are in the story. Sam recalls how he used to think that people in tales went looking for adventure because their lives were dull. But, he reflects, "that's not the way of it with the tales that really mattered." Frodo enjoys the story Sam starts to tell about their own adventure. But then he stops his friend: "We're going on a bit too fast. You and I, Sam, are still stuck in the worst places of the story, and it is all too likely that some will say at this point 'Shut the book now, dad; we don't want to read any more.'"[10]

The hobbits do not know how their story will end. If it ended in this moment, it would be bleak and hopeless. But the story goes on. Tolkien takes them through darkness and suffering and loss to a

---

10. J. R. R. Tolkien, *The Lord of the Rings*, 50th anniversary ed. (Boston: Mariner, 2005), 711–12.

painful victory, as Gollum bites the ring off Frodo's hand. The story leaves Frodo scarred in body and mind. But it is a victory nonetheless, and one of which he and Sam hear songs sung and stories told. Finally, changed and matured, Frodo goes with the elves to their land across the sea. Tolkien's work was sculpted by his Christian faith, and that was a faith not just in Jesus's death but also in his resurrected life. The journey of all the central characters is through darkness—even death—to new life. But tap them on the shoulder at the darkest moment, and none would know where they are in the story.

If you are in the midst of suffering now, hope of a happy ending may feel crass. A friend who lost his first child to miscarriage shared with me that for a long time, he and his wife could only pray Psalm 88, which ends with darkness. The panacea platitude "Everything happens for a reason" is often cold comfort to an anguished heart. But another friend, whose teenage son was brain damaged in a sport accident, shared his perspective on suffering like this: "People often think that the reality of suffering is an embarrassment to the Christian faith. But I think suffering is the greatest apologetic for Christianity there is."

From an atheist perspective, not only is there no hope of a better end to the story; there is no ultimate story. There is nothing but blind, pitiless indifference. From a Christian perspective, there is not only hope for a better end; there is intimacy now with the One whose resurrected hands still bear the scars of the nails that pinned him to his cross. Suffering is not an embarrassment to the Christian faith. It is the thread with which Christ's name is stitched into our lives.

Genesis to Revelation

This perspective on suffering helps us understand the grand sweep of the biblical narrative. The beginning of the Bible paints a picture of Paradise: human beings in relationship with God and with each other, unstained by sin or suffering or death. Many people conclude from this that the end point of Christianity is a return to Eden. But when we examine this idea, we realize that it renders the whole of human history a cosmic waste of time. God could just have stopped Adam and Eve from sinning in the first place. And even if there were reasons to allow sin—granting human free will, perhaps—one can imagine a much shorter, straighter line to draw between the beginning and the end than the Scriptures describe. But the Bible's "new creation" is not just a return to the idyllic old. It is far better.

In the early Genesis narrative, Adam and Eve knew God as Creator and Lord—perhaps, even, as friend. But Christians know Jesus far more intimately: as Savior, Lover, Husband, Head, Brother, Fellow Sufferer, and their Resurrection and their Life. The first humans could not have dreamed of this earth-shattering intimacy with God. It was an intimacy best glimpsed in their experience of each other before they turned from their Maker. But the lack of that intimacy with God himself explains the strange declaration that it was "not good that the man should be alone" (Gen. 2:18). The original vision of humanity was very good. But it was not the best. The best, from a biblical perspective, was yet to come. And the way to get there would be through suffering.

My eight-year-old is an avid reader and an aspiring writer. Her vocabulary is broad, her imagination is wild, but her stories are dull. Why? Because she strives for happiness throughout. Without suffering, her characters cannot develop. Without fellowship in suffering, they cannot truly bond. The Bible begins and ends with happiness, but the meat of the story is raw. Christians are promised that one day, God "will wipe away every tear from their eyes, and death shall be no more, neither shall there be mourning, nor crying, nor pain anymore" (Rev. 21:4). But we are not promised that God will not allow us to cry in the first place. What end could possibly be worth all this pain? Jesus says he is.

Suffering and Christian Ethics

In Jesus, Christians have the promise of a lover who will never leave them or forsake them, who sits with them in suffering to the bitter end—and beyond. As Jesus's "body" on earth, therefore, Christians must throw themselves into fellowship with sufferers. This is not a fellowship devoid of practical help. Christians were the first to found hospitals and—for all their moral failure—have done more in global terms to alleviate suffering than any other movement. We see this historically and we see it today.

In 2018, ISIS victim and humanitarian Nadia Murad, whose story we encountered in chapter 4 (p. 59), shared the Nobel Peace Prize with Congolese physician Denis Mukwege. Dr. Mukwege, nicknamed "Doctor Miracle," is a pioneering surgeon who has treated thousands of victims of sexual violence for the medical aftereffects of gang rape and brutality. Recognizing Jesus's relentless call on Christians to serve the suffering, Mukwege urges fellow believers, "As long as our faith is defined by theory and not connected with practical realities, we shall not be able to fulfil the mission entrusted to us by Christ." "If we are Christ's," Mukwege continues, "we have no choice but to be alongside the weak, the wounded, the refugees and women suffering discrimination."[11]

Those living in the slums of Calcutta know this from Mother Teresa and the Missionaries of Charity. Mother Teresa's goal was profoundly theological—"seeing and adoring Jesus . . . in the distressing disguise of the poor"[12]—but not at all theoretical. It meant caring for people no one else cared for, touching people no one else would touch. Christians are not called to compassionate detachment. Christians truly following Jesus are deeply attached, and covered in tears—their own, and those of others—just like their Lord.

"I Am the Resurrection and the Life"

Believing that Jesus is the resurrection and the life is not a one-time posture of the mind. Rather, it is a daily battle of the heart. As with a kid riding a rollercoaster, all our senses scream otherwise. I'm routinely tempted to believe that something or someone else is in fact my life. I look to the things I desire to fill me up. And those things, those people, can feel so real compared with this impossible God who calls me to crucify my desires and throw myself into his arms.

In those moments, when I don't believe, I recall Martha's story. Her heart yearned for her brother. His restoration felt like life to her. But Jesus stood before her, looked into her eyes, and said, "I am the

---

11. Denis Mukwege, "Liberated by God's Grace" (keynote address delivered at the twelfth assembly of the Lutheran World Federation, Windhoek, Namibia, 2017), 51, 54, https://www.lutheran world.org/sites/default/files/2018/documents/lwf-12th-assembly-keynote-dr-mukwege.pdf.
12. Mother Teresa, *In the Heart of the World: Thoughts, Stories and Prayers*, ed. Becky Benenate (Novato, CA: New World Library, 1997), 23.

resurrection and the life." Sometimes I win the battle. Sometimes I lose. At times I feel Christ's presence flooding my meager heart. At other times I cling on for dear life, not knowing the end of the story. But I must stake my life on this claim: that Jesus is the resurrection and the life.

12

How Could a Loving God Send People to Hell?

On April 15, 2013, two brothers from our local high school attended the Boston marathon. Others had come to run or cheer, but these boys came to kill. They detonated two homemade explosives near the finish line. Three people died. Sixteen lost limbs. Hundreds were injured. After the FBI released images of the brothers, Dzhokhar and Tamerlan Tsarnaev killed two policemen. Tamerlan was shot several times in the exchange of fire and died shortly after his brother ran him over in a scramble to escape. An unprecedented manhunt ensued. Dzhokhar was eventually discovered hiding under a boat cover in nearby Watertown. As the helicopters circled and the infrared outline of his body was revealed, I wondered what we would make of this young man.

We twenty-first-century Westerners hate judgment. We fear being judgmental and blame horrific crimes on mental health problems, religious extremism, or educational deficits. To be sure, all these things can be factors. And yet, when we hear of callous murders, carefully planned terrorism, or systematic abuse, part of us still yearns for justice. Perhaps these brothers were too young and impressionable to be held accountable. But others who kill are mature. Perhaps they were under the sway of Islamic radicalism. But others who kill are not. Perhaps they had early life experiences that left them scarred and vulnerable. But other killers come from happy homes. Each time we try to extract the hook of evil from humanity, at least one barb digs in.

In this chapter, we will explore the hardest question in this book: How could a loving God send people to hell? Every other question pales in comparison. This one is about the end of the story, and it is the most difficult thing Christians are called to believe—harder by far than believing in miracles or prophecies, or that the God who made us has the right to tell us what to do with our bodies. We will unearth what the Bible says about judgment and hear a strange tale in which love and judgment are intertwined, and in which our vague ideas about heaven and hell become rooted in a person. We will unpack how these concepts are often misunderstood in ways that make God's actions seem illogical, arbitrary, and unjust. To do this, we will examine whether good and evil, hatred and love stand up under scientific scrutiny, and we will train biblical light on the logic of the cross to see what the humiliating death and supposed resurrection of a first-century, Palestinian Jew has to do with you, or me, or Dzhokhar Tsarnaev.

Has Science Murdered Sin?

Sam Harris begins his book *Free Will* by recounting a set of callous crimes committed by two men against an innocent family. The crimes included rape, child sex abuse, robbery, and indiscriminate murder. The account is hard to read: it turned my stomach and brought tears to my eyes. Harris recognizes that our natural response when we hear of such crimes is to demand justice. These men deserve punishment. But he argues that these criminals in fact had no real choice in the matter. Their actions were entirely determined by their past experiences and neurological states. While we may seek restorative justice to prevent them from committing other crimes, we cannot hold them morally accountable. Indeed, Harris claims, "The idea that we, as conscious beings, are deeply responsible for the character of our mental lives and subsequent behavior is simply impossible to map onto reality."[1]

---

1. Sam Harris, *Free Will* (New York: Free Press, 2012), 13.

Perhaps we can breathe a sigh of relief. Now, according to Harris, we can invoke science to untie the noose of judgment from the worst criminal's neck and go back to believing that humans are fundamentally good. But there's a catch. If Dzhokhar Tsarnaev had no real moral agency in his actions, if he did not in any meaningful sense decide to kill the marathon runners and spectators, shoot the policemen, and run over his own brother, then no act of moral courage is real either. Sophie Scholl, whose anti-Nazi pamphlets fluttered down from the top of the university atrium, did not decide to resist—just as the janitor who reported her to the gestapo and the Nazi guards who beheaded her cannot be judged for their crimes. If the ISIS judge who held Nadia Murad as a sex slave, raping and abusing her night after night, cannot be judged for his actions, neither can Harriet Tubman be commended for her courage as she risked her life night after night to help black slaves go free. If Larry Nassar, the USA national gymnastics team doctor who is serving multiple life sentences for sexually abusing more than 250 young girls, cannot be held accountable for his callous crimes, then neither does Rachael Denhollander—the first woman to accuse him—truly love her children.

Harris's scientific determinism scratches away at our deepest beliefs: that there is a moral fabric to the universe, that right and wrong are more than dreams, and that you and I—weak and contingent as we are—are capable of love, just as we are capable of cruelty. Our circumstances, genetics, and deep pasts are certainly factors in our decisions. But unless we are willing to rob humans entirely of their moral agency, we must sometimes say that evil is evil, and that it comes from the heart. And if we cannot say this, we must also never say that love is love.

The #MeToo of Judgment

This connective tissue between love and judgment has been recently exposed by the justice-bringing scalpel of #MeToo. The #MeToo movement has gained traction because we are finally willing to say that sexually harassing or abusing women can no longer be excused or covered up—whatever the status and accomplishments of the abuser. For some, this means public disgrace. For others, it means prison. As

I write, film producer and Miramax cofounder Harvey Weinstein, whose record of alleged sexual abuse triggered the movement in 2017, has just been arrested on charges of rape.

But as the waves of #MeToo have swept through Hollywood, industry, finance, and the church, it has often felt less like a celebratory "ding-dong, the witch is dead" and more like the troubling fall of our would-be heroes. Bill Cosby went from being the widely loved dad in America's most popular fictional family to being a hated sex offender. Morgan Freeman, whose voice alone inspires our trust, has been accused of sexual harassment. And New York attorney general Eric Schneiderman, who was known for his outspoken support of the #MeToo movement, has now been accused by four women of physical abuse. We long for the vindication of women who have been abused and traumatized. But as we grasp for justice, we find even seeming advocates succumbing to the wave of judgment. And we start to wonder, *Who is next? Is anyone incapable of exploiting power?*

What if the answer is no? Christian leader Andy Crouch expressed this universal vulnerability well in a 2018 article on the dangers of celebrity power in the church. Calling for ongoing accountability, he wrote, "If you knew the full condition of my heart, my fantasies and grievances, my anxieties and my darkest solitary thoughts, you would declare me a danger to myself and others. I cannot be entrusted with power by myself, certainly not with celebrity, and neither can you."[2] The #MeToo movement has exposed a painful truth: that there is no ultimate "them" and "us" when it comes to exploiting power over others; there is only a sliding scale. And while arguments from circumstance can exonerate, they can equally condemn. Indeed, as we saw in chapter 4, there is ample evidence to suggest that most of us are capable of evil and cruelty, given the right peer pressure. And the rot goes deep.

It has been said that no friendship in the world would last a day if we could see each other's thoughts. Run that test on yourself between now and tomorrow. Think of everyone you spend time with and ask, would I let them see a transcript of my thoughts? My marriage would

2. Andy Crouch, "It's Time to Reckon with Celebrity Power," The Gospel Coalition, March 24, 2018, https://www.thegospelcoalition.org/article/time-reckon-celebrity-power/.

die. My children would be crushed. My friends would leave. My thoughts are not all bad: many are good and kind and true. But like a bag of flour infested by maggots, no part of me is pure. This dawned on Aleksandr Solzhenitsyn as he was lying on rotting straw in a Soviet gulag: "Gradually it was disclosed to me that the line separating good and evil passes not through states, nor between classes, nor between political parties either—but right through every human heart."[3] This realization leaves us with another problem: all our relationships hinge, to some extent, on hiding.

Longing to Be Known and Loved

Much of our modern heartache flows from the search for identity. We are told that being our authentic selves is the key to happiness: "You do you" is our self-loving battle cry. Any sense that the authentic "me" may not be a beautiful thing is repression, and guilt must be shed like a snakeskin. We are worth it. We are enough. But what if Larry Nassar was living out of his authentic self as he abused young gymnasts? Should he not have suppressed the part of himself that desired children's bodies? How do I know when my authentic self is speaking? And why should I believe that the love and kindness in me is truly "me," while the selfishness and jealousy are alien invasions? Part of me longs to be more known. But what would happen if my "true self" were revealed?

Going deeper into someone's identity can breed empathy. In the 2018 blockbuster *Black Panther*, we rethink Killmonger's actions when we realize who he is. The film begins with a showdown between two brothers. Killmonger turns out to be Erik, the son of the brother who died, and who was left as an orphan when his uncle killed his dad. His actions are driven by a two-pronged drive for justice: he longs to avenge his father; and—having grown up as a poor, black orphan in America—he longs for justice for African Americans. The revelation of his identity makes us empathize, even with a brutal killer. But in other stories, revelation breeds disgust. The brilliantly manipulative song "Mother Knows Best" in the 2010 animation

---

3. Aleksandr Solzhenitsyn, *The Gulag Archipelago, 1918–1956*, trans. Harry Willetts, vol. 3 (New York: Basic Books, 1997), 615.

Tangled typifies how the woman Rapunzel thinks her mother controls and exploits her. When Rapunzel discovers who the witch really is—not her mother but an evil child abductor—the maternal bond dies. Indeed, Rapunzel appears to feel no sadness at the death of the woman who raised her.

The last time I had my hair cut, my stylist had a tattoo on her right arm. It read, "If you can't handle my worst, you don't deserve my best." These words stuck in my mind. Ultimately, they express a desire to be known and loved. But as we invite people in, we must navigate a minefield. Dig in some places in my heart, and you will find rich soils that will help you know me better and, perhaps, love me more. But scratch on other turfs, and your positive view of who I am will explode in your face. We all manage our self-disclosure. In varying degrees and ways, we find ourselves making a choice: to be known or to be loved. How does the Bible speak into this?

Found Out

Christianity acts like a searchlight. On the one hand, it confronts us with a God who sees our thoughts. He knows our hearts and our pretense, our words and our deeds. The parts we work so hard to hide are laid bare before him, and the one person with the right to judge has all the evidence. Like the infrared sensors that revealed Dzhokhar Tsarnaev hiding under the awning of a boat, the God of the Bible is the God from whom we cannot hide. And yet the searchlight that could expose us as fugitive criminals is trained on us as lost children. This God is looking for us, longing for us, calling to us to come home.

Three years ago, my younger daughter disappeared from the park. First, I looked for her myself. I searched the play structures and scoured the bushes. Then, I recruited other parents to help. Panic rising in my blood, I imagined my beautiful three-year-old gone forever. I called the police. But as I was describing my lost child, an officer showed up. He had come because a little girl had been discovered wandering around the parking lot of the local store. On the few other occasions when I have called the police, it has been to report a criminal. This time, I called because my little one was lost. When I saw her at last, I could not stop holding her. I cried and hugged her and kissed her and told her never, never, never to leave a park alone again. I searched for her because I loved her. And that is how God searches for us.

In one of Jesus's most famous parables, a wastrel son who has taken his father's money and run is welcomed home. Seeing his prodigal child still far off, his father runs to him, kisses him, hugs him, and calls for a party to celebrate, not because his son is innocent—which he is not—but because he is loved. The son was lost and now he is found (Luke 15:11–32). As my friend Rachel (whom you met in chap. 9) eloquently puts it, "In Christ, we are not pursued like wanted criminals, but like wanted children, or like wanted lovers, because wrath is replaced by desire."[4]

But if God cares about justice, and all our mixed motives and manipulative thoughts are exposed before him, why isn't the searchlight trained on us as criminals?

The Logic of the Cross

On the night Jesus was arrested, he went up to the Mount of Olives to pray. He was profoundly distressed. Walking away from his disciples, he fell on his knees and pleaded: "Father, if you are willing, remove this cup from me. Nevertheless, not my will, but yours be done" (Luke 22:42).[5] An angel came to strengthen Jesus. But it was not enough. "Being in agony he prayed more earnestly; and his sweat became like great drops of blood falling down to the ground" (Luke 22:44).

Why was Jesus so afraid?

Some have speculated that he was afraid to die. Crucifixion was designed to maximize torture and humiliation so onlookers would be cautioned to avoid the kind of offense against Rome that got you nailed to a cross. This would be quite enough for you or me to fall on our faces and beg to be spared. But for Jesus there was more. Just as human marriage is an illustration of a deeper love, the physical agony of the cross was an illustration of a deeper pain—a pain Jesus packaged in a metaphor.

---

4. Rachel Gilson, "Who Is Rest?," *Born Again This Way* (blog), August 31, 2017, https://rachel gilson.com/blog/2017/8/20/who-is-rest.
5. See also Matt. 26:39; Mark 14:36; John 18:11.

The image of the cup of the Lord cuts through the Hebrew Scriptures with the jagged force of a lightning bolt. Job, the Psalms, Isaiah, Jeremiah, Lamentations, Ezekiel, Obadiah, Habakkuk, and Zechariah all use this metaphor to communicate God's judgment.[6] Some passages proclaim destruction for those about to drink the cup. Others herald salvation for those from whom the cup is being removed. Just as the image of God as Husband presents the whole nation of Israel as his bride, so the cup of God's wrath is served up to whole nations whose sinful abuses, child sacrifices, rejection of God, and exploitation of the poor have incurred the Lord's judgment. And here is Jesus, kneeling on the ground, begging for "this cup" to pass him by. To the first Gospel readers, the meaning would have been clear: Jesus faced drinking down the righteous anger and judgment of God against sin on an epic scale.

The idea of the wrath of God seems alien to us—a psychologically damaging relic from a bygone era. But just as we cannot absolve people of moral accountability without also erasing their ability to love, so God's love and God's judgment cannot be pulled apart. Think of the anger you feel when you see school children shot, women raped, or people beaten because of the color of their skin. Think of your anger at the slave trade, the Holocaust, and global sex trafficking. When you analyze that anger, its root is love. No one who regards those of other races as subhuman cares about racial exploitation. No one who believes that women or children are property cares about sexual abuse. And the more we love, the more easily our anger is kindled. We rush to defend our children from the least attack because we love them: anyone who harms them inspires our fury.

Imagine that this kind of love-motivated anger is so deeply entrenched in the heart of God that your own commitment to justice is like a drop in the ocean, like the justice of a child dressing up in a police outfit compared with a high-court judge. God is—as Hagar recognized—the God who sees (Gen. 16:13). God's anger at the Holocaust, God's anger at the slave trade, God's anger at abuse and murder and cruelty and neglect was all poured out on Jesus on the cross. That was what he dreaded: not the nails in his hands.

---

6. See, e.g., Job 21:19–20; Pss. 60:3; 75:8; Isa. 51:17–23; Jer. 25:15–29; 49:12; 51:7–8, 39, 57; Lam. 4:21; Ezek. 23:31–34; Obad. 16; Hab. 2:15–16; Zech. 12:2.

But this alone does not explain the logic of the cross. Even if there is a world of sin to pay for, why would an outpouring of anger against a totally innocent man make a difference? Is this not the worst form of *injustice*? Before we can grasp the logic of the cross, we must understand who Jesus is in relation to God and who he is in relation to us.

First, according to the Bible, Jesus is not the passive victim of God's wrath. He is God himself. Thus, on the cross, Jesus is both executioner and condemned. People sometimes associate God the Father with the Old Testament, seeing him as angry and vengeful, and God the Son—Jesus—with the New Testament, preaching love and mercy and forgiveness. But while God certainly acts in judgment in the Old Testament, he is also "merciful and gracious, slow to anger, and abounding in steadfast love and faithfulness" (Ex. 34:6). He is like a loving husband, extending mercy after mercy to his unfaithful wife (Isa. 62:4–5); like a nursing mother, clutching her infant (Isa. 49:15); like a father, lifting his little child to his cheek (Hos. 11:3–4). Conversely, while Jesus expounds God's love and mercy again and again, he also hammers on God's judgment more than any Old Testament prophet. And Jesus is clear: he is the one who will judge all humanity.

In the last book of the Bible, the tender, vulnerable metaphor used to depict Jesus as the sacrifice becomes an image of terrifying judgment. Revelation describes a time when people will say to mountains, "Fall on us and hide us from the face of him who is seated on the throne, and from the wrath of the Lamb, for the great day of their wrath has come, and who can stand?" (Rev. 6:16–17). The wrath of God is the wrath of Jesus, the Lamb. On the cross, the one perfectly righteous, perfectly loving, perfectly innocent man who ever lived faced the full force of God's judgment, drank it down, and threw away the cup. In biblical shorthand, he went to hell.

Second, just as Jesus is not separable from the God whose wrath he faces on the cross, so he is not separable from us, if we but put our trust in him. In chapter 9, we explored the stunning biblical metaphor of the church as Jesus's body and what that means for Christians in relation to each other. But a yet more vital implication of this truth is that if we trust in Jesus, we are as inseparable from him as our bodies are from our heads.

As I write these words, my fingers are typing. But they are not acting independently. If you find what I have written offensive, you cannot blame my fingers alone. The offense is mine. Likewise, Jesus is not a random bystander, hauled in to pay for our sin. If we have put our trust in him, he is our Head: every evil of our hearts has been laid on him and paid for by his death, and each of his beautiful acts of love is credited to our account. We have all rejected God and deserve his rejection in return. The choice we have is this: to face hell by ourselves or to hide ourselves in Christ.

The Real Meaning of Heaven and Hell

We tend think of heaven and hell primarily as places to be sent. Some imagine our destination depends on our deeds: if we are, on balance, "good people," we can expect heaven, while bad people like Hitler and Stalin languish in hell. Others think Christianity sorts people into heaven or hell on the apparently arbitrary basis of their assent to certain statements. Those lucky enough to have been told about Jesus and credulous enough to believe he died in their place are sent to heaven. Those who have not heard, or have other religious preferences, or are simply too smart to believe this crazy story of a resurrected man are capriciously dispatched to a place called hell. But the Bible tells a different story.

Heaven, in biblical terms, is not primarily a place. It is a shorthand for the full blessing of relationship with God. It is the prodigal son come home. It is the bride being embraced by her husband with tears of joy. It is the new heavens and the new earth, where God's people with upgraded, resurrection bodies will enjoy eternity with him at a level of intimacy into which the best of human marriage gives us no more than a glimpse. Heaven is home: an embodied experience of deep relationship with God and his people on a recreated earth.

Hell is the opposite. It is the door shut in the face of the wastrel son, the divorce certificate delivered at the moment of remorse, the criminal receiving his just deserts. If Jesus is the Bread of Life, loss of Jesus means starving. If Jesus is the Light of the World, loss of Jesus means darkness. If Jesus is the Good Shepherd, loss of Jesus means wandering alone and lost. If Jesus is the resurrection and the life, loss of Jesus is eternal death. And if Jesus is the Lamb of God, sacrificed for our sins, loss of Jesus means paying that price for ourselves.

In the classic Russian novel *Eugene Onegin*, a jaded aristocrat, Onegin, meets an innocent young girl in the countryside. The girl, Tatyana, writes him a letter, offering him her love. Onegin does not reply. When they meet again, he turns her down: the letter was touching, he tells her, but he would soon grow bored of marriage to her. Years later, Onegin enters a St. Petersburg party and sees a stunningly beautiful woman. It is Tatyana. But she is now married. Onegin falls in love with her. He tries desperately to win her back. But Tatyana refuses him. Once, the door was open: she offered him her love. Now it is shut.

For many of us, it is easy to reject Jesus now. Like Tatyana's letter to Onegin, his offer is touching. But we believe we will be happier without such a commitment. We worry he will cramp our style, so we move on with life and leave him in the spiritual countryside. One day, the Bible warns, we will see Jesus in all his glory, our eyes painfully open to his majesty. We will know in that moment that all our greatest treasures were nothing compared with him, and we will bitterly regret that decision. But it will be no more unfair than Tatyana's rejection of Onegin. If we accept Jesus now, we will live with him forever in a fullness of life we cannot imagine. If we reject him, he will one day reject us, and we will be eternally devastated. The choice is ours.

But is it?

Freedom, Life, and Love

The possibility of unity with Christ unpicks one final knot in the human condition—a challenge that confronts Christians and atheists alike. Are we really free to choose at all? Sam Harris believes that free will is a delusion: a belief impossible to map onto reality. Christianity holds out an alternative. Yes, our actions are informed by our circumstances (experiential and neurological), but we are moral agents nonetheless.

Multiple biblical texts suggest that our wills are in a state of bondage in some ways similar to that described by Harris: we are free to do what we want to do, but we cannot determine the wanting itself.

Paul calls us "dead in our sins" until we are made "alive in Christ."[7] And corpses cannot choose. But whereas in Harris's worldview there is no true free will, in a Christian worldview there is. God himself is entirely free, just as he is completely alive. And just as our lives are contingent on his life, and our loves are contingent on his love, so our wills are contingent on his will.

We get a hint of this relationship in pregnancy. The child in my womb right now is truly alive, even though his life is utterly contingent on mine. He moves freely within my womb. But he does not control his location: where I go, he goes. Likewise, I am truly alive and truly free not independently from Jesus but enfolded in him. And just as escaping from me right now would mean not life to my child but death, so escaping from Christ would mean not freedom and life to me but a brief writhing before stillness. Enclosed in my body, dependent on my blood, protected by my immunity, and housed in my love, my son is, in a tangible sense, united with me. Because I trust in Jesus, I am similarly dependent on him. Where Jesus goes, I go. If he lives, I live. He died my death and took my punishment. He is my resurrection and my life.[8]

The Scandal of Grace

Harris argues that our recognition that human beings do not have free will should make us more compassionate for murderers. They were just unlucky in their circumstances, not morally culpable. Christianity also demands that we identify with the worst criminals, but on different grounds: not because they (like us) are innocent but because we (like them) are guilty.

In a moving speech at the trial of Larry Nassar, Rachael Denhollander, the first woman to file sex-abuse charges against Nassar, faced the man who took her innocence and pleaded with him to turn to Christ. The Bible, she explained,

> carries a final judgment where all of God's wrath and eternal terror is poured out on men like you. Should you ever reach the point of truly facing what you have done, the guilt will be crushing. And

---

7. See, e.g., Eph. 2:1–7; Col. 2:13–14.
8. See, e.g., Col. 3:2–3.

that is what makes the gospel of Christ so sweet. Because it extends grace and hope and mercy where none should be found. And it will be there for you.[9]

Denhollander, a victim of child abuse, knows that she ultimately stands in the same dock as her abuser. The cross of Christ serves justice: through Jesus, Nassar's sin could be expunged. The crushing weight could be lifted. He is serving multiple life sentences for his crimes, as he rightly should. But—as it has been for many before him—the prison door *could* be a door to freedom, love, and life in Christ. This is the ultimate scandal of the Christian faith. The worst criminal can be welcomed. And that is good news for us, because we are more sinful than we realize. But in Christ we can be more known, more loved, and more truly alive than we have ever dreamed.

Two Worlds

In chapter 1, I confessed that my all-time favorite TV show was the British sci-fi series *Doctor Who*. The Doctor faces life-threating situations on an almost daily basis. Near-death for him is like breakfast for you or me. But in one episode, the terms of engagement change. The Doctor and his friends experience two worlds: one is a dream; the other is real. If they die in the dream world, they wake up in reality. If they die in the real world, they're dead. But the problem is this: they don't know which is which.

The Bible also offers us another world, another claim on reality. It tells us that the only way to truly live—now and for eternity—is to die. And time is running out. "If anyone would come after me," says Jesus, "let him deny himself and take up his cross and follow me. For whoever would save his life will lose it, but whoever loses his life for my sake will find it" (Matt. 16:24–25).

Every day I struggle to believe in Jesus's world. I do not mean this in the sense of mental assent. For the reasons laid out in this book, I find the alternatives less compelling. But I struggle in the heart sense of living this truth: denying myself, taking up my cross, believing that

9. "Rachael Denhollander's Full Victim Impact Statement about Larry Nassar," CNN, January 30, 2018, https://www.cnn.com/2018/01/24/us/rachael-denhollander-full-statement/.

Jesus *is* my life. And yet every day I find the fingerprints of this impossible man in my life, calling me into a story so much greater and more exhilarating than my own little life could ever be.

In Jesus's world, we find connective tissue between the truths of science and morality. We find a basis for saying that all human beings are created equal, and a deep call to love across diversity. We find a name for evil, and a means of forgiveness. We find a vision of love that is so much deeper than our current hearts can hold, and a true intimacy better than our weak bodies could ever experience. We find a diagnosis of human nature as shot through with sin and yet redeemable by grace. We find a call to care for the poor, oppressed, and lonely, a call springing from the heart of God himself and grounded in the hope that one day every tear will be wiped away, every stomach will be filled, and every outcast will be embraced. But we do not find glib answers or an easy road. Instead, we find a call to come and die.

I want to end this book with the words of a woman who encountered this world in the strangest of circumstances. Joy Davidman was a Jewish American atheist poet. As a young woman, she became a Communist to slake her thirst for justice. She married a fellow writer, Bill. And she went on to be the woman whose death broke author C. S. Lewis's heart. "Of course, I thought atheism was *true*," Joy recalls, "but I hadn't given quite enough attention to developing the proof of it. Someday, when the children were older, I'd work it out."[10] But between marrying Bill and meeting Lewis, Joy met God.

Bill was a workaholic, an alcoholic, and unfaithful. One day, he called Joy from his New York office and told her he was having a nervous breakdown. Then he hung up. There followed a day of frantic telephoning. By nightfall, Joy recalls, "there was nothing to do but wait and see if he turned up, alive or dead." She put her children to sleep and waited. And in that silence, something happened:

> For the first time in my life, I felt helpless; for the first time, my pride was forced to admit that I was not, after all, "the master of my fate" and "the captain of my soul." All my defenses—all the walls of arrogance and cocksureness and self-love behind which

10. Don W. King, ed. *Out of My Bone: The Letters of Joy Davidman* (Grand Rapids, MI: Eerdmans, 2009), 94.

I had hid from God—went down momentarily—and God came
in. . . .

There was a Person with me in that room, directly present to
my consciousness—a Person so real that all my previous life was
by comparison a mere shadow play. And I myself was more alive
than I had ever been; it was like waking from sleep.[11]

Friend, if you are settling for deferred beliefs, hoping that the
universe has a plan, believing human equality is self-evident but not
knowing why, wondering if anyone who knew your secret thoughts
could ever truly love you, come to Jesus. Come to the man who
brought hope to oppressed slaves. Come to the man who calls dead
people from their graves. Come to the man who could have covered
Dzhokhar Tsarnaev's guilt when the boat cover in Watertown could
not. Come to the man who found my friend Rachel in a library at Yale
when she realized how little she deserved mercy and how much Jesus
loved her, and her heart swelled with thankfulness as she surrendered
herself to him.

"I am the resurrection and the life," said Jesus to Martha. And he
says the same to you: "Whoever believes in me, though he die, yet shall
he live, and everyone who lives and believes in me shall never die. Do
you believe this?"

---

11. King, *Out of My Bone*, 94.

Acknowledgments

This book was built like the mythical magpie's nest: I am grateful to the friends who let me thieve their bright ideas and steal their shining stories. It would all be dry twigs without them.

Each chapter has been scoured by expert eyes, including those of Ian Hutchinson, Tyler VanderWeele, Christian Miller, Andra Gillespie, Ronald Osborne, Senganglu Thaimei, Patrick Smith, Rachael Beale, Dominic Erdozain, Peter Williams, Fenggang Yang, Ard Louis, Laura Sanderson, Curtis Cook, and Nicole Garcia. Their comments have improved my work. Any enduring errors are my own.

Collin Hansen at the Gospel Coalition took a chance on a rookie writer and has supported me at every turn. At Crossway, Dave DeWit backed this book, while Thom Notaro and Samuel James have labored tirelessly over my text. I'm thankful for their guidance and encouragement.

My writing running mates, Rachel Gilson and Lydia Dugdale, have kept me fueled intellectually and emotionally, and been my first readers and sounding boards. If I am ever asked for advice by aspiring writers, the first thing I will say is find your comrades.

My parents, Nicholas and Christine Beale, raised me to believe that Christians should be the most intellectually curious people in town, and have supported me in this project from caring for my kids to spotting my mistakes. My in-laws, John and Carol McLaughlin, have helped in a hundred practical ways. My wonderful sister, Rose Beale, was the first to read the whole manuscript, and flew to Boston to be my research assistant in the final phase. May their names be a blessing.

I am profoundly grateful for three people who have hindered my progress: my daughters, Miranda and Eliza, who have begged to read "mummy's book" (suggesting I use Post-it notes to cover the age-inappropriate parts); and my son, Luke, who was co-gestated with this book, and who reminds me daily of my utter weakness, which is—in the Christian worldview—the place where we find God's strength.

Finally, I thank God for my husband, Bryan. He dared to take me on (when no British man in his right mind would have) and has always supported my work and pushed me to do better. He brings me down to earth, tolerates my mess, and loves me when I fail. This side of eternity, I'm thankful I can call him mine.

General Index

Scripture Index

THE GOSPEL COALITION

The Gospel Coalition is a fellowship of evangelical churches deeply committed to renewing our faith in the gospel of Christ and to reforming our ministry practices to conform fully to the Scriptures. We have committed ourselves to invigorating churches with new hope and compelling joy based on the promises received by grace alone through faith alone in Christ alone.

We desire to champion the gospel with clarity, compassion, courage, and joy—gladly linking hearts with fellow believers across denominational, ethnic, and class lines. We yearn to work with all who, in addition to embracing our confession and theological vision for ministry, seek the lordship of Christ over the whole of life with unabashed hope in the power of the Holy Spirit to transform individuals, communities, and cultures.

Join the cause and visit TGC.org for fresh resources that will equip you to love God with all your heart, soul, mind, and strength, and to love your neighbor as yourself.

TGC.org